24.99

Jean Toomer's Years with Gurdjieff

Jean Toomer's Years with Gurdjieff

PORTRAIT OF AN ARTIST
1923–1936

Rudolph P. Byrd

THE UNIVERSITY OF GEORGIA PRESS
Athens and London

© 1990 by the University of Georgia Press
Athens, Georgia 30602
Designed by Erin Kirk
Set in Palatino by Tseng Information Systems, Inc.
Printed and bound by Thomson-Shore
The paper in this book meets the guidelines
for permanence and durability of the Committee on
Production Guidelines for Book Longevity of
the Council on Library Resources.

Printed in the United States of America

94 93 92 91 90   5 4 3 2 1

Library of Congress Cataloging in Publication Data

Byrd, Rudolph P.
Jean Toomer's years with Gurdjieff: portrait of an artist,
1923–1936 / by Rudolph P. Byrd.
p. cm.
Includes bibliographical references.
ISBN 0-8203-1248-7
1. Toomer, Jean, 1894–1967–Philosophy.   2. Toomer, Jean,
1894–1967–Criticism and interpretation.   3. Gurdjieff, Georges
Ivanovitch, 1872–1949–Influence.   4. Philosophy in literature.
I. Title.
PS3539.O478Z59   1990
813'.52–dc20   90-10778
                                                            CIP

British Library Cataloging in Publication Data available

To My Parents: Meardis Cannon and Rudolph V. Byrd

By habit
cultivate your name;
the dead spoken
remembered habitual.

MICHAEL S. HARPER

Contents

Acknowledgments

THE PUBLICATION OF this book is not solely a personal triumph—very far from it. Many have shared in the difficult, daunting, and discouraging work of creating a book that corresponds to certain truths, to certain realities, to certain expectations.

First, I thank members of my family who supported me in what doubtless seemed to them a bewildering and interminable project. Perhaps the book will serve as some compensation for the many years during which I was sometimes distant, but more often absent, from the beat and pulse of their living.

I offer special thanks to my teachers: to Susan Kirschner, whose example persuaded me that one could have a full life with books; to John F. Callahan, who introduced me to African-American literature and who lovingly watched an undergraduate essay become a book; to Michael S. Harper, who gave me my first copy of *Essentials* and who established standards I hope one day to meet; to Charles T. Davis, who advised me that the only way I could make sense of Toomer's later fiction was to study the writings of George I. Gurdjieff; to Robert B. Stepto, John Blassingame, and R. W. B. Lewis, who, as members of my dissertation committee, provided leadership, encouragement, and much useful advice in the early stages of my research.

This book benefited enormously from the insight and careful reading of Vera M. Kutzinski, Herman Beavers, and Marcellus Blount, whom I had the good fortune to meet during my years of study in Yale's American Studies Program. I owe a special thanks to Nellie Y. McKay, whose close reading also improved this book and who generously assisted and supported me in securing a publisher for it.

In gratitude I acknowledge the loving support of many friends who were steadfast in their belief that I would one day bring this project to fruition. In exchange for my irritability, diffidence, and monomania, they cheerfully provided me with diversions that only broadened the scope of my research, renewed my faith in my peculiar talents and abilities (such as they are), and offered me a very rare fellowship. In *Essentials* Toomer wrote that "human relationships are matters of skill and art." Those whose names are listed here have demonstrated the truth of this assertion in deeds: Richard A. Benson and his family in New Haven, Robert C. Carwell, John C. Covington and his family in Baltimore, Derrick Dowell and his family in Nashville, Brenda Files, Dorothy Fleming, Craig Fort and his family in New Haven, Phyllis Fraley, Gregory Gammons, Earl Gordon, Cecilia Hunter, Ellis Mack, Ana Malinow, James D. Manning, Walter L. Miller, Barry Nelson and his family in Los Angeles, Michael Oby, Edward H. Sarrett, Ingrid Saunders, Jean Shifres, Garth Tate, Jack Tatum, Fred Tyson, Jonathan Walton, Dewitt Webster, Tal Ben-Dashan Widdes, and Jerome Wright. A very sincere thanks is tendered to Henry A. Leonard, who introduced me to the work of P. D. Ouspensky and who sustained me in all phases of this project.

During various stages of the research and writing I was supported by fellowships. Though this book had a long gestation period, it would have been even longer without the support of the Danforth Foundation, whose funds were administered with humanity by Robert E. Bunselmeyer, Etta Onat, and Deborah G. Thomas of Yale University. I wish also to thank the Center for African-American Studies at the University of California at Los Angeles, where I completed most of the revisions of the manuscript as a visiting scholar under the able stewardship of Claudia Mitchel-Kernan.

I began my teaching career at Carleton College, and to my friends and colleagues there I am deeply indebted for their high standards and fine examples in both teaching and scholarship. I wish to thank members of the Department of English and the Program of African/African-American Studies, most notably Elizabeth Ciner, Mary Easter, Keith Harrison, Ray Kea, Cherif Keita, Stephen R. Lewis, Jr., Arthur L. Little, Jr., James McDonnell, Jane T. McDonnell, Susan Jaret McKinstry, Frank Morral, May Okada, Clare Rossini, Carolyn Soule, George Soule, Dana Strand, and Robert Tisdale. Many thanks to Joseph Byrne and Fred Hagstrom of the Department of Art, Angelique Dietz of Off-Campus Studies, Roy Elveton of the Department of Philosophy, Michael Flynn of the Department of Linguistics, and Humberto R. Huergo of the Department of Romance Languages. Saul Zelan and Jim Pence of Electronic Services provided me with lifesaving advice concerning the use of my sometimes intractable computer. A special thanks is due Jewelnel Davis, my sister and spiritual adviser in that frigid place.

I wish also to thank Kenneth E. Gadomski for his patience and wizardry with the computers at the University of Delaware.

Finally, I wish to thank the able staff of the University of Georgia Press. Many thanks to Angela G. Ray for the many improvements she made to this book as copy editor: she is a devoted soldier of the word. I also wish to thank Mary Murrell for her very sound advice during the final stages of editing this book. A very special thanks to Karen Orchard, Executive Editor, whose faith in the value of this book brought it successfully through all the stages of review and editing.

I ask the pardon of those whose contributions I have failed to mention here. And, of course, what is abiding and fine in the pages to follow is a gift from those named here; for everything else, the dross and infelicities, I accept full responsibility.

Introduction

IN MY WORK on Jean Toomer, I have discovered a fascinating pattern of a poet, playwright, and fiction writer obsessed by and completely committed to an "ideal of Man"—man as a psychologically and spiritually whole being—that was his lifelong inspiration and theme. This pattern assumed greater significance and definition after a careful study of the life and writings of George Ivanovich Gurdjieff, a Russian psychologist and philosopher who, in the years following the publication of *Cane*, dominated Toomer's mind and imagination. As I argue in the pages to follow, it is in Gurdjieff's theories on human development that Toomer discovered the "intelligible scheme" that gives precision, structure, and authority to his "ideal of Man," and it is only through these theories that the large body of work Toomer produced after *Cane* can be understood.

Like other writers of his generation—Waldo Frank, Gorham Munson, Sherwood Anderson—Toomer was deeply troubled by what he perceived as the decline of modern civilization as a consequence of the rather exciting, but nonetheless disturbing, possibilities of American technology. Unlike many of his contemporaries, Toomer searched for a means to address and arrest this decline, and his search led him to Gurdjieff. The discovery had far-reaching effects for Toomer as a writer. After the discovery of Gurdjieff, the philosopher-poet of *Cane* vanished and in his place appeared a spiritual reformer and social critic whose obsession with Gurdjieff's theories weakened and then wasted his great talent.

In this effort to examine the influence of Gurdjieff's theories on Toomer's development as a writer, the sometimes peculiar interests of the biographer and the preoccupations of the literary critic converge. While I am interested in examining, interpreting, and evaluating the works that Toomer's experiments in esotericism produced, I am also interested in examining the particular life experiences that created in the young author of *Cane* a predisposition toward spiritualism and psychology. I have not, as might be expected, excluded *Cane* from this study. Some may wonder why a study of Toomer's works written during the period of his greatest involvement with Gurdjieff includes *Cane*, but such an undertaking would be incomplete without it. Thematically, *Cane* is much closer to the later works than most scholars of Toomer realize. In fact, *Cane* is the first in a series of works joined together by a theme of great importance to Toomer: human development, or, more precisely, man's lack of and search for wholeness.

As I argue in chapter 1, *Cane* was Toomer's first and most successful attempt to give artistic significance to this cherished theme. While Toomer believed firmly in the value of his later writings, most efforts subsequent to *Cane* failed because of Toomer's unfortunate tendency to utilize the forms of literature as a platform to promote the theories of the Gurdjieff system. (*The Sacred Factory* and "The Blue Meridian" are the most obvious exceptions.) Gurdjieff the man, his psychological system, and Toomer's discovery and promotion of both are the subjects of chapter 2. My objective in this chapter is to provide some sense of the educational background and personality of Gurdjieff, the purpose of his psychological system, and the significance of both to Toomer. In chapter 3, I return to an examination of the major literary works in Toomer's canon. Here I examine "The Gallonwerps" and "Transatlantic," unpublished novels that illustrate the extent to which Gurdjieff's theories are essentially the foundation for Toomer's later fiction. In chapter 4, I examine the dramatic works in Toomer's rather uneven canon, giving special attention to those works written during the apex of his involvement with the Gurdjieff work. The principal work examined in this chapter is *The Sacred Factory: A Religious Drama of Today*. Here again my intention is to reveal the thematic links between the later works and *Cane*, as well as the influence of Gurdjieff's theories on Toomer's conception of drama. In chapter 5, my objectives are the same, but this time the subject is verse, not fiction or drama. Here I examine "The Blue Meridian," the most unified statement of Toomer's racial, philosophical, and spiritual convictions. My analysis of this magnum opus reveals not only the influence of Walt Whitman but also the supreme importance of Gurdjieff's theories to Toomer's vision of the function of poetry. Reading the chapters that follow, one should have not only a clear sense of the relationship *Cane* has to the later works but also a portrait of a philosopher-poet whose acceptance of Gurdjieff's theories transformed him into a spiritual reformer and social critic. I will argue that this transformation occurred to the detriment of Toomer's work as a writer.

With the exceptions of Nellie Y. McKay, Cynthia E. Kerman, and Richard Eldridge, Toomer scholars have focused their critical efforts chiefly upon *Cane*, Toomer's relationship with such writers as Sherwood Anderson and Waldo Frank, and the importance of *Cane* to the writers of the New Negro movement. While this is clearly a valid and ambitious attempt to understand and locate Toomer in a seminal and extremely self-conscious artistic community, many scholars seem unaware of the thematic unity within Toomer's canon and do not emphasize sufficiently the importance of Gurdjieff's theories in its creation. Further, many scholars have failed to come to terms with *Cane*'s prophetic relationship to the later works, as well as with Toomer's legacy to and influence upon contemporary writers. My objective is to continue the discussion on Toomer in these and other important areas, to start near the point where the discussion generally ends and to fill in some of the gaps, both biographical and textual, that the growing body of Toomer scholarship has left vacant.

Finally, I suppose my objective is to demonstrate the unity and complexity of Toomer's canon as well as its theoretical underpinnings. If I succeed in doing this, then I will have realized my aim in undertaking this study.

1

Cane: *The Search for an Ideal of Man*

❦

ALFRED KREYMBORG ONCE described Jean Toomer as "one of the finest artists among the dark race, if not the finest."[1] This dubious pronouncement was made in 1929, nearly ten years after Kreymborg's first meeting with Toomer at the Rand School in New York City.[2] Kreymborg referred mainly to the critical success and acclaim that Toomer enjoyed after the appearance of *Cane,* and he cited "Reapers" as one of the best poems in Toomer's first and last book of fiction and verse. While we may be offended by the tone of Kreymborg's statement, not to mention the language he used to place and to describe African-American writers, the sentence that immediately follows it is, for the purposes of this study, more deserving of our attention. "A philosopher and psychologist by temperament," wrote the editor of *The Second American Caravan,* "the Washington writer is now fascinated by the larger, rather than the parochial interests of the human race, and should some day compose a book in the grand manner."[3] What is important about Kreymborg's statement is that it anticipates and subverts the view, one implicit in so much of the criticism on Toomer, that Toomer's life and work are an amalgam of discrete parts. One part is Toomer the philosopher and psychologist; the other is Toomer the imaginative artist whose life and literary interests changed dramatically after *Cane,* that is, after his experimentation with the philosophical and psychological system of George Ivanovich Gurdjieff.

Although Kreymborg's statement wisely discourages it, we might be justified in adopting this dualistic view of Toomer's life and writings. Toomer divided his own life into two separate phases: "Before Being Consciousness," the period before 1923 and the discovery of Gurdjieff, and "After Being Consciousness," the period following it.[4] But as we are interested in complexity and in charting the stages of an artist's evolution, the limitations of such divisions are all too obvious. Actually, Toomer only created these categories in order to dramatize certain developments that occurred during a particularly rich and eventful period in his life, and he himself would be opposed to the division of his life into such phases or episodes.

The majority of critics, however, struck by the dissimilarities between *Cane* and the works that followed it, not to mention the mistaken belief that Toomer did not become interested in philosophy and psychology until after his discovery of Gurdjieff, have thought only in terms of parts, phases, and episodes. Nearly all the studies on Toomer's fiction and verse begin and end with *Cane,* and this is proof of the unfortunate tendency in literary criticism to separate Toomer's first book from the works that follow it. Although there are many obvious and quite striking differences between *Cane* and the later works, there are also some profound similarities. Here we return to Kreymborg.

In describing Toomer as a "philosopher and psychologist by temperament," Kreymborg called attention to an extremely important and interesting point, one on which my argument depends to some extent. By suggesting that Toomer, because of a curious turn of the mind or because of certain novel intellectual predilections, was constitutionally more receptive to philosophy and psychology than to other disciplines, Kreymborg, unlike the critics of his day and many since, identified an important feature of Toomer's sensibility that links *Cane* with the body of writing that emerged from it. As we shall see, *Cane* was the firstborn in a family of works joined together by a common theme.

Although always a writer, Toomer, as Kreymborg suggested, was essentially and temperamentally a philosopher and psychologist. He was a philosopher because he sought to address the problems of his age through reason and rational investigation; he was a psychologist because, like Carl Jung, he believed that man himself was the source of all evil.[5] Determined to overcome this self-originating evil with its antithesis, Toomer devoted himself to a formal study of various psychological systems and theories. Viewed within the context of his lifelong search for meaning and order, Toomer's acceptance of the Gurdjieff system is not a non sequitur, or a frantic search for a new base, as Robert Bone suggests, but an inevitable and predictable stage in a long evolutionary process.[6] *Cane,* the beautiful book that rocketed Toomer to intellectual and artistic prominence, is part of this evolutionary process. It is, among other things, Toomer's first attempt at a search for values, his first attempt to utilize the forms of literature to address the spiritual and psychological problems of the modern age. As will be seen in later chapters of this study, the sensitive poet of *Cane,* upon accepting the worldview embodied in the teachings of Gurdjieff, was transformed into a zealous social critic and spiritual reformer. But this transformation would have been impossible without a foundation for belief, without, as Kreymborg wrote, a certain temperament.

We may find the basis for Toomer's special temperament, for his preoccupation with the condition of man and man's development, in particular childhood and adult experiences. Darwin T. Turner is mistaken in suggesting that Toomer's interest in such matters did not emerge until after he discovered Gurdjieff.[7] S. P. Fullwinder comes closer to the mark than Turner when he writes that "Toomer's overriding concern for the human condition grew out of an early lack of self-esteem, a concomitant tendency towards introspection and soul-searching, and a loss of childhood absolutes."[8] Although Fullwinder wisely turns our attention backward in time to Toomer's childhood, we cannot accept all the reasons he offers for Toomer's emergence as a writer committed to solving the spiritual and psychological problems of his age. Fullwinder states, for example, that Toomer was thrust forward into this progressive posture as a consequence of "an early lack of self-esteem." If we read the various versions of Toomer's unpublished autobiographies—thanks to the efforts of Turner, some of the most fascinating sections from each now have been assembled into a single volume—we discover that nothing could be further from the truth.

Toomer seems to have had a rather inflated, indeed an exaggerated, sense of his own importance. Recalling his earliest remembrances of himself, Toomer wrote: "I had an attitude towards myself that I was superior to wrong-doing and above criticism and reproach." No lack of self-esteem or poor self-image here. Even Norman Mailer, the swag-

gering younger counterpart of Ernest Hemingway, could not have
exhibited at so young an age more aplomb and such an overween-
ing pride in his real or fancied gifts. Toomer wrote that he retained
this superior posture, this "older-than-thou attitude," as he called it,
throughout his childhood, and because of it he seemed to exercise a
strange power over adults. "I myself," wrote Toomer, "seemed to induce in the grownups an attitude which made them keep their hands
off me; keep, as it were, a respectful distance." [9] To illustrate this point,
Toomer recounted the story of how his mother, worried and angry
because he had been out playing past dark, administered her last
spanking:

> Mother was waiting for me in the front hall. She was so angry that
> grandmother thought she also should be present to intercede for me.
> The minute I entered I was yanked off my feet and given a thrashing.
> I did not cry. Something had happened in me and I was beyond tears
> and beyond anger. Mother was somewhat appeased. Grandmother was
> sorrowful. I got to my feet, faced them without a quiver, and heard the
> strangest words come from me. 'She can do no more than kill me.' I
> spoke to my grandmother, but it was meant for my mother. . . . Both
> were taken back. . . . I went upstairs, and, still without feeling resent-
> ment or anger, I would have nothing to do with them for the next few
> days. . . . That was the last spanking I ever had. [10]

Although we may question the accuracy of this story, retold with a
good deal of drama and bravado from the perspective of adulthood, it
nonetheless conjures a picture of Toomer that stands in marked contrast to the one painted by Fullwinder. Toomer's early sense of superiority and his curious ability to project a baffling sense of power even
in the presence of adults were early manifestations of characteristics
that would serve him well not only as the leader of his neighborhood
gang but also as a social critic and spiritual reformer. [11]

Fullwinder, however, is correct when he writes that Toomer at
an early age exhibited a tendency toward "introspection and soul-
searching." Toomer wrote that "something happened which swiftly
transferred my interests from the world of things to the world of ideas
and imagination." The event that triggered this abrupt change in ori-
entation was Toomer's discovery of his Uncle Bismarck. Bismarck,
the elder brother of Nina, Toomer's mother, is the individual whom
Toomer credits with introducing him to the larger world of ideas and

fantasy. As he joined Bismarck in his room in the evenings to read folklore and mythology or to pore over maps and globes, Toomer was "growing a sense and forming an attitude towards my and our position on earth and in the universe." [12] Because of the special attention Toomer received from Bismarck, the young author of *Cane* discovered a "new way of seeing things." His range of interests broadened, and a reflective nature emerged and deepened.

But the event that followed these sessions with Bismarck and intensified an already deeply contemplative nature was an illness that confined Toomer to his bed for several weeks. At the age of ten, Toomer fell victim to a painful and enervating stomach disorder that brought him close to death. During this illness he luxuriated in the attention he received from his grandparents but more especially from his mother. Toomer wrote that the origins of this illness were largely psychosomatic, and he referred to it as "the climax of the long train of my experiences with mother." Toomer was alluding to his abandonment by his father, his parents' subsequent divorce, and his mother's decision to resume a life with other men. Throughout this unusually stressful and confusing period, Toomer, as any child would, felt isolated, hurt, and angry. Having lost his father, Toomer feared losing his mother. The illness was then, as he wrote, "a means of securing . . . what I unconsciously feared I would not be able to secure in any other way; namely the complete concerned attention of my mother." [13]

Although Toomer achieved his desired aim, albeit at great risk to himself, the illness had disastrous consequences for him in other areas of his life. When the "little Napoleon," as Toomer called himself, emerged from his sickbed, he discovered that the illness that had brought him closer to his mother had driven a wedge between him and his playmates. Toomer's playmates were sincerely concerned about his health, but, not surprisingly, they adjusted quickly to his absence. The seat of power within the gang was now occupied by someone else. The "little Napoleon" had met his Arthur Wellesley. His stature within the group diminished greatly by his long absence, Toomer found himself relegated to the hated position of follower. Recalling the pain and the deep sense of abandonment caused by this experience, he wrote that the reversal in status had far-reaching effects:

> I had been by nature a leader. Now I was deposed. I was compelled to make effort myself to become a self-made leader. . . .

> I had experienced the collapse and loss of a world. . . . I had been
> active mainly externally. Now I could not be so. I gradually became
> active mainly internally and built up an inner world of my own in which
> intangible things were more real than thoughts.
>   I had been a member of a group, a participant in a common existence.
> Now I was different. . . . I was in all ways compelled to differentiate
> and to learn to stand independently. In short, the entire experience and
> its consequences were the shock and the circumstance which started my
> individualization.[14]

The illness, then, not only altered Toomer's status within his peer
group but also turned his attention inward. It "energized [him] in a
new way" and forced him, as he recalled, to "struggle" with himself.
Toomer wrote that his illness was a "turning point, a radical deflection
of the course of [his] developing essence."[15] In an autobiographical
fragment, Toomer, glancing back to this time, linked this particular
childhood experience to later adult behavior and inclinations: "That
early I acquired towards myself an attitude that was partly curative,
partly developmental. The interest in human development, based on
my own need and desire, dates from that time. . . . Ever since I have
had recurrent occasions for taking myself in hand, making effort to
change myself in line with some self-impelled standard or ideal."[16]
    As a consequence of the change in status brought on by his illness,
Toomer now assumed a position within his peer group that would
serve as the foundation for his growth and development as a creative
artist. He became an observer:

> I sat on my post. This post was the brown-stone post of our front steps,
> the steps leading to the porch. Occasionally before, I had climbed up and
> perched on it. . . . Now I made a regular habit of it.
>   I had even come to like the spectator's role, watching them play and
> do things, making comments to myself, or my mind going wandering far
> off along some path of its own.[17]

Unbeknownst to himself at the time, Toomer was developing habits
and practices that would benefit him enormously when he turned his
mind to the difficult task of writing. But equally as important, this
habit of introspection, this tendency to look inwardly toward the self
for solutions and companionship are characteristics of an individual
who would find satisfaction in an intellectual approach to life, who

would be attracted to theories and abstractions, who would seek to address his own personal dilemmas and those of his time through analysis, theoretical frameworks, elaborate rational schemes, and "some self-impelled standard or ideal." In this childhood disappointment, we see plainly the outline of that special temperament that Kreymborg identified so early in Toomer's career.

It was not too long, however, before Toomer turned his own burgeoning intellectual powers upon himself in order to address a personal habit he felt sure possessed the potential to destroy him. During his third year at Paul Dunbar High School (now, M Street High School) Toomer fell prey to an "avalanche of sex indulgences." Recalling the chaos and anxiety of this time, Toomer wrote: "I saw myself falling to pieces. Some strength of my nature arose to fight, and I took myself in hand. I began searching to find a way of building myself up. I hit on a physical means; and this was the beginning of my self-imposed discipline."[18] The physical means Toomer discovered to cope with what Turner has identified as Toomer's spell of masturbation was a regimen of physical training and diet advocated by Bernarr McFadden, at the time a nationally known figure in health and physical education. Toomer was convinced of the effectiveness of McFadden's methods and prescriptions. As was characteristic of Toomer whenever he discovered anything that excited him, he began, as he wrote, "talking and arguing [McFadden's] ideas with everyone." He purchased McFadden's encyclopedia and following the dietary and training methods described there, increased his physical strength and general sense of well-being. Toomer, however, fell prey to another "spell of sex" and this time added breathing exercises to his already highly structured dietary and physical fitness regimen. In time Toomer overcame these sexual urges and became, he wrote, "an exceptionally strong and healthy young man."[19]

What is fascinating about this episode from Toomer's high school years is the means by which he sought to address a particular personal difficulty. Rather than wring his hands and retreat further into himself, Toomer searched for a plan of action, an intellectual scheme and method to cope with a personal crisis. The success and relief Toomer enjoyed as a consequence of his application of McFadden's methods doubtless instilled in him a firm belief in the usefulness of intellectual methods as well as a belief that many of the problems of his generation could be addressed through the application of similar cerebral inventions. In this particular experience, more than in any other from the early period in Toomer's life, we see the emergence of a characteristic bent toward the application of a theory to address a particular personal or social disorder. In later years the marriage of this impulse to the Gurdjieff system produced a spiritual reformer and a social critic who used his skill as a poet to call attention to a human condition whose seriousness he had only glimpsed, so he believed, in *Cane*.

As is revealed in Toomer's several autobiographies, he was deeply interested in a number of schemes and theories. During what Toomer described as his period of wandering, the period from 1914, when at the age of seventeen he set out for the University of Wisconsin, to 1920, when he again found himself in Washington, D.C., with his aging grandparents, his intellectual base expanded to embrace everything from atheism to theories of human intelligence. Recalling the impact of socialism and the unconscious behavior the acceptance of this theory revealed, Toomer wrote:

> I had been, I suppose, unconsciously seeking—as man must ever seek—an intelligible scheme of things, a sort of whole into which everything fit, or seemed to fit, a body of ideas which held a consistent view of life and which enabled one to see and understand as one does when he sees a map. Socialism was the first thing of this kind I had encountered. I responded accordingly. It was not so much the facts or ideas, taken singly, that aroused me, though certainly I was challenged and stimulated by them. More it was the body, the scheme, the order and inclusion. These evoked and promised to satisfy all in me that had been groping for form amid the disorder and chaos of my personal experiences.[20]

Although the principles and theories of socialism appealed to Toomer, the "body, the scheme" appealed to him more. But Toomer's passion for socialism was soon supplanted by an equally engrossing passion for psychology. It seems that Toomer perceived more value in his readings in psychology than in socialism. He was convinced that in psychology "lay the key, and the one fundamental approach to life."[21] Since at this early date the author of *Cane* believed that psychology possessed such great power and promise, his later acceptance of Gurdjieff's psychological system should not come as much of a surprise.

During his nearly six-year period of wandering Toomer, in his search for an "intelligible scheme," read widely. He discovered Goethe, Rolland, Whitman, Frost, Sandburg, and, immediately in the years following, Crane and the Imagists. Toomer read all the modern writers of fiction, but chiefly enjoyed Anderson, Munson, Burke, and Frank, a writer who exercised a great influence over him. But as Toomer continued to write and to immerse himself in American and European literature, there were of course the expected diversions into other areas. For a period of eight months Toomer set aside his readings in literature and read extensively in "Buddhist philosophy, the Eastern teachings, occultism, [and] theosophy." Toomer was fascinated by this new turn in his intellectual peregrinations. He wrote that these materials had an appeal he had yet to discover in other readings: "These ideas challenged and stimulated me. Despite my literary purpose, I was compelled to know something more about them. So, for a time, I turned my back on literature and plunged into this kind of reading." Toomer soon became dissatisfied with just reading and searched for a "personal all-around experience of the world these books seemed to open." Since there were few opportunities for such experiences in Washington, D.C., in 1920, Toomer set aside his readings in Eastern thought and returned, so he wrote, to the "physical, tangible, earthly world." [22]

But these readings, to which Toomer would return with renewed interest after discovering Gurdjieff, made a deep impression upon his developing mind and imagination: "From this reading, but not so much from it as from the ponderings and gatherings-up of impressions and experiences which it stimulated, there swung to the fore my picture and ideal of Man, of a complete and whole individual who was able to function physically, emotionally, and intellectually. This ideal was much fuller, with more substance and detail than that formed by my reading of Goethe, but it was in the same line and order of desirable and valuable human life." [23] Although we have the sense of an old man looking back to his youth, this passage is particularly revealing because it provides indisputable evidence of Toomer's early interest in psychological and philosophical matters at a level most believed possible only *after* his involvement with the Gurdjieff work. The Gurdjieff work provided Toomer with direction and a mission at a time in his life when he had neither, but it is clear that this decisive involvement had an intellectual precedent. In spite of the importance of this interesting fact, Gurdjieff remains more a mentor than a catalyst, since Toomer, in the manner of all disciples, sought the respect and approval of his teacher, a teacher whom Marjorie Content (Toomer's second wife) described as "greedy and untrustworthy" but about whom Toomer wrote with affection and respect: "With certain notable exceptions, every one of my main ideas has a Gurdjieff idea as its parent." [24]

The childhood experiences and adult aspirations outlined here were not discarded or forgotten; they found their way into Toomer's fiction. The precocious child who was unimpressed by the authority of adults reminds us of the mischievous Karintha who stoned the cows and beat her dog. Toomer's introspective bouts call to mind the dreamy Esther and the remoteness of the protagonist in "Calling Jesus." Toomer's struggle to master warring sexual urges is a conflict at the center of "Karintha," "Carma," "Fern," and "Avey"; the teenager who found relief from these sexual urges in the theories of Bernarr McFadden would later, when faced with more complex challenges, discover a way out of his malaise through the psychological theories of Gurdjieff. The adult who achieved this release appeared in the later fiction as Hugh Langley and Prince Klondike. Plainly, Toomer's "ideal of Man" and the various experiences that led to its creation remained with him as material and the governing principle not only for *Cane* but also for the major works that emerged from it.

Every writer, as can be seen clearly by the works that have been preserved for our study and pleasure, is bedeviled by certain preoccupations. For James Fenimore Cooper it was the terror and the mystery of the American frontier; for Herman Melville it was all the possibilities of human experience as symbolized by the sea; and for Charles Chesnutt it was the issue of race in a changing American landscape. As we move into the twentieth century, we find William Faulkner struggling to give form to the South's massive, complex legacy; Ernest Hemingway elevating the code of American manhood to the level of ritual; and Ralph Ellison, armed with the best elements from European, American, and African-American cultural traditions, revealing and celebrating the unity and diversity of human experience. As we turn our attention to the contemporary scene, we see many of the same preoccupations reemerging through different voices. Norman Mailer improvises upon Hemingway's best themes; Ernest J. Gaines, with the invaluable perspective of one who knew women like Dilsey in their kitchens, extends, amplifies, and clarifies the conflict of a region that baffled and preoccupied Faulkner; and Alice Walker is redefining, with unbelievable depth and vision, what it means to be black and female in America.

As these examples indicate, all writers are plagued by certain themes, certain concerns. Toomer is no different from the writers I have named and others I have not named. As Kreymborg has stated and as I have attempted to demonstrate, Toomer was essentially a philosopher, a psychologist, a writer preoccupied with an "ideal of Man." This ideal, this interest in man's possibilities and in man's development, is not only at the center of the fiction and verse written during the height of Toomer's involvement with Gurdjieff but is also, disguised in some of the most beautiful stories and poems written in this century, at the center of *Cane*. It is in *Cane*, the work that mystified W. E. B. Du Bois and over which, according to Arna Bontemps, an entire generation of writers "went quietly mad," that we behold the early outline of Toomer's "ideal of Man."[25]

The widely accepted view of *Cane* as the work in which Toomer sought to come to terms with the past and with his own racial makeup is one with which we are all familiar. In this vein, Robert Bone has described *Cane* as Toomer's "reconciliation to the painful history of the black man in America." Similarly, Nathan Huggins has described *Cane* as a "forthright search for the roots of the Negro-self; the son to know the father."[26]

Both Bone and Huggins are correct in emphasizing these elements, for history and ancestral encounters are an integral part of the fabric of Toomer's first book. They are, however, only elements within a larger, more complex pattern. In his own remembrances of Sparta, Georgia, the town that served as the inspiration for *Cane*, Toomer himself seemed to be at cross-purposes with Bone and Huggins. He suggested that his masterpiece was neither about his reconciliation with history nor a search for his forefathers but a farewell to a vanishing folk culture. Recalling his responses to the people and the town of Sparta, Toomer wrote:

The setting was crude in a way, but strangely rich and beautiful. . . . There was a valley of 'Cane,' with smoke-wreaths during the day and mist at night. A family of back-country Negroes had only recently moved into a shack not too far away. They sang. And this was the first time I'd ever heard the folk-songs and spirituals. They were very rich and sad and joyous and beautiful. But I learned that the Negroes of the town objected to them. They called them 'shouting.' They had victrolas and player pianos. So, I realized with deep regret, that the spirituals . . . would be certain to die out. . . . The folk-spirit was walking in to die on the modern desert. That spirit was so beautiful. Its death was so tragic. . . . And this is the feeling I put into 'Cane.'[27]

So Toomer's sorrow at witnessing the dissolution of a fecund African-American folk culture provided him with the inspiration for *Cane*. Bone and Huggins, it seems, are mistaken. But Toomer's own remarks do not provide us with a completely satisfactory framework for an examination of *Cane*, because they do not illuminate, to my satisfaction, such stories as "Karintha," "Esther," "Fern," and many of the stories in the middle section. The differing views of *Cane*—and there are many—only attest to the work's great complexity and to Toomer's ability to speak anagogically.

Aside from *Cane*'s meaning, nothing has puzzled readers more than its form. Although Bone assumes that *Cane* is a novel, I must agree with Turner when he says it is not.[28] Before Toomer added the middle section, I suppose that an interesting case could have been made for *Cane* as an experimental novel. Without the middle section, the work possesses a marvelous kind of symmetry. Without the middle section, it becomes clear that Karintha, Burlow, Louisa, and Kabnis are all members of the same community—Sempter. But Horace Liveright, Toomer's publisher, did not believe that Toomer, with just the Georgia pieces, had enough material for a book and insisted that the work be expanded. Of this Toomer wrote that he had "said all [he] had to say about [Georgia]" and, hence, the "middle section of 'Cane' was thus manufactured."[29] When Toomer added the stories set in Chicago and Washington, D.C., he increased the diversity and depth of *Cane*, but he also altered radically its original design and structure.

I have wondered often if Toomer, before or after adding the middle section, conceived *Cane* as a novel. Nowhere did Toomer refer to his first book as a novel, but the fact that critics are not in agreement on this point forces us to address the important question of form. The novel has been defined by both critics and novelists in a number of ways, but E. M. Forster's general and workable definition will, I believe, suffice. Actually, the definition Forster advanced is not his own but was the invention of the French critic Abel Chevally, who defined the novel as: "a fiction in prose of certain extent."[30] Forster expanded Chevally's tight and marvelously pure definition by adding that a fictional work, if it was to be called a novel, should not be less than fifty thousand words. *Cane* meets Forster's requirement for length, but like its author, the work does not conform completely to established categories. Forster's belief that a novel is always a work of prose I suppose disqualifies *Cane,* for what does one do with all the poems within the work, not to mention Toomer's fluid prose style that is actually, like so much of Whitman's verse, a calculated mixture of poetry and prose?

We could argue, if we were interested in building a case for *Cane* as a novel—which I am not—that Toomer set out to do something that Forster, so rigidly grounded in the English novel of the nineteenth century, never dreamed of doing, that is, to adapt a given form to suit his own purposes. If we allow Toomer a certain latitude, a certain freedom of choice, then the poems of *Cane,* exquisite expressions in verse modeled after the best experiments of the Imagists, become subtexts within a larger text. These relationships would exist, however, even if we were satisfied, as I am, that *Cane* is not a novel.

A critic whose ruminations have done much to illuminate the interconnectedness between the various parts of *Cane* is Bernard Bell, who writes that the poems "elucidate or set the stage or provide a transition between sketches."[31] The poems "November Cotton Flower" and "Reapers" are, as Bell argues, companion pieces to the story "Karintha." Further, "Portrait in Georgia" foreshadows the action of "Blood-Burning Moon," and "Face" recalls the misery of "Becky." Moreover, the poems—this is a point Bell fails to make—increase our appreciation of the mystery and beauty of the region. They heighten our sense of place. We feel this most deeply in poems such as "Georgia Dusk," "Nullo," "Evening Song," and "Song of the Son." The poems of the middle section of *Cane* do not, however, function in quite the same manner. The relationship between the poems and the stories of the middle section is not as clearly defined, for the poems function quite independently of the stories.

Although there is some interrelation between some of the poems and stories, this is not a consistent feature. This fact weakens any argument of *Cane* as a novel, and we come now to an issue that was not emphasized in Forster's definition. This issue is not central to our effort to determine *Cane*'s formal identity, but it is one that we are required at least to clarify. I am thinking now of voice and of point of view. Whose voice do we hear in *Cane*? Who tells the story of Karintha, Avey, and Kabnis? Charles T. Davis has argued quite persuasively that the speaker of "Song of the Son," a poem that celebrates a son's return to the land of his forefathers, is the consciousness that stands behind the varied verbal structures in *Cane*. It is the son's voice or consciousness, Davis claims, that "imposes unity upon the verse, sketches, narratives, and symbolic signs that make up the body of the work."[32] The speaker in the poem is from the North, and as Toomer was interested in contrasts, in analyzing, in Davis's words, "the factors that have shaped the Northern mind," we have therefore a justification for the existence and inclusion of the middle section of *Cane*.

If we accept Davis's argument, then the speaker of "Song of the Son" becomes the "I" in "Becky," "Fern," and also "Avey." But is this true? Davis makes a strong case, and his argument gives the stories and poems a unity that they might not otherwise have. It does not, however, satisfactorily explain certain inconsistencies within the work. We observe, for example, that the sensibility of the narrator in "Avey," the obnoxious, self-centered young man impressed with his own achievements, is markedly different from the more generous, mature sensibility of the narrator of "Fern." And what do we make of the narrative shifts that occur in the middle section? Davis suggests that the increase in the difficulty and complexity of language reflects the difficulty and complexity of northern urban life. I could not agree with him more on this point, but might the shift in narration also suggest the presence of another voice? Although it is probable that *Cane* possesses only one voice, a voice that changes as the setting changes, we plainly do not know the face and name of the speaker, and we can only speculate about the nature of his relationship to the community he describes with so much passion and accuracy.

But in order to call *Cane* a novel, we need something more than a single unifying point of view. We need a conflict that would integrate one story with another, a conflict that would bring the action of the stories and poems to resolution. This we do not have. Although there is some integration in the Georgia sections—for example, David Georgia appears in "Becky" and again in "Blood-Burning Moon," and Barlo appears in "Becky" and in "Esther"—it is minimal. Further, there is no such integration in the middle section or between it and the sections by which it is bound. The complex integration of character and action as well as the achievement of a resolution that would, in its force, evoke past patterns and developments that point toward an orchestrated climax of thought and action are elements absent in *Cane*. These elements, however, are essential to any work we would call unreservedly a novel.

Cane also lacks the structural unity characteristic of the novel. Each story and poem is self-contained; the meaning of one is not dependent upon another. Although the various parts function beautifully as a whole, their structural independence is underscored when we remember that many of them were first published separately in such journals as *Double Dealer*, *Liberator*, *Nomad*, *Broom*, and *S4N*. When these stories and poems first appeared, they were accepted and read as separate, independent, self-contained units of meaning and not as fragments of a larger work. Although *Cane* meets, if we wish to be generous, the general requirements of Forster's definition of the novel, for structural reasons we could never view Toomer's book in quite the same manner as we would such works as Melville's *Moby Dick*, Wharton's *Summer*, or Wright's *Native Son*, works that are, structurally, novels from start to finish.

Cane, then, is not a novel. It is instead a unified series of stories, sketches, poems, and a semidramatic piece that individually addresses a whole range of issues but that collectively gives voice to Toomer's most important theme—human development, or man's lack of and search for wholeness. This theme assumes a fixed form in the book's narrator, who, after describing his mood and condition in "Song of the Son," reveals, in the lyric manner of a poet, his own desire for fusion, for wholeness, as well as the nature and force of the influences (Toomer called them "tensions") that thwart the same hope in the men and women he encounters during his regional odyssey. Further, this theme of a search for wholeness emerges again in Toomer's writings before and after *Cane* in the attitude and function of such characters as Nathan Merilh, Prince Klondike, and Hugh Langley, who are, like Dan Moore of "Box Seat," messianic figures who yearn for connection and who have "come to a sick world to heal it." But *Cane* was Toomer's first successful attempt to give artistic significance to this important theme and to wrestle with the factors that violated and corrupted his "ideal of Man." As Toomer strove to understand the causes for the fragmentation of the modern age, as he strove to reveal to us the value of human life and human development, his concerns in *Cane* were, as in all his works, essentially spiritual. These concerns emerged and crystallized in Toomer's meditations on *Cane*'s design and movement.

In a well-known letter to Waldo Frank, Toomer outlined *Cane*'s complex organization, and he also indicated the existence of an organizing principle that reflected his spiritual and psychological concerns:

> From three angles, 'Cane's' design is a circle. Aesthetically, from simple forms to complex ones, and back to simple forms. Regionally, from the South up to the North, and back into the South again. Or, from North down into the South and then a return North. From the point of view of the spiritual entity behind the work, the curve really starts with 'Bona and Paul' (awakening), plunges into 'Kabnis,' emerges in 'Karintha,' etc., swings upward into 'Theatre' and 'Boxseat' and ends (pauses) in 'Harvest Song.'[33]

In his letter to Frank, Toomer provided us with four different angles from which to decipher *Cane*'s meaning. The first two are rather straightforward and require little, if any, elucidation. The aesthetic and regional approaches are clearly favorites of critics, as a reading of almost any critical essay on *Cane* will demonstrate. The regional shifts that occur in *Cane* are, as Robert B. Stepto shows, a common feature in African-American literature. Stepto cites the slave narratives, Du Bois's *The Souls of Black Folk*, and James Weldon Johnson's *The Autobiography of an Ex-Coloured Man* as examples of works that contain this complexity of movement.[34] Although he did not identify the works of Johnson and Du Bois as models, Toomer, who read widely, was doubtless familiar with them, for the influence of both is apparent in *Cane*.

While Toomer's letter gives us a clue to *Cane*'s structural complexity, it is clear that his concerns were more thematic than structural. In fact, he indicated quite plainly the extent to which his theme determined *Cane*'s form. *Cane* is a circle, a broken circle symbolizing the fragmentation Toomer believed was the condition of modern man, a condition that is his overriding theme. Although Toomer provided us with several different angles from which to approach *Cane*, he said that from "the point of view of the spiritual entity behind the work" —this "spiritual entity" is his theme of human development, of man's lack of and search for wholeness—the "curve really starts" in "Bona and Paul" and ends, or pauses, in "Harvest Song." Toomer's assertion regarding the origin and end of the "curve" corresponds to the arrangement of materials in the work, for "Harvest Song" does follow, in the path of the curve, "Bona and Paul." This beguiling structural arrangement indicates the importance of theme to Toomer. Indeed, it establishes in this particular instance the interdependency of theme and structure.

Toomer's thoughts on form and the assumptions that dictate and inform it, contrary to Northrop Frye, possess more than just a "peculiar interest," but a "peculiar authority."[35] Toomer's remarks possess such authority for the simple reason that we, during our first reading of the work, even if we were interested in or aware of what Toomer calls the "spiritual entity behind the work," would not have begun with "Bona and Paul," as Toomer's remarks suggest we should, but with "Karintha." Further, unaware of the internal design, we would not have concluded our reading of the work with "Harvest Song," but with "Kabnis."

Toomer's stance in the letter was a daring one, for he suggested several possible approaches to his first book; but the work itself to some extent belies Toomer's outline. Although one may object to this effort to lead the reader down a particular critical path, it is important to remember that these instructions do not reside within the work but revolve around it. They are not essential to our interpretive task, and we may use or discard them in accordance with our tastes and objectives. But it is probable that we, after several close readings, would have discovered the interrelationships Toomer outlined in his letter. Toomer no doubt expected us to make this discovery, and this expectation only increases the power and importance of his words to Frank.

Given the thematic importance Toomer attached to the third circle, the obvious question is, why does *Cane* begin with "Karintha" and end with "Kabnis," not begin with "Bona and Paul" and end with "Harvest Song"? To open and close *Cane* in this manner would destroy, I believe, the subtle interrelationship based upon circles. The ambiguity the current arrangement of materials creates would be lost. Toomer obviously recognized this and preserved the original order of the different parts of *Cane*.

Because I see *Cane* as essentially a spiritual work, as an attempt by a philosopher-poet preoccupied with an "ideal of Man" to focus our wandering attention upon the causes of our psychological and spiritual fragmentation, I will, like Davis, begin my analysis of the stories at the start of the "curve." I choose to begin here for several reasons. First, with the exception of Davis every critic has begun his or her analysis of Toomer's masterpiece with "Karintha," and although this is certainly a logical point of departure, I prefer an atypical approach because it spares me and the reader the tedium of beginning at what *appears* to be the beginning. Second, I can think of no other literary work in which it is possible to begin one's ruminations in the middle, and frankly I find the possibilities of interpretation and discovery which this approach affords too intriguing to ignore. Third, Toomer himself certainly invited such a radical reading of *Cane* and to some extent implied—"the curve really starts with 'Bona and Paul' " —that if one was interested in the "spiritual entity behind the work" it might actually be more fruitful to begin with his story of "awakening." Finally, beginning at the start of the "curve," that is, with "Bona and Paul," underscores the brilliant balance and interdependency between form and theme, since the broken circle is both *Cane*'s design and Toomer's metaphor for the psychic and spiritual condition of his age and our own.

As I trace the emergence of the curve from "Bona and Paul" to its dramatic descent in "Harvest Song," my readings of the various parts of *Cane* will be amplified by excerpts from *Essentials* (1931), Toomer's slim but dense volume of definitions and aphorisms.[36] *Essentials* is the abstract, quintessential expression of concerns and themes to which Toomer gave a human face and form not only in *Cane* but also in the works that followed it. *Cane* contains Toomer's fully developed meditations on the "tensions," that is, the powerful, disruptive influences that flow from "artificial oppositions, . . . unnatural prejudices, preferences, mutual antagonisms, . . . [as well as] class and caste lines." In Toomer's view, these "tensions" eventuate in "destructive crises," or, to restate this conclusion in language that reveals the thematic concerns and philosophical assumptions of Toomer's canon, they thwart our sense of wholeness.[37] Indeed, they are the principal causes of our sense of fragmentation as well as our growing sense of alienation in this violent and technological age.

Chicago's American College of Physical Training, where Toomer was enrolled as a student during the winter of 1916, is the setting for "Bona and Paul." The awakening that takes place in this story occurs within Paul Johnson, a handsome, athletic youth, who, finding himself at a nightclub called the Crimson Gardens, comes into a racial awareness that transforms his self-conception, an awareness that gives form and vigor to a life very much in need of these things. The catalyst that brings Paul to the knowledge of himself as a black man of beauty and potential is Bona Hale, a rather complex southern beauty who also undergoes an awakening of sorts, but with vastly different consequences.

Bona is attracted to Paul: "The dance of his blue-trousered limbs thrills her."[38] But her attraction is not without tension, ambivalence, and a certain grotesqueness. Dazzled by the precision and sensuality of Paul's movements as he goes through the paces of a basketball drill, Bona struggles with the truth of her attraction: "He is a harvest moon. He is an autumn leaf. He is a nigger. . . . That's why I love" (134–35). The truth, however, is too much for Bona, and she cannot complete the sentence that would give clarity and exactness to her thoughts and feelings. Bona can neither admit, even to herself, that she is attracted to Paul because he is black, nor is she able to transcend a tradition that defines and limits an individual on the basis of race. Although Bona is ambivalent about Paul, she is not completely paralyzed, and through mutual friends, she provides Paul with incontestable proof of her interest in him—she arranges a date.

Paul is aware of Bona's interest. He did not miss the point of her aggressive, petulant behavior on the basketball court, and, as the following passage indicates, he is not without some feelings for her as well:

Paul is in his room of two windows. . . . Bona is one window. One window Paul. . . . Paul follows the sun to a pine-matted hillock in Georgia. He sees the slanting roofs of gray unpainted cabins tinted lavender. A Negress chants a lullaby beneath the mate-eyes of a southern planter. Her breasts are ample for the suckling of a song. She weans it, and sends

it, curiously weaving, among lush melodies of cane and corn. Paul follows the sun into himself in Chicago. He is at Bona's window. With his
own glow he looks through a dark pane. (137–38)

This is a curious and dense passage. In it we find not only evidence of
Paul's interest in Bona, but we realize the gulf that separates them—
"Bona is one window. One window Paul." We also find confirmation
of Paul's regional and racial origins. We discover that Paul, as he "follows the sun to a pine-matted hillock in Georgia," is, like Bona, a
southerner. We also learn that Paul, as he listens to a "Negress [chant]
a lullaby beneath the mate-eyes of a southern planter," is aware of the
racial difference that separates him from Bona. And we are also given,
however cryptically, omens that adumbrate the story's denouement,
for as Paul comes to accept his ancestry, his "glow," he will find Bona
to be distant and then gone—"a dark pane."

As Paul comes to terms with the truth of his life, as he moves
closer to awakening, he understands better the complexity of Bona's
attraction. On their first and last date, Bona is "nervous, and slightly
afraid"; Paul is "critical." Bona's confidence rises and falls. She insists
that Paul "tell her something about himself," but the request is dis-
ingenuous, because she fears what Paul might really tell her—that
he is black. She eschews the truth and clings instead to half-truths
and labels: "Colored; cold. Wrong somewhere" (144). "We assume,"
as Toomer wrote in *Essentials*, "that because we have the label we have
the understanding" (lxi). This is certainly Bona's view of the world,
not to mention her chief stumbling block in her relationship with Paul.
Bona assumes that she understands Paul because she has labeled him
"colored," but, as we shall see, certain events prove her wrong. Paul's
understanding of himself is circumscribed neither by Bona's racist,
exotic fantasies nor by the hostility and confusion he encounters at
the Crimson Gardens. These competing, potentially dehumanizing
attitudes do not thwart Paul's awakening but induce it.

When Bona and Paul arrive at the Crimson Gardens, the stares of
the crowd increase Paul's awareness of race, and they deepen the
sense of pride he has begun to feel about himself and the physical
differences that separate him from others: "Suddenly he knew that
people saw, not attractiveness in his dark skin, but difference. Their
stares, giving him to himself, filled something long empty within him,

and were like green blades sprouting in his consciousness. There was fullness, and strength and peace about it all. He saw himself, cloudy, but real" (145). All the action of the story has led us to this moment. In a hostile, almost menacing, environment, Paul sprouts new life. Unlike Chesnutt's John Warwick who seeks to evade his mixed ancestry and Faulkner's Joe Christmas who is destroyed by it, Paul is transformed and strengthened by his bloodlines. He plucks confidence and resolve out of the hateful gazes of the whites at the Crimson Gardens. Their contempt, ironically, brings him "into life," into an appreciative awareness of his mixed ancestry, into manhood. Paul "awakens," to use Toomer's verb, to himself and to life's possibilities, and this new knowledge separates him from the people around him in the same manner as his dark skin. Paul now feels connected with himself. He can now assert, like the narrator of Ellison's *Invisible Man:* "I yam what I am." [39] It is in this new spirit of confidence, inner strength, and pride that Paul leaves the Crimson Gardens with Bona.

As Paul leaves the club, he exchanges glances with the black doorman. He sees presumption and perhaps even disdain in the doorman's "knowing" eyes and stops to disabuse him:

> Youre wrong.
>   Yassur.
>   Brother, youre wrong.
>   I came back to tell you, to shake your hand, and tell you that you are wrong. That something beautiful is going to happen. . . . That I came into the Gardens, into life in the Gardens with one whom I did not know. . . . I came back to tell you, brother, that white faces are petals of roses. . . . That I am going out and know her whom I brought here with me to these gardens. (152–53)

This passage is particularly important because within it Toomer provides us with proof of Paul's growth and maturity, of his awakening. It is significant that during the course of Paul's exchange with the doorman he addresses the man as brother. The salutation brings them closer together and bridges the gap created by Paul's fair skin and the doorman's assumptions about his racial position. The doorman is forced to confront the error in his thinking, because he assumes that Paul is passing for white. Paul, firmly but gently, assures the doorman that he is mistaken. After shaking hands with the doorman, a gesture that is proof of his sincerity, Paul returns to the spot where he left Bona. But he finds her gone.

Why does Bona leave? It seems that she is more at home with ambiguity than with the truth. Paul's exchange with the doorman provides Bona with indisputable proof of his mixed ancestry, of his blackness, and, equally important, proof of his refusal to deny it. Paul's uncompromising stance changes everything. Bona abandons him because she is bound completely to a tradition that forbids a white woman to feel anything but revulsion and superiority for black men and that scornfully terms intimacy between blacks and whites as miscegenation.

As stated earlier, the awakening that occurs in "Bona and Paul" possesses a different meaning for each protagonist. Bona discovers that she cannot shake off the well-defined, controlling code of her southern upbringing. Conversely, Paul discovers a new pride in his blackness, a new faith in himself and in life's possibilities. By accepting and affirming the facts of his ancestry, Paul takes the first steps toward wholeness.

In this story of awakening, Toomer suggests that the first step toward wholeness—and here I am thinking of his "ideal of Man"— is the complete and total acceptance of self. Without this unequivocal acceptance and the capacity to affirm all aspects of the self, the possibility of wholeness and of growth of any kind is impossible. Paul's acceptance and affirmation of self is total, and at the story's conclusion we feel that his new racial consciousness has deepened, broadened, and enriched his life.

As we "plunge," to use Toomer's verb, into "Kabnis," the long semi-dramatic piece that is the third section of *Cane,* and look ahead to its conclusion, we can assert with some confidence that Ralph Kabnis shares the psychological and spiritual achievement of Paul Johnson. "Kabnis" extends Paul's dilemma, as Davis writes, beyond the realm of race into history. Toomer would have us understand that an individual is not whole until he accepts and affirms the facts of his ancestry and embraces the historical forces that give them meaning and resonance. This is the dilemma, the agony, and the drama of "Kabnis."

Ralph Kabnis, "an atom of dust in agony on a hillside," is the "promise of a soil-soaked beauty; uprooted, thinning out." He is a man detached from history, "suspended a few feet above the soil whose touch would resurrect him" (191). Kabnis is a northerner with literary pretensions who has come south to teach in a black school. The school is located in the rural, fictitious town of Sempter, Georgia, and it resembles Sparta Agricultural and Industrial Institute where Toomer was acting principal in 1921. Kabnis is on the faculty for what seems only a brief period of time when he is roundly dismissed by a Mr. Hanby, the school's headmaster. Kabnis's misdeeds are not enumerated, but we assume, based upon Hanby's scorching, Booker T. Washington–like dismissal, that his behavior was less than exemplary. After his dismissal, Kabnis is taken in by Fred Halsey, a blacksmith who inspires our respect, not only because he comes to the aid of Kabnis and in the process reduces the pretentious Hanby to blathering but also because he is a strong, proud man who appears to have made the most of extremely discouraging circumstances.

Unfortunately, the move to Halsey's home does not help Kabnis. He is as inept at blacksmithing as he is at teaching. His ineptitude becomes painfully apparent when Toomer compares Kabnis to Halsey as the two move about Halsey's workshop: "Halsey, wonderfully himself in his work overalls, stands in the doorway and gazes up the street, expectantly. . . . Kabnis passes the window and stoops to get in under Halsey's arm. He is awkward and ludicrous, like a schoolboy in his big brother's new overalls" (196). Kabnis is quite unable to complete even the simplest tasks. When asked to repair a damaged handle for Ramsay, a white customer, he is sadly inadequate: "Kabnis burns red. The back of his neck stings him beneath his collar. He feels stifled. Through Ramsay, the whole white South weighs down upon him. The pressure is terrific. He sweats under the arms. Chill beads run down his body. His brows concentrate upon the handle as though his own life was staked upon the perfect shaving of it. He begins to out and out botch the job" (201–2).

But we did not expect a change in setting to effect a change in Kabnis. Far more than that is needed. As Kabnis says to Carrie K., Halsey's sister, who helps him up from the floor after an evening of booze and abusive talk: "But twont do t lift me bodily. You dont understand. But its th soul of me that needs th risin" (234). It is indeed the soul of Kabnis that needs the "risin"; it is his spirit that so badly needs healing and renewal. And the restoratives—Lewis, Carrie K., Father John—

who might induce this spiritual healing and renewal are all around Kabnis, but he, in his great pain and vanity, scorns and rejects them.

But even as Kabnis rejects help, he is aware of the capacity and desire of others to give it. For example, Kabnis senses that Lewis, a northern black whose confident and critical manner has inspired fear and envy in Sempter's black community, can give Kabnis's life the meaning and direction it so desperately needs: "There is a swift intuitive interchange of consciousness. Kabnis has a sudden need to rush into the arms of this man. His eyes call, 'Brother' " (191–92). But in the same instant Kabnis rejects Lewis. Unable to admit he needs help and anxious to conceal his confusion and vulnerability, he mocks Lewis: "And then a savage, cynical twistabout within him mocks his impulse and strengthens him to repulse Lewis. His lips curl cruelly. His eyes laugh" (192).

We are not surprised at Kabnis's disdain for Lewis. Lewis is a mirror image of Kabnis, "what a stronger Kabnis might have been," and as such he throws Kabnis's pathetic condition into even greater relief. Curiously, Lewis is aware of this bond that connects him to the confused, disgruntled Kabnis. Lewis articulates, at Halsey's behest, the source and nature of Kabnis's misery: "Life has already told him more than he is capable of knowing. It has given him in excess of what he can receive. I have been offered. Stuff in his stomach curdled, and he vomited me" (200). Plainly, Lewis is sensitive to Kabnis's suffering and in his own way reaches out to him. Lewis understands the "form" that is "burned int [Kabnis's] soul," the "twisted awful thing that crept in from a dream, a godam nightmare, an wont stay still unless" Kabnis feeds it (224). The "twisted awful thing" is history, the history of African-Americans, a history that reveals the systematic efforts by European-Americans to twist and distort the humanity of African-Americans for economic and political gain. "History begins," wrote William Carlos Williams, "with murder and enslavement, not with discovery." [40] Until Kabnis embraces this dark side of history and finds his place in it, the "form" will continue to torture and devour him.

It is in Lewis's attraction to Father John, who is described as the "symbol, flesh, and spirit of the past" (217), that Kabnis is offered a way out of his misery. Unlike Lewis, Kabnis spurns his historical connection to Father John and vehemently denies the possibility of one: "An besides, he aint my past. My ancestors were Southern blue-bloods" (217). Lewis, possibly amused by and expecting this denial, completes Kabnis's sentence by adding, "And black." Though Kabnis asserts that "there is not much difference between blue and black," Lewis, growing impatient with Kabnis's refusal to accept the facts of history, counters: "Enough to draw a denial from you. Cant hold them, can you? Master; slave. Soil; and the overarching heavens. Dusk; dawn. They fight and bastardize you" (218). Lewis's honesty and strength are at this juncture of no use to Kabnis. He rejects Lewis and, for the moment, seeks refuge from history in sarcasm, hedonism, and illusions of superiority.

But Kabnis cannot escape the past. It stands before him in the figure of Father John and demands full acceptance. The morning after the party at Halsey's, Kabnis, with all the rage and pain within him, verbally assails Father John. Just at the moment when Kabnis appears to have emptied himself of all his hostilities, Carrie K. enters with Father John's breakfast. Carrie K. is "lovely in her fresh energy of the morning, in the calm untested confidence and nascent maternity which rise from the purpose of her present mission" (233). Carrie K.'s mission is not just to feed Father John but also to bring Kabnis some relief from his suffering. Kabnis, driven to distraction over Father John's interpretation of sin, continues to insult and abuse the old man. At this point Carrie K., shocked at Kabnis's behavior, administers to his pain: "She turns him to her and takes his hot cheeks in her firm cool hands. Her palms draw the fever out. With its passing, Kabnis crumples. He sinks to his knees before her, ashamed, exhausted. His eyes squeeze tight. Carrie presses his face tenderly against her. The suffocation of her fresh starched dress feels good to him" (238). For the moment Carrie K. provides Kabnis with some relief from his suffering by "drawing the fever out." The "fever," a metaphor for the fears, illusions, and denials that have been an unending source of conflict for Kabnis, has left him. With its passing he collapses at the feet of Carrie K., exhausted and ashamed.

In *Essentials* Toomer tells us that "Shame of a weakness implies the presence of a strength" (ii). It is at the point in Toomer's drama when Kabnis is ashamed that we witness this belief in action. We see the expression of Kabnis's new strength not only in the shame he feels before Carrie K. but, more important, in the symbolic removal of his robe. In the shedding of the robe, Kabnis casts off the lies, illusions, and subterfuges he has employed all his life as a shield against the truth and the meaning of the past. Kabnis has come through his ordeal with history whole and sane. In celebration, Toomer concludes his drama on a hopeful, confident note: "Outside, the sun arises from its cradle in the tree-tops of the forest. Shadows of pines are dreams the sun shakes from its eyes. The sun arises. Gold-glowing child, it steps into the sky and sends a birth-song slanting down gray dust streets and sleepy windows of the southern town" (239). It appears that Kabnis, purged of his illusions, can now move forward. The "birth-song" that the sun sends "slanting" down the streets of the town is Kabnis's birth-song, a song that carries a message of his passage from a consciousness at odds with history and the past to one that finds its strength and being in both.

In "Bona and Paul" and "Kabnis," Toomer suggests that racial and historical awareness is essential to our growth and development, to our sense of wholeness, and that without it we exist at only the most primitive level. But the refusal to accept the facts of history and one's personal and racial past is not the only force, or "tension," as Toomer called it, that may undermine one's sense of wholeness.[41] In "Karintha," for example, that force, or tension, is sex.

Another aphorism from *Essentials* helps us to understand better Toomer's aim in "Karintha." Approaching sex and human relationships from a philosophical point of view, Toomer writes: "We are stimulators, not satisfyers" (xxix). This, in fine, is the tragedy of the beautiful Karintha. She is not a "stimulator," because her great intellectual and spiritual potentialities are undeveloped and ignored. Karintha is reduced to the role of "satisfyer," to the role of concubine. Toomer writes that Karintha, even as a child, was pursued by the young and old men of Sempter: "Men had always wanted her. . . . Old men rode her hobby-horse upon their knees. Young men danced with her at frolics when they should have been dancing with their grownup girls. God grant us youth, secretly prayed the old men. The young fellows counted the time to pass before she would be old enough to mate with them. This interest of the male, who wishes to ripen a growing thing too soon, could mean no good to her" (1). Karintha suffered as a consequence of this "interest of the male . . . to ripen a growing thing too soon." The opening paragraph of "Karintha" sets the mood of the story and prepares us for the violation we sense is inevitable.

In temperament and outlook, Karintha is different from the adults and other children in Sempter. She is "a wild flash that told the other folks just what it was to live" (1). Toomer tells us that "her sudden darting past you was a bit of vivid color" and that her "running was a whir" (2). Because of her beauty, Karintha is regarded as special by the townspeople, and this generous attitude leads to indulgences and privileges the other children in the town never enjoy. Although she "stoned the cows, and beat her dog, and fought the other children," she is never punished. Even the preacher, struck by her beauty, looks with favor upon her mischief and "told himself that she was as innocently lovely as a November cotton flower" (2).

We search in vain for a logical explanation that would shed some light upon the community's refusal to impose upon Karintha accepted standards of conduct. Clearly, her extraordinary beauty is a factor in the community's laxity, but perhaps the people of Sempter also realize that Karintha possesses something more precious than mere external beauty—a rare vitality and force that they, cast from a different mold, do not possess. It is Karintha's life force, the "flash," "color," and "whir," that increases her attractiveness to the men, and it is her life force that they, in a fever to possess her body, trample upon and violate.

As Karintha grows older, her predicament worsens. The young and old men continue to exploit her, and she, out of weakness, fear, habit, or desire—we do not know which—continues to indulge them. The inevitable soon occurs. Karintha, after several marriages, gives birth to a child and leaves it to die on "a bed of pine-needles in the forest." We are saddened but not surprised by the indifference Karintha feels for the new life she brought into the world. She does not feel a sense of responsibility toward her child and remains oblivious, so it seems, to any biological or spiritual bond. Karintha feels nothing for the child she leaves to die in the forest, because experience has taught her that life, particularly female life, is neither sacred nor meaningful.

Toomer tells us in the last paragraph of this story that the soul of Karintha "was a growing thing ripened too soon" (4). Plainly, Karintha's premature initiation into certain adult pleasures was harmful to her development. Perceived as nothing more than an object of sexual desire and gratification, "a satisfyer," Karintha lives a life that is fragmented and incomplete. She lives only to give pleasure; though she is beautiful, her life is without beauty. The perception of women as "satisfyers" is a recurring concern of Toomer, and it reemerges with equal force and urgency in "Fern" and "Avey."

"Becky" gives fictional significance to another "tension" and an old taboo of the South: miscegenation. As Toomer wrote in *Essentials;* "Races are real; but, to men, races are prejudices" (xxxv). Because races inspire fear and prejudices and lead to the creation of bizarre, life-threatening codes of behavior, because races are not accepted for what they are—real and interesting facts that are proof of the diversity and range of human types—because children of mixed ancestry can never be white, Becky is known in Sempter as the "white woman who had two Negro sons." The townspeople, both black and white, outraged by what they regard as Becky's reckless, illogical behavior, have cast her out. It is terrible enough to have a child out of wedlock, as we know from reading the *Scarlet Letter,* but for a white woman to bear two such children by a black man in a southern town is, judging from the reactions of Becky's neighbors, an outrageous and unforgivable offense. For the people of Sempter, such indiscretions defy reason and represent a threat to the moral order by which they live and judge everyone.

But Becky, like Hester Prynne, exhibits remarkable strength as she endures the bigotry of the town.[42] She is spared the pillory and the wearing of the scarlet letter—in her case it would be "M" for miscegenation—but, like Hester, she meets her tragic end without revealing the patrimony of her sons. But Sempter, like Hester's Boston, at least initially, does not turn its back on Becky. When word spreads through the town that Becky has given birth to the first boy, John Stone, a white landowner and the father of Bob Stone, whose interracial drama is played out with disastrous consequences in "Blood-Burning Moon," has a neighbor build a cabin for her. The rest of the people in town, in their own way, follow Stone's example: "Folks from the town took turns, unknown, of course, to each other, in bringing corn and meat and sweet potatoes. Even sometimes snuff" (10). Old David Georgia, grinding cane and boiling syrup, never goes her way without some sugar sap.

It seems that the people of Sempter, realizing that they themselves are not without sin and remembering also that this is not the first time a child was born of black and white parents, secretly continue to bring Becky food and anything else she might need. But when Becky's first boy is seen carrying an infant, the helping hand the town had extended, however sheepishly, is withdrawn.

Toomer tells us that the two boys, raised with the knowledge of their difference, grow "sullen and cunning." Resenting deeply their pariah status, they are often violent. In a fusillade of bullets, blood, and curses, the boys, no longer able to endure the judgment of the town, leave their mother and are never heard from again. Shortly after their departure, the townspeople, apparently concerned about Becky's well-being, resume taking food to the cabin, but their concern, if it can be called that, is short-lived: "They quit it soon because they had a fear. Becky if dead might be a hant, and if alive—it took some nerve even to mention it" (11). Although the townspeople are superstitious, it is not fear of the supernatural that forces them to cast Becky out a third time but rage at the possibility that she might again be pregnant. Curiously, a supernatural event puts Sempter and Becky out of their miseries. A "ghost train" passing by Becky's cabin weakens the foundation of the chimney, and the chimney crashes down, crushing Becky.

"Becky" is a strange, sad story of bigotry and fear. The peculiar force and success of this story repose upon the fact that Becky, even when alive, is largely a phantom. We are neither introduced to Becky, nor are we given a physical description of her. As Houston A. Baker, Jr., perceptively explains, Becky "is primarily a psychological presence to whom the community pays an ironical homage: a spectral representation of the southern miscegenatory impulse".[43] Becky's predicament is a reminder of things that are better left unsaid and unseen. Toomer, keenly aware of the South's (and the nation's) inability to deal truthfully with certain human facts, replicates this historical blindness by presenting the story's heroine as an abstraction, as a vague gnawing fear. From the first word of the story to the last, Becky is as remote and as immediate as the conflict that frames the tale.

Following the curve of the spiritual entity that started in "Bona and Paul," we continue in our rise upward to "Carma." Carma's tale, as Toomer tells us, "is the crudest melodrama" (18). Again, unrestrained sexuality is Toomer's subject, but here we discover a novel and subtle variation in his treatment of it. Unlike Karintha, Carma, who is as "strong as any man. Stronger," is not victimized by her suitors and

appears to exercise more control over her relationships. As a consequence, Carma seems not to suffer to the degree that Karintha does,
because she possesses a physical strength that functions as a buffer
against the advances of unwelcome suitors.

The concerns Toomer deemed most important in "Carma" are revealed through the story's title. I have indicated already the depth of
Toomer's interest in Eastern teachings, and in "Carma" he returned
to them as a storyteller. With the ancient Hindu belief of karma as
his frame of reference, Toomer examined the effects of adultery upon
a marriage. It should be noted that *karma* is a Buddhist term that
translates as deed or act. Since melodrama is a genre characterized
by sensational and thrilling actions (here I am thinking of Carma's
adultery and feigned suicide), it seems that Toomer succeeded in com-
bining the salient features of a literary genre with the expression of a
philosophical concept.

Because Carma does not exercise *samvara*, or restraint, the force generated by her actions is negative. The law governing deeds is patent
and inflexible—negative actions beget negative effects. Carma's infi-
delity leads to bloodshed, disorder, and the sentencing of her husband
Bane, whose name is a clue to the only possible outcome of the story,
to hard labor on the chain gang.

Toomer ends his story with a question that is really a kind of plea
for understanding: "Should she not take others, this Carma, strong as
a man, whose tale as I have told it is the crudest melodrama?" (20). The
narrator is clearly sympathetic to Carma's plight. He seems to ask that
we not look unfeelingly upon Carma's predicament, for her decision
to take lovers, in view of her lusty nature and Bane's long absences,
seems understandable. Although each reader will judge Carma differ-
ently, it is clear that she neither exhibits, during the crisis with Bane or
during the events that precipitate it, the self-control that we assume is
a feature of her great physical strength. Unfortunately, Carma is weak
at the precise moment when she should be strong. But we do not
despise Carma for her weakness, because Toomer, without assuming
the indignant air of an offended moralist, teaches us that it is one thing
to be physically strong and quite another to be spiritually so.

Of all the stories in *Cane*, "Fern" is easily the most memorable, for
it possesses a mystery and power not found in the others. A haunting
tale of a beautiful woman possessing prodigious, but thwarted, spiri-

tual powers, "Fern" in its opening paragraph contains some of the best writing in *Cane*. In simple, elegant, and evocative language, Toomer describes a woman who functions as both a concubine and a virgin: "Face flowed into her eyes. Flowed in soft cream foam and plaintive ripples. . . . The soft suggestion of down slightly darkened, like the shadow of a bird's wing might, the creamy brown color of her upper lip. . . . Her nose was aquiline, Semitic. If you have heard a Jewish cantor sing, if he has touched you and made your own sorrow seem trivial when compared with his, you will know my feelings when I follow the curves of her profile, like mobile rivers, to their common delta" (24). Toomer's description of Fern suggests that she is of mixed ancestry, but this is not, we discover, the source of her misery. In this story, as in "Bona and Paul," Toomer spares us the absurd portrayal of the mulatto as a tortured and tragic figure, a common feature in much of the literature of the South, and suggests instead that Fern's suffering springs from a different source.[44]

Like Karintha, Fern is a "satisfyer," but she is one who, in spite of the sexual exploitation, exercises unusual power over her lovers. Toomer writes that men "were everlastingly bringing [Fern] their bodies" but "got no joy from it" (25). After evenings with Fern, the men, "(quite unlike their hit and run with other girls), felt as though it would take them a lifetime to fulfill an obligation which they could find no name for. They became attached to her, and hungered after finding the barest trace of what she might desire" (25). Lust, in the case of the men who become involved with Fern, has strange and surprising consequences. The men, out of a feeling of guilt, passion, love, possessiveness, we do not know which, feel bound to Fern. Toomer suggests that these men hope that they will one day return in equal measure what they took—to fill, with a gift or a "magnificent something," the space in Fern's soul "left vacant by the bestowal of their bodies" (29).

The narrator tells us that "nothing ever came to Fern," and, like the other men in the town, he too succumbs to her irresistible powers (33). In doing so he becomes not only a candidate for a beating at the hands of the men "who'd set themselves up to protect" Fern, but, in a surprising break in the narrative pattern, he becomes a character in a story of his own telling (32–33). Some have argued strongly against such narrative shifts, insisting that "intimacy is gained at the expense of illusion and nobility."[45] But in "Fern" the narrator's move from the role of observer to that of participant does not produce these results. Toomer uses the device to good effect, for it brings the narrator closer to the community he describes and permits him to engage the reader in a dialogue, which in turn narrows the distance between the reader and the narrator, giving the reader the sense that he or she is a participant in the story's unfolding drama.

The story's ending comes as no surprise. The narrator and the men of Sempter cannot give Fern what she needs; they are not a means, a vehicle, to her fulfillment but the chief cause of her profound spiritual malaise. In their helplessness, the narrator and the other men of Sempter remind us of John Hardy and Doctor Reefy in Sherwood Anderson's *Winesburg, Ohio*, men who stand as simpletons before the complex psychological and spiritual needs of the woman whom they love but whom they cannot help or understand. The sense of sadness that permeates Toomer's story stems in part from the realization that Fern, endowed with the capacity to inspire change in the lives of the men who surround her, cannot harness her own tremendous physical and spiritual resources to bring about similar changes in her own life.

As we continue to follow the path of the spiritual entity originating in "Bona and Paul," we come now to "Esther." Esther Crane possesses neither the beauty of Karintha and Fern nor the strength of Carma. What she does possess in ample measure is an imagination so active and powerful that it has supplanted the life and rhythm of actual events. Esther is a dreamer, a woman who finds the world of phantoms more desirable than the world of the flesh and more real than the goods that line the shelves of her father's store. Esther's condition is one that Toomer remonstrates against in *Essentials*, where he writes, "We do not have states of being; we have states of dreaming" (lv). Esther is not rooted in the spirit of her context, nor is she a self-conscious participant in even the most marginal community activity. This sense of connection and awareness is at the core of what Toomer terms "states of being," or, to return to his principal theme and preoccupation in *Cane*, a sense of wholeness. Esther's somnambulistic states are an obstruction to this sense of wholeness, and Toomer, as he has in other parts of *Cane*, in "Esther" tenders us yet another example of what we must struggle against to achieve it.

The only person in Sempter who possesses sufficient strength and presence to penetrate the imaginary wall Esther has erected against the boredom and narrowness of town life is King Barlo. We first meet King Barlo in "Becky"; he is the preacher who manages to overcome his fear of the supernatural long enough to place his Bible on Becky's grave of bricks. Barlo is a handsome man of powerful build, whose popularity is perceived as a threat to the authority of Sempter's black and white leaders. Esther's first memories of Barlo originate in childhood. Walking from her home to her father's store, she encounters Barlo on his knees in the town square in the grip of some fantastic vision. Although Barlo's vision of an African enslaved by "white-ant biddies" has some relevance for Esther, at the time she is far too young to grasp its meaning and importance. Unbeknownst to Barlo, his inspired preaching makes a tremendous impact upon Esther, and she carries with her the memory of that experience for eighteen years. Describing the impression Barlo made upon Esther's developing mind, Toomer writes: "He left his image indelibly upon the mind of Esther. He became the starting point of the only living patterns that her mind was to know" (40).

As Esther grows into womanhood, she cherishes the memory of Barlo, and in her dreams of love and sex, she gives birth to his "black, singed, woolly, tobacco-juice baby" (41). Although Esther attracts the attention of a few men in town and others who pass through it, she does not form relationships with any of them. It seems that Esther, lacking spirit and sophistication, cannot hold these men, but it also seems that she prefers her imaginary life with Barlo to the company of these occasional suitors. When Barlo's image loses its luster for want of actual contact with him, Esther "spices it by telling herself his glories" (42). She soon decides that she is in love with Barlo and vows to declare her love to him when he returns to Sempter.

When Barlo returns to town a rich man from speculating in the cotton industry, Esther gathers up her courage to call on him, with the expectation of bringing her dreams of marriage and childbearing to fruition. Although the intoxicated Barlo is flattered by her boldness and slightly interested in her proposal, Esther, struck by the thought that "conception with a drunken man must be a mighty sin," leaves Barlo's apartment and returns home, oblivious to the "jeers and hoots" that follow her down the stairs and into the street (48).

In this story of loneliness and sexual frustration, Toomer explores the dangers and pitfalls of a dreamer's rejection of the real world as well as the failure of dreams, when not guided by reason, pragmatism, and effort, to engender in us the sense of purpose and possibility that marks the difference between living and merely existing. Like Anderson's Alice Hindman, Flaubert's Madame Bovary, and Austin's Emma Woodhouse, Esther chooses illusion over reality. Unable or unwilling to view the world in realistic terms, Esther, spurned by Barlo, retreats further and further into an imaginary world of her own making.

"Blood-Burning Moon" is the last story in the first section of *Cane*. Just as we are about to leave the South, Toomer, by returning to an issue examined in "Becky," seems determined that we should not leave the region without becoming acquainted with some of its most brutal and horrifying features. In "Blood-Burning Moon," Toomer, without sensationalism and false sentiment, details the fury, waste, and chaos that unfold when race collides with love and the supernatural.

In this story Toomer creates a situation that is doomed from the start. A black woman living in a southern town is being courted by two men, one black, the other white. As we might expect, this love triangle is fraught with tension at every angle. Louisa is the first angle of this triangle of passion and race. Louisa is a beautiful woman; her body and voice are equivalent to the land and the wind: "Her skin was the color of oak leaves on young trees in fall. Her breasts, firm and up-pointed like ripe acorns. And her singing had the low murmur of winds in fig trees" (51). Louisa, as these lines suggest, is a woman of remarkable beauty. Like Karintha's and Fern's, her beauty is both a bane and a blessing.

As Louisa returns home from her day's work, she thinks of Tom Burwell, her black suitor whom the town calls Big Boy, and of Bob Stone, her white suitor and a descendant of slaveholders and cotton kings. Louisa feels affection for both men, but we sense that Tom's chances of winning Louisa's heart are greater. As Louisa thinks of Tom, his "black balanced and pulled against the white of Stone" (52). Louisa is not unaware of her ambivalence toward Bob or of the extreme difficulty of her situation, but she mistakenly believes that she can continue to see both men and avoid the dangerous confrontation she senses is inevitable: "To meet Bob in the Canebrake, as she was going to do an hour or so later, was nothing new. And Tom's proposal which she felt on its way to her could be indefinitely put off. Separately, there was no unusual significance to either one. But for some reason, they jumbled when her eyes gazed vacantly at the rising moon" (52). Louisa senses that the situation cannot continue to remain unresolved, but she does nothing to facilitate or achieve closure. The difficulty posed by her relationships with Bob and Tom requires Louisa to take action of some kind, but she is helpless before the currents of race, gender, and history. The moon, evil and "blood-burning," is an omen forecasting a violent resolution.

Tom has heard stories concerning Louisa's relationship with Bob, but until now he has dismissed them as gossip. In his great confidence and infatuation, he does not perceive Bob as a rival. While visiting Old David Georgia, Will Manning laughingly suggests that Louisa is Bob's girl. A scuffle ensues, but Manning and his friends, aware of Tom's facility with his knife, decide that it is not in their best interest to press the matter further. Manning's courage to speak so freely of Louisa and Bob confirms Tom's worst suspicions. As Tom sets out to find Louisa, he senses the meaning and possible danger of Manning's talk: "Tom felt funny. Away from the fight, away from the stove, chill got to him. He shivered. He shuddered when he saw the full moon rising towards the cloud-bank. He who didnt give a godam for the fears of old women" (55). In this moment a curious change comes over Tom. Rejecting the truth of the change he feels as "the fears of old women," Tom denies that he is moonstruck (55). The shudder and the shiver indicate the alteration of his mood and consciousness set in motion by the power of the "blood-burning moon." As Tom makes his way to Louisa, he is anxious and vexed. Finding Louisa at home, his fears are allayed. Settling down beside her, Tom sings along with Louisa and the rest of the town in an effort to ward off the evil influence of the moon:

> Red Nigger moon. Sinner!
> Blood-burning moon. Sinner!
> Come out that fact'ry door.
> (58)

In spite of their singing the inevitable occurs. Bob, on his way to meet Louisa in the canebrake, overhears his name mentioned in connection with Louisa and Tom and sets out to find them both. Finding Louisa and Tom together, Bob is enraged. Although Bob loves Louisa—"Beautiful nigger gal, why nigger? Why not, just gal?" (61)—during his confrontation with Tom he assumes the consciousness of a white man protecting his honor and property against a black man who has forgotten his place. Bob sees in Tom's proud, confident manner and his public demonstrations of affection for Louisa evidence of his family's altered status. In this violent confrontation with Tom, Bob seeks to restore his family to its former prominence. But Bob, a stubborn unreconstructed southerner, is about to have a revelation. The whole town senses the significance of this contest and braces itself for the impact: "Chickens cackled. Roosters crowed, heralding the bloodshot eyes of southern awakening. Singers in the town were silenced. They shut their windows down" (63).

The results of Bob's awakening are very different from those of Paul Johnson's. Paul's realization that he is not like Bona leads to life; Bob's realization that time has altered the world of his father and grandfather prefigures his own death. Although Tom does not fear Bob, he is anxious, being keenly aware of the possible repercussions, to avoid an altercation. But Bob's insults bring the situation to its bloody, destructive end. Bob is no match for Tom, who dispatches him quickly and efficiently. Unfortunately, this is not the end of the matter, for the white men of the town accomplish collectively what Bob could not do individually. Like "ants upon a forage," they descend upon Tom and drag him to the town's factory, where they beat him and burn him at the stake (65).

The lesson of "Blood-Burning Moon" is painfully obvious. As Toomer tells us in *Essentials*, "Races are real; but, to men, races are prejudices" (xxxv). This aphorism, cited earlier during my discussion of "Becky," is the refined expression of a recurring theme in *Cane:* racism and racial strife. Because the white men of Sempter are governed by prejudices, they do not perceive Tom as a man whose interests in Louisa are real and legitimate. Instead, they perceive him as a brash and presumptuous fieldhand who has forgotten his place and whose strength and recalcitrance are matched only by the violence of their wish to destroy him. We have in this love story of the South harsh evidence of the insidious, evil influence of race and its terrible effect upon the lives of those who would defy and challenge its influence. Like Copper Laurent in Ernest J. Gaines's *Bloodline*, Tom has the courage to defy the established order, to break the rules by which the white South lives.[46] Although Tom dies at the hands of the town's white men, men who are frightened and intimidated by his courage, he dies secure in his manhood.

After "Blood-Burning Moon," we leave Sempter and return North, not to Chicago, the setting of "Bona and Paul," but to Washington, D.C. The setting for Toomer's philosophical meditations has changed from rural to urban, and this change provides him with an opportunity to examine a whole new species of maladies that undermine our sense of wholeness. The pressures of an urban existence are great, and as they increase, so do the chances and forms of annihilation. The spiritual and psychological annihilation of which I speak often assumes attractive forms, as revealed in the sketch "Seventh Street."

"Seventh Street" opens and closes with a poem:

> Money burns the pocket, pocket hurts
> Bootleggers in silken shirts,
> Ballooned, zooming cadillacs,
> Whizzing, whizzing down the street-car tracks.
>   (71)

In this short poem Toomer seeks to convey the spirit and intensity of street life, its speed and its dangers, and the frippery that passes for elegance. The poem's most important line is its first: "Money burns the pocket, pocket hurts" (71). The line contains meanings that reverberate throughout the sketch. It first suggests the importance of money and the power it exercises over the bootleggers, pimps, and other hustlers of Seventh Street. Second, the verb "burns" suggests the violence and intensity of Seventh Street. Toomer writes that Seventh Street "is a bastard of Prohibition," and we therefore conclude that the money of Seventh Street is bootleg money. Finally, the phrase "pocket hurts," suggests that not only is there always the desire for greater wealth but also that it is never commensurate to the effort and energy expended to acquire it. Moreover, the money and the ruthless pursuit of it do not bring peace or a release from the dangers and chaos of the streets but only hurt and pain.

But in spite of the dangers of street life, Toomer suggests that the

blacks of Seventh Street have something that white Washington does
not have and needs: "A crude-boned, soft-skinned wedge of nigger
life breathing its loafer air, jazz songs and love, thrusting unconscious
rhythms, black reddish blood into the white and whitewashed wood
of Washington" (71). This is the contradiction of Seventh Street, for
it contains the best (laughter, jazz, passion) and the worst (death,
violence, crime) of Washington. The "blood," or, in other words, the
vitality, movement, and magic, of Seventh Street energizes the rest of
Washington with new life, but it is a life so strange and so potent that
its origins defy comprehension: "Who set you flowing?" (71).

The vitality of Seventh Street is everywhere. It is in the "shanties,
brick office buildings, theatres, drug stores, restaurants, and cabarets"
(71–72). The vitality of Seventh Street is as omnipotent as it is omni-
present, for all who come in contact with it are changed by it. The
blood that flows through the veins of the bootleggers, dancers, and
jazz musicians of Seventh Street is a rich and powerful brew, so rich
and powerful that even "God would not dare to suck black blood"
(72). The sporting life of Seventh Street, where men live by their wits
and fists and women live by their wits and good looks, is unlike anything else in Washington. Although it possesses a certain fascination
for hedonists in search of new pleasures, it possesses little more than
that, for the solutions of Seventh Street are shallow and short-term.
They lead not to understanding but to madness. The following aphorism from *Essentials* best describes Toomer's attitude toward the life
of Seventh Street: "I think there is no evil in the human world save
that which causes—to our modes of perception—the essential to be
transient, the nonessential to be lasting" (xii). Even though Toomer
to a certain extent admires the rich and fantastic quality of Seventh
Street and offers it as a contrast, indeed as a criticism, of the values
and modes of being of "official" Washington, he also laments the tendency of the bootleggers and dancers to value or celebrate what is
transient and to miss or dismiss what is lasting.

In "Rhobert" Toomer continues to ridicule the preoccupation with
comfort and materialism and to criticize the elevation of the nonessential above the essential, but his target is not, as in "Seventh Street," the
pimps and bootleggers of Washington but its homeowners, its middle
class. Rhobert, the sketch's protagonist, is an "upright man whose
legs are banty-bowed and shaky because as a child he had rickets"

(74). Since Rhobert's legs are so weak, we wonder how he is able to support the tremendous weight of the house that he wears "like a monstrous diver's helmet on his head" (73). Plainly, Rhobert's love for his house and his wish to be identified as its owner add muscle and fiber to his weak legs. Rhobert's self-image is inextricably linked to his house, hence the image of the diver's helmet.

Toomer describes Rhobert's house as "dead," and so it is. The impulse to acquire it did not spring from a love of life and living things, from a wish to house and protect his family, but from an obsession with matter—dead matter—and a perverse materialism. Rhobert does not find pleasure in the contact he could have with his wife and children, whom he sees only in his dreams, but in his house. For Rhobert meaning and love are not to be found in family and in the companionship of other human beings but in inanimate objects. Rhobert has chosen matter over life, and the choice has dehumanized him, hence the unmistakable similarity between his name and the word "robot."

Although Rhobert is sinking, although it is clear that his extreme materialism will destroy him, he is oblivious to the fate that awaits him. Like all other materialists, he is totally convinced of the importance of his possessions. He has been fooled and seduced by P. D. Ouspensky's devil who arrogantly declares that "the kingdom of matter is eternal."[47] Rhobert has accepted this false declaration as the ultimate truth, and as a consequence, the house and the "pressure it exerts is enough to convince him of its practical infinity" (74).

As we continue to trace the path of the spiritual entity behind *Cane*, we come now to "Avey." This story takes place in the sections of Washington, D.C., that Toomer knew best: Soldier's Home, U and V streets, N.W., and the Potomac River. The story contains an obvious autobiographical reference, for, like the narrator, Toomer, after graduating from Dunbar High School just a few years ahead of Sterling A. Brown, spent a year at the University of Wisconsin studying agriculture. In "Avey" Toomer returns to a concern of some importance to him, one to which we were first introduced in "Karintha"—sex and sexual excess.

Avey is a young woman who has become, for various and complex reasons, a prostitute. Avey, like Karintha, Fern, and the other women in *Cane*, is not permitted to tell her own story, and we can only speculate about the causes that led to her dissipation. The narrator, however, when he is able to control his own egotism and sexual urges, does provide us with intelligent, and even illuminating, insights into the causes of Avey's decline. Meeting after a seven-year separation, the narrator and Avey settle down upon a grassy spot at Soldier's Home, and there he, believing that for once he has her attention and maybe even her admiration, discusses in a bold, knowledgeable manner her own nature, needs, and feelings: "I described her own nature and temperament. Told how they needed a larger life for their expression. How incapable Washington was of understanding that need. How it could not meet it. I pointed out that in lieu of proper channels, her emotions had overflowed into paths that dissipated them. I talked, beautifully I thought, about an art . . . that would open the way for women the likes of her. I asked her to hope, and build up an inner life against the coming of that day" (86–87).

Although the narrator is perhaps swept away by his own eloquence and extreme presumption, he succeeds in conveying the possible origins of Avey's decline. In this passage we sense the narrowness of Washington life and the limits of its appeal for Avey. The young trees that grow in boxes along V Street, "the young trees that whinnied like colts impatient to be let free," are a metaphor for Avey's condition (76). The trees will eventually die if they are not taken out of their boxes and placed in the ground. Avey too needs a larger setting in which to grow and develop. The box of Washington is much too small. But lacking direction and courage, she, like the trees, remains a prisoner. Sensuality is her means of escaping the limitations of her environment, but clearly it has not brought her the release she originally thought it would or the sense of accomplishment promised by more conventional pursuits.

Avey, so the narrator tells us in a voice filled with scorn and the frustration of unrequited love, is an "orphan-woman" (88). Avey's decision to live as a prostitute has made her a social outcast. The community, as in Becky's case, has essentially broken ties with her, and she is left to exist on its fringes. As for the art of which the narrator speaks, the art that will "open the way for women the likes of her," it is obvious that if such an art were to come into being it would fail to attract or even to hold Avey's attention and it would certainly fall short of expressing her pain, longing, and confusion (87).

Following the path of Toomer's curve, we come now to "Theatre." In this particular story, doubtless shaped by his experiences as an usher at the Howard Theatre in Washington, D.C., Toomer examines the class prejudices that structure and regulate the lives of Washington's black middle class. Here again an aphorism from *Essentials* prepares us for the histrionics of "Theatre." Concerning class snobbery and all other false and misleading indexes of an individual's worth, Toomer writes that acceptance of "prevailing standards often means we have no standards of our own. Adjustment to the external world may mean maladjustment to oneself" (xii). As we shall see, this aphorism contains the essence of the conflict at the center of Toomer's story.

When Dorris, a chorus girl, asks Mame, her dance partner, about the handsome man sitting alone in the audience during rehearsal, Mame answers: "Th manager's brother. Dictie. Nothin doin, hon" (95). Mame's reply, crude but honest, is a prophecy pointing toward the story's conclusion. Although attractive and talented, Dorris cannot overcome the class barriers that separate her from John, a well-educated man of the middle class. Try as she might, Dorris only becomes embittered, and her sense of frustration increases. Her question, "Aint I as good as him?" expresses the anger she feels at the insult implicit in Mame's friendly advice and makes the falseness of class distinctions all the more galling and obnoxious (95).

Although Dorris attempts to minimize John's importance and social status by disdainfully referring to him as the "manager's brother," her emotions get the better of her. She cannot deny or repress her interest in John and sets out to woo him through her dance: "Dorris swings to the front. The line of girls, four deep, blurs within the shadow of suspended scenes. Dorris wants to dance. . . . The girls, catching joy from Dorris, whip up within the footlights' glow. . . . Dorris dances. . . . Glorious songs are the muscles of her limbs. And her singing is of canebrake loves and mangrove feastings" (96–98). Dorris's wild and beautiful dance of love and sensuality does not produce the desired effect. At the conclusion of her dance, a dance punctuated by dreams of marriage and childbearing, she examines John's face for traces of the same dreams and discovers only a "dead thing" (99).

John finds Dorris talented and desirable, but he is a prisoner of class snobbery and class distinctions. He struggles with his attraction to Dorris and considers the difficulties that would attend any effort to bring it to fruition: "Stage-door johnny; chorus-girl. No, that would be all right. Dictie, educated, stuck up; show-girl. Yep. . . . It wouldnt work. Keep her loveliness. Let her go" (94). Although John is interested in Dorris, he decides that a relationship with her is out of the question. In doing so, he swallows whole the bogus, elitist distinctions of his class. But the decision to reject Dorris also ignites a terrible conflict within John, a conflict in which passion and desire engage will and intellect in a battle for control over his actions and emotions: "You're going wrong. Here's right: get her to herself—(Christ, but how she'd bore you after the first five minutes)—not if you get her right she wouldn't. . . . Hell no. Cant be done. But the point is, brother John, it can be done. . . . Cant be done. Let her go. . . . And keep her loveliness" (96). Passion and desire are subordinated to will and intellect. John's internal conflict does not advance his interest in Dorris but kills it.

Toomer writes that "John's body is separate from the thoughts that pack his mind" (92). John is powerless to bring them together, and as a result he is unable to act on his desires for Dorris but will "keep her loveliness," that is, he will achieve in his imagination what his background and class pretensions make impossible in reality. The story's irony, strength, and ingenuity repose upon the fact that at no point do Dorris and John actually speak, meet, or interact with one another. Their opinions of one another are based solely upon fantasy, hearsay, and appearance. Toomer could not have made his point about the arbitrary and superficial nature of class distinctions more effectively, for John rejects Dorris not because he knows her but because he feels he knows her type. Toomer returns to the limitations of John's narrow conclusions about Dorris in the following aphorism from *Essentials:* "Types are real; but, to men, types are prejudices" (xxxv).

"Calling Jesus" is the shortest sketch in *Cane,* but in it Toomer expresses his theme of psychological and spiritual fragmentation with a simplicity and depth of feeling not found in other stories. In three short paragraphs, Toomer describes the life of a woman who is "large enough . . . to find a warm spot" for her soul, a small "thrust-tailed dog that follows her, whimpering," but each evening she leaves it alone in the vestibule of her house, "filled with chills," until morning (102). The narrator states that he has seen the little dog "tagging on behind her" up streets and alleys but never establishing contact with her. The woman is oblivious to the presence of the dog and to the life of the spirit that contact with the dog would give her. Unaware of the dog, she is unable to care for it. Every evening a spectral figure sees to its comfort and carries it to where she sleeps, "cradled in dream-fluted cane" (103).

Although technology has provided the woman with certain comforts—"storm doors"—it has provided little else and indeed has taken away something precious and irreplaceable in the process: her soul. During her waking moments the woman has no consciousness of the loss, but she returns each night in her dreams to a region where she at least has some contact with the regenerative forces that hold the promise of the reunification of her body and soul. But this reunification does not occur, and she remains, as Toomer writes in *Essentials* concerning the general condition of his and our own generations, "a nerve of the cosmos, dislocated, trying to quiver into place" (xx). Since the woman is unaware of the existence of the dog and the great spiritual possibilities for which it is a metaphor, she remains "dislocated," apart from the forces of the cosmos that would give her life significance and unity.

"Calling Jesus," as the title of the sketch suggests, is a call to the land and to the life of the spirit and a rejection of technology and materialism. Technology and materialism are not a means to our salvation. They will not bring us wholeness but, as evidenced by this woman's sad predicament, only profound fragmentation. Toomer suggests that it is through nature—"dream-fluted cane"—that we regain our lost spirituality and come to know Christ as he moves across "bales of southern cotton" (103). Nature is our way back to the spirit, for nature, as Emerson tells us, "always wears the colors of the spirit."[48]

In "Box Seat" Toomer returns to the pernicious influence of class, conventions, and elitism first examined in "Theatre." Dan Moore, the story's protagonist, is an attractive and strong figure. In his great energy, confidence, and sensitivity he reminds one of Lewis in "Kabnis." Both men share a deep and abiding respect for the past. The admiration Dan feels for the old former slave who saw not only the first Oldsmobile but also Walt Whitman calls to mind Lewis's attraction to Father John. As evidenced by his fascination for the "portly Negress" seated beside him at the theater, Dan's acceptance of the past is total: "Her strong roots sink down and spread under the river and disappear in blood-lines that waver south" (119). Dan derives his strength from these "blood-lines," from his "blood-intimacy," as D. H. Lawrence would say, with the gods who inhabit the past and the land. "I am Dan Moore," he declares. "I was born in a canefield. The hands of Jesus touched me. I am come to a sick world to heal it" (105–6).

Dan is a kind of modern messiah whose mission is to restore society's connection with the curative forces of nature and to destroy the "zoo-restrictions and keeper taboos" that threaten to defeat and enslave it (112). Dan senses the tragedy of the age in which he lives. He has walked through its ruins, but the gods within him have grown stronger. But Dan, for all his strength, is powerless before the forces that have enslaved Muriel. Dan fails not because he is weak, for he has done all he can, but because Muriel is not strong.

A thought cited earlier from *Essentials* fits exactly the unfortunate circumstances of "Box Seat": the acceptance of "prevailing standards often means we have no standards of our own. Adjustment to the external world may mean maladjustment to oneself" (xii). The tragedy of Muriel is her uncritical acceptance of prevailing standards. She has accepted the standards of society not only because she lacks the courage of an independent thinker but also because she has no standards of her own. Although Dan believes that Muriel's "animalism [remains] unconquered," by the story's conclusion it is caged, and Muriel herself is responsible for its imprisonment (112). Muriel finds Dan and his message extremely attractive—"Something awfully good and fine about him"—but she cannot break free of the pernicious, suffocating hold of Washington and its Mrs. Pribbys: "I wont let myself. I? Mrs. Pribby who reads newspapers all night wont. What has she got to do with me? She *is* me, somehow. No she's not. Yes she is. She is the town, and the town wont let me love you, Dan" (110).

Even with Dan there to support her and to lead the way, Muriel holds back. She "wont let" herself hear and respond to the meaning of Dan's message. Like John of "Theatre," Muriel is dominated completely by the community and its Mrs. Pribbys, and their dominion over her is apparent in all aspects of her life: "Teachers are not supposed to have bobbed hair" (116). The town and Mrs. Pribby completely dominate Muriel, and her acceptance of the dwarf's blood-stained rose, a grotesque symbol of the artificial life of middle-class Washington, is proof of their complete control over her. By accepting the rose, Muriel also rejects the values and ideals for which Dan is both a symbol and an advocate. Muriel's capitulation to the will of the community destroys Dan, for as he leaves the theater and enters the street he "is as cool as a green stem that has just shed its flower" (129).

Having completed the journey through the landscape of Sempter, Washington, and Chicago, having come as close to full circle as is possible, we pause at "Harvest Song." We recall that Toomer's curve emerges in "Bona and Paul" and ends, or pauses, in "Harvest Song," because it is within this poem that the concerns addressed in each story, sketch, and poem are given their final, metaphoric expression.

The poem's title is an ironic comment upon the mood and condition of its central figure and speaker:

> I am a reaper whose muscles set at sundown. All my oats are cradled.
> But I am too chilled, and too fatigued to bind them.
> And I hunger.
>
> (132)

After the harvest, the reaper not only lacks the energy and the strength needed to complete the process of harvesting and storing his crops, but he also lacks the joy and the sense of accomplishment that follows the completion of a great and difficult task. The reaper's efforts have not brought him peace, pride, and security, but fear, pain, and an emptiness that manifests itself as a deep and consuming hunger. We are reminded of Richard Wright's *American Hunger*, in which Wright also uses hunger as a metaphor to convey the alienation, fragmentation, and extreme frustration he feels as an African-American searching for his voice and place in a sometimes hostile, frequently bewildering northern landscape. At the conclusion of the autobiographical fragment that completes the journey started in *Black Boy*, Wright states that "all my life I had been full of a hunger for a new way to live."[49] Throughout his life, Wright yearned for the sense of connection and completion that is the theme of "Harvest Song." Interestingly, Toomer shared deeply Wright's "hunger for a new way to live," as Cynthia E. Kerman and Richard Eldridge have demonstrated for us in their superb biography, *The Lives of Jean Toomer: A Hunger for Wholeness*. Plainly, Toomer and Wright, in their "hunger for a new way to live," in their hunger for wholeness, embody the inner conflict and fragmentation so characteristic of many Americans of the modern era.

The reaper of "Harvest Song" describes himself as a "blind man who stares across the hills, seeking / stack'd fields of other harvesters" who are also "dust-caked and blind" (132). He wishes to call to the other reapers, he desires to bridge the distance between them, but he is unable to do so and remains silent. He is unable to call to them and fears that contact with them will bring him knowledge of his hunger. As the poem unfolds, we discover that the reaper feels not only blind but also deaf. In his deafness, he longs to hear the songs of his fellow reapers, even though the "strangeness of their voices," would deepen and intensify his deafness. The reaper's need for fellowship is so great that the physical threat that such contact poses does not diminish his desire for it. At the poem's conclusion, the reaper, having summoned enough courage to call to the other reapers, stands with his harvest that has now turned to "stubble" and waits for a response that does not come.

It is clear, as Charles T. Davis argues, that the reaper yearns for emotional connection. I would expand Davis's argument and add that the reaper yearns not only for emotional connection but also for the sense of wholeness such a connection would bring. As I stated at the beginning of this chapter, in *Cane* Toomer is essentially concerned with spiritual matters, with the peace of the mind and the soul, and with the fragmentation that follows when this peace is violated or undermined by forces whose origins are both internal and external. The struggle of the individual to achieve a sense of wholeness in an environment inimical to such aims is the overriding theme of *Cane*, and it is this theme that joins and binds Toomer's first major work to the ones that follow it. In *Essentials*, Toomer writes:

> We should have a strong and vivid true sense of ourselves as wholes, made up of both actualities and potentialities.
>
> I would call this last mentioned sense a sense of oneself. Also, I would call it a sense of reality.
>
> Modern man is losing his sense of potentiality as regards himself. Hence he is losing his sense of himself and of reality. (iii)

The imminent loss of potentiality of which Toomer speaks in *Essentials* is expressed lyrically in the various stories and sketches and also in the poem that brings the movement of *Cane* to the pause that serves as its conclusion. The harvest of the reaper, the oats he has "cradled" but is "too chilled, and fatigued" to bind, is the potentiality we fear losing. The reaper is deficient in the knowledge of the many uses of the oats, of the process of transforming the oats into a food suitable for consumption, a food that would bring him knowledge of and an end to his hunger. Lacking the ability to exploit the creative potential symbolized by the harvest, the reaper's hunger only grows, his throat becomes dry, and his harvest turns to "stubble."

Looking back over the stories and sketches of *Cane*, we realize that each character shares the anguish of the reaper because each one lacks that sense of wholeness for which the reaper yearns. We see this plainly in the beautiful, but sad, stories of Karintha, Fern, and Avey, women whose lives have been defined and restricted by the sexual needs of the men in their community. The source of Carma's distress is not external but internal, for her unrestrained sexuality leads to her separation from Bane. Becky, Tom, Louisa, and Bob are victims of the oldest fears and hatreds of the South, and, as Davis argues, Esther, Dan Moore, and John of "Theatre" suffer because they are unable to achieve the desired union with their love objects. The people of Seventh Street, Rhobert, and the woman in "Calling Jesus" unfortunately choose the world of matter over the world of the spirit, and in doing so they reject even the possibility of the kind of fellowship that the reaper stands prepared to receive.

Clearly, the world of Toomer's *Cane* as seen through the prism of "Harvest Song" is bleak, but it is not enshrouded completely in darkness. Although Paul loses Bona, we rejoice in his discovery that he is not like her, and we sense that there is hope and a better world for Kabnis. We also feel that there is a part of Karintha that remains untouched, unsullied by her premature initiation into sex, and above Carma is suspended the hope that her strength and resourcefulness will sustain and fortify her during the enforced separation from Bane.

Although the particular experiences of these characters to some degree negate the great feeling of fragmentation that abounds throughout *Cane*, the condition of the reaper prevails. This melancholy fact is reflected in the broken circle that appears before "Kabnis," a broken circle that indicates not only *Cane*'s structure but its theme as well. The circle, Toomer's symbol for wholeness, remains broken, because he, as Davis writes, "is not prepared to explore completion or to celebrate a triumphant ending—nor was that his intention—because completion would mean nothing less than the promise of a redeemed [and I would add whole] America." [50]

In writing his first book, Toomer did not set out to give the world a false image of itself but to record life as he perceived it, to remake life as he experienced it. In the process he produced the book that Kreymborg asserted he had yet to write. In each section of *Cane,* we hear the voice of a remarkable and sensitive poet who is saddened, perplexed, and sometimes frightened by the world about which he writes so beautifully. In *Cane* Toomer wished, without resorting to the didacticism so common in his later works, to indicate the variety, character, and complexity not only of the dangers posed by the modern age but also of the dangers that are not bound by time. These dangers—sexual exploitation, racism, materialism, elitism, denial of our personal and racial past—are an ever-present threat to that sense of wholeness, to that "ideal of Man" Toomer cherished. Plainly, this "ideal of Man" was uppermost in Toomer's mind as he wrote *Cane,* but during and after the completion of this masterpiece he was also engaged in a search for that "intelligible scheme," that "body of ideas" that would give form, clarity, and depth to this all-consuming ideal. The fact that Toomer was still searching for this "scheme" as he wrote *Cane* explains the open-ended quality of the work. But Toomer soon found what he had spent so much of his life searching for. He found it, as we will see in the following chapter, in the philosophical and psychological system of George Ivanovich Gurdjieff.

2

The Years with Gurdjieff

NINETEEN TWENTY-TWO was an important year in the strange and eventful life of George I. Gurdjieff. After an international search that led him through such world capitals as St. Petersburg, Istanbul, Berlin, and London, Gurdjieff selected Paris as the base and center for the diffusion of his psychological system. In October of the same year Gurdjieff purchased the Château du Prieuré after much haggling with the owner, Madame Labori. Located not far from the famous Château du Fontainebleau, the Prieuré served as the international headquarters for Gurdjieff's Institute for the Harmonious Development of Man until its closing in 1939.

The year 1922 was as important for the young Jean Toomer, because it was the year in which, after much encouragement from his friend and mentor Waldo Frank, he saw several of the stories and poems of *Cane* published in such prestigious journals as *Double Dealer, Liberator, Modern Review* and *Broom*. The same year also marked the beginning of friendships with Gorham Munson and Sherwood Anderson. Although framed by mutual respect and admiration, Toomer's friendship with Anderson would not bear much fruit. Even though the author of *Winesburg, Ohio* was confident of the lasting value of Toomer's work and offered to write the foreword to *Cane*, an honor that would later fall to Frank, Anderson, so Toomer complained in his letters to Frank, insisted upon limiting him to the category of "Negro writer."[1] For personal and artistic reasons, Toomer rejected all traditional classifications of race. Toomer's radical stance on an issue that inspired only the most conservative declarations in others was based on a precise knowledge of his varied ancestry. Toomer was physically white but racially mixed; therefore, he defined himself as "neither black nor white" but as an American. Anderson's rigidity, blindness, or lack of sophistication on this important issue annoyed Toomer. The irony, however, is that Frank, the individual whom Toomer expected to rise above Anderson's narrow divisions, introduced Toomer to the reading public as an African-American poet.[2] Frank's omission of African-Americans in *Our America* should have been warning enough.

This all underscores the fact that 1922 was the year in which the twenty-eight-year-old Toomer, after much twisting and turning, decided to try writing as a possible career, and through a redoubtable combination of luck, contacts, and talent, he emerged as a vital, respected, if not faintly controversial, member of New York City's literary scene. For the ambitious and talented Toomer, literary life in New York City did not, as many have supposed, include Harlem. On the contrary, it was limited almost exclusively to Greenwich Village, where his circle of friends included not only Munson, Anderson, and Frank, but also Kenneth Burke, Malcolm Cowley, and Hart Crane.

Plainly, 1922 was an eventful year for both Toomer and Gurdjieff. Although these two very different men were, as evidenced by their activities, moving down paths that would have seemed to have kept their lives separate, it would not be too long before their shared interests and objectives would bring their seemingly divergent paths to a fateful point of intersection. We come now to 1923, another eventful year for both Toomer and Gurdjieff, the year in which the paths of these two men born on different continents would begin the slow, but inevitable, process of merging.

Nineteen twenty-three was an auspicious year for Gurdjieff for two reasons. First, Gurdjieff's institute was flourishing. Since settling the institute at the Prieuré, enrollment had increased dramatically. The core of Gurdjieff's followers, comprised initially of his family and a small group of students who had been with him since the founding of the first institute some years earlier in the city of Tiflis in the Russian republic of Georgia, had now expanded to include a large number of new students from Europe and America. As many as one hundred fifty to two hundred students were at the institute at any one time. There was never a great deal of money in the institute's treasury, but as the institute was largely self-sufficient since food and other necessities were produced on the grounds, there were periods when the needs of the institute did not exceed its budget.

The year 1923 was also significant for Gurdjieff because during the year he began planning his famous tour of the United States. Then well-known in Europe, Gurdjieff had been contemplating a visit to the United States for some time. The purpose of Gurdjieff's trip, which was scheduled for the spring of 1924, was twofold: he planned to generate international interest in his psychological system and the institute and to increase the financial resources so necessary to its survival. Gurdjieff realized his objectives in both areas. More about the success of his visit to the United States and its significance to Toomer will follow.

The year in which Gurdjieff laid the foundation for his triumphant visit to what he doubtless perceived as the new psychological frontier was also important for Toomer for several reasons. We need only be concerned with two, however. This was the year in which *Cane* was published. After nearly two years of intensive work on the manuscript, Toomer, with the assistance of Waldo Frank, had found a publisher for his stunning collection of stories, sketches, and poems. The dream had become a reality. The young man who had bounced around from college to college, never staying long enough to earn a degree, had succeeded where so many had failed. Recalling the pleasure and excitement of that season, Toomer wrote: "My words became a book. At long last I had written a book, parts of which at least I felt measured up. A book! I had actually finished something. The fellow who had seldom carried any one specific project through to a conclusion had done it at last."[3]

It was a sweet victory. The reviews were filled with praise for Toomer's craftsmanship, and he was hailed as a young man of letters of prodigious skill and promise. The fact that *Cane* sold only about five hundred copies did not seem to trouble Toomer. Although it must have pained him to know that the majority of the reading public was not the least bit interested in his work, he no doubt found some consolation in the fact that his fellow writers—Frank, Anderson, and Munson—whose opinions he valued more, were reading and praising it. So Toomer had "arrived," as he put it, "tardily, but surely." With the publication of *Cane* he felt part of a "living world of great promise." But this feeling of fellowship, of a deep connection with a "regenerative life which transcended national boundaries and quickened people in every country of the post-war world," would not last long.[4]

This brings us to the second reason why 1923 stands apart as special from the others in Toomer's long and interesting life. Just after Horace Liveright informed Toomer of his decision to publish *Cane,* Toomer's mood changed from elation to something approaching a depression. Toomer described his feelings at the time: "During the winter of 1923, owing to a complex of causes, my writing stopped; and my disharmony became distressingly prominent. So it became clear that my literary occupations had not worked deep enough to make of me an integrated man. Had it done so for others?"[5] We may find one answer to Toomer's rather pointed question in the strident, tumultuous careers of such writers as Hart Crane, Ernest Hemingway, and Sylvia Plath. These writers were, to borrow and extend the sardonic phrase Alice Walker has employed to describe Plath, "fatally self-centered."[6] Sadly, the profession Toomer believed would give his life meaning and order, clarity and precision, had not. Although he was proud of his accomplishment in *Cane,* he soon discovered, when the process of writing, revising, and publishing his first book had come to a grinding halt, that writing in and of itself would not bring his life the meaning and structure he intended it to have. Something more was needed.

At the precise moment when it would seem that Toomer could luxuriate in the well-deserved attention that follows the publication of an important and influential book, he felt a deep and growing sense of estrangement from the process and product that had brought him to such an enviable position. As Toomer struggled with the emptiness and confusion that were again creeping into his life, he began to look "questioningly not at the book, but at the writer of it." It was through this painful, revealing process of self-examination that Toomer began to apprehend the character and magnitude of the "complex of causes" that made him stop writing and that made his "disharmony . . . distressingly prominent."[7] As revealed in the following excerpt from one of his autobiographies, Toomer was unprepared for the shocks and occult inversions this crisis occasioned:

> It was curious. To all outward appearances I was going well, if not strong. I had recently written, my publisher had just brought out my first book. Critics were praising me. I was, it seemed, one of the promis-

ing writers of the younger generation. All I had to do was to write more books. A series of works, a name, a place. The world was before me, so it appeared. But all of this was outside. It existed in the minds of those who did not know my inner condition. To me who knew, it was ironic and strange. That I, who had just begun as a figure in American letters should find myself in the big blind alley of my life.

In prison. In prison on every plane and in every way of which I was sensible. Imprisoned in my ego—which is the first and last prison. . . . Personal problems overshadowed all else. . . . I was not a whole man.[8]

This passage suggests something of Toomer's mood following the publication of *Cane* in September 1923. It is strange that Toomer, at so glorious a point in his literary career, would think of himself as "imprisoned," but the strangeness of his condition can be explained.

Cane was a difficult book to write, and the immensely lonely and trying process of composition, though past, was still vivid in Toomer's memory. It is probable that the young, talented author of *Cane*, unprepared for the critical success of his first book, may have had doubts about his ability to produce a second book of comparable beauty and force. Moreover, it is likely that Toomer was undergoing the painful, necessary process of separating himself from a book in which he had invested so much of himself, a book that created opportunities for deeply personal, intensely private revelations. The writing of *Cane* and the special context from which it emerged provided Toomer with experiences and inspirations that would never be repeated. Sparta, Georgia, and its peculiar, rich life were behind him now, along with the unity of feeling and sense of wholeness the place and the effort to write about it engendered. The absence of such powerful, regenerative influences and the later failure to continue to link an artistic impulse with a region possessing personal and historic significance certainly help to explain Toomer's autumn angst, as well as why so much of his writing after *Cane* falls short of eloquence.

There are other reasons that perhaps explain Toomer's crisis of confidence in the fall of 1923. It is probable that Toomer, though heartened by *Cane*'s critical reception, may have been disappointed with his efforts to address, through the prism of African-American life and culture, what he had identified as the causes of the spiritual malaise of his generation. In a letter to Liveright on 27 February 1923, Toomer voiced a budding sense of having missed the literary mark: "The book is done. I look at its complacency and wonder where on earth all my groans and grunts and damns have gone. It doesn't seem to contain them. And when I look for the power and beauty I thought I'd caught, they seem to thin out and elude me. Next time, perhaps."[9] Plainly, Toomer was his own most demanding, exacting critic. With Frank as his mentor, Toomer held himself to only the highest artistic standards. Thus, the young Washington poet may have brooded secretly over what he regarded as the defects of a work that has become an American classic.

As Nellie Y. McKay has explained in her fine book, *Jean Toomer, Artist*, the publication of *Cane* raised publicly for Toomer the complex issues of race, and this fact, for a man adverse to simplistic explanations and overly confident of his powers to explain and persuade, also contributed to what I have termed his "crisis of confidence." With the publication of his stories and poems in *Broom*, the *Dial*, and other leftist, experimental literary magazines, Toomer's race, that is to say, whether he was an African-American or a European-American, was debated more and more. The style, content, and mood of his work gave rise to these debates, since many assumed, only because of the style, content, and mood of his work, that Toomer was not African-American. But Toomer's well-developed racial position, formulated as early as 1914 before he enrolled as an undergraduate at the University of Wisconsin, did not correspond to the definition that others, namely the reading public and publishers, imposed upon him.

For Toomer there were two definitions of race: one was biological, and the other sociological and psychological. In the former definition, race is determined by a knowledge of what Toomer termed "organic heredity, . . . [by] the physical composition of people," in other words, by the "organic actuality which exists in its complex identity as a thing distinct from our opinions of it." In the latter definition, however, race is determined by "labels, together with ideas, opinions, beliefs, emotions and their associated behavior." Toomer held that all "races are mixed races—and so mixed that no one can unravel them in all their blended complexity. No one knows for sure," postulated Toomer, "but guesses have been made as to the strains which make up the present day peoples of Germany, of France, of England—and the layman would be surprised at the results of such guesses. They lead back to Asia—into Africa."[10]

Toomer himself was physically white but racially mixed, and by hearsay (doubtless in conversation with the Pinchbacks, his maternal grandparents), he concluded that the following strains were in his heredity: Scotch, Welsh, German, English, French, Dutch, Spanish, Negro, and Indian. Because of his own varied ancestry and the blending of races he believed had been taking place in America for hundreds of years, Toomer was convinced that in this country "we are in the process of forming a new race, [and] that I was one of the first conscious members of this race." Rather than accept existing racial classifications, Toomer created one more: American. He labeled himself an American, but an American who was "neither white nor black." [11]

Plainly, Toomer rejected as ludicrous the theory of the mighty drop, that is to say, one drop of Negro blood doth a Negro make, and defined himself in terms that reflected the complexity of his racial makeup. Having come of age in an era when the rigid divisions of race were underscored by lynchings and segregation, Toomer's contemporaries, as well as the writers and critics who succeeded him, did not always understand or accept his racial position. But through all the questions, accusations, and cynical expressions of disbelief, Toomer defended the logic and validity of his position. As Toomer's reputation as a writer grew, however, so did the questions about his racial background. One of the first to write to Toomer for clarification of this point was Claude A. Barnett, director of the Associated Negro Press.

Barnett wrote to Toomer on 23 April 1923, six months before the publication of *Cane*, and the first paragraph of his unsolicited letter reveals the nature of the divisions that were forming in literary circles owing to the manner and ambiguity of Toomer's writing:

> For some time we, and by we I mean a group of three friends, the other two of which are literary men, one colored the other white, have wondered who and also what you are. There have been several arguments, the literary men contending that your style and finish indicated that you were not Negroid, while I, who am but the business manager of a news service, felt certain that you were—for how else could you interpret "us" as you do unless you had peeked behind the veil.[12]

In this racial debate, Barnett's position was that Toomer, owing to his ability to interpret certain aspects of African-American experience and culture, was African-American. Barnett's colleagues, on the other hand, primarily for stylistic reasons, held the opposite view. It is curious, indeed absurd, that Barnett's colleagues would assume that Toomer was white for reasons of style and technique alone. Behind this assumption lurk other insidious assumptions about the role of race in the creation of literary works. Over time, these assumptions have led to clashes in literary circles, the most famous of which is the thorough thrashing that Irving Howe received at the pen/hand of Ralph Ellison.[13] But let us return to Barnett's diplomatic effort to achieve a consensus in his newsroom and move on to the intricacies of Toomer's reply.

Toomer's reply is subtle and complex, but these traits are not conveyed in the excerpt McKay cites to advance her claims that Toomer was ambivalent about his Negro ancestry.[14] It is obvious that if Toomer had been ambivalent about his Negro ancestry he would have featured it neither in his many autobiographical sketches and letters to editors nor in his several autobiographies. Since this fact was never suppressed, we can only conclude that if Toomer was ambivalent about anything at all, then it was the racial climate of his generation, which rejected as absurd his right and decision to define himself in terms that correspond to his actual condition. I have found no evidence to support McKay's view in this exchange between Barnett and Toomer; indeed, the overwhelming evidence is to the contrary. Toomer insisted upon complexity in all things, particularly in matters of race, and his reply to Barnett's query illustrates this fact. I have reproduced not only the often-quoted passage that appears in McKay's book, but, more important, the passages that precede and follow it. It is in these passages that the complexity and consistency of Toomer's racial position emerge:

> The arguments you have had with your friends, the different points of view and the consequent contentions, are not at all peculiar to your group. The fact is that I have had inquiries of like nature come in from New Orleans, New York, Milwaukee, and Hollywood. The true and complete answer is one of some complexity, and for this reason perhaps it will not be seen and accepted until after I am dead. (This sounds quite solemn, but I assure you that I am capable of the saving smile.) The answer involves a realistic and accurate knowledge of racial mixture, of nationality as formed by the interaction of tradition, culture and environment, of the artistic nature in relation to the racial or social group, etc. All of which of course is too heavy and thick to go into now. Let me

state then, simply, that I am the grandson of the late P. B. S. Pinchback. From this fact it is clear that your contention is sustained. I have 'peeped behind the veil.' And my deepest impulse to literature (on the side of material) is the direct result of what I saw. In so far as the old folk-songs, syncopated rhythms, the rich sweet taste of dark skinned life, in so far as these are Negro, I am, body and soul, Negroid. My style, my esthetic, is nothing more nor less than my attempt to fashion my substance into works of art. For it, I am indebted to my inherent gifts, and to the entire body of contemporary literature. I see no reason why my style and finish could not have come from an American with Negro blood in his veins. The pure fact is that they have, and hence your friends' contentions are thrown out of court.[15]

As we examine the various parts of this racial declaration, a declaration of personal origins and allegiances, one of our first discoveries is that Toomer quickly distanced himself from Barnett and the conflicting views of his office debate. Toomer created distance through language, specifically through the phrase "your group." It is not exactly clear what Toomer's intentions were, but it seems that he wished to draw distinctions. Toomer wished to draw distinctions between himself and those who practice journalism, between himself and African-Americans (now we are on to something). Since Barnett identified one member of the debate team as white, it is plain, when we examine the cluster of sentences that follow the designation "your group," that Toomer sought to draw a distinction between himself and the mass of people who did not share his enlightened view of race.

Formulating his reply to Barnett, Toomer was careful to emphasize that the "true and complete answer is one of some complexity," since it "involves a realistic and accurate knowledge of racial mixture, of nationality as formed by the interaction of tradition, culture and environment, of the artistic nature in relation to the racial or social group." Plainly, such an answer would have resulted in a letter of considerable length and complexity. Rather than attempt such an answer in a short business letter, Toomer elected to take a shortcut. His shorthand has created, as we know from the scholarly debate concerning Toomer's racial position, enormous difficulties for him.

Toomer identified himself as the grandson of P. B. S. Pinchback, the first governor of African-American descent in the United States. Toomer offered this fact to Barnett as evidence that he had "peeped behind the veil." But what is extremely important here is that although Toomer identified Pinchback as his grandfather and implied that this fact provided him with certain experiences and insights into African-American culture and experience, he did not identify himself as an African-American. Plainly, Toomer understood and drew a distinction between *being* and "peeping" behind the veil. The former implies a complete identification with and allegiance to African-American history and culture, while the latter implies a sympathetic, but nonetheless disconnected, position toward these traditions.

In this effort to suggest the complexity of his racial position and background, Toomer went on to write the sentence that, at the very least, when taken out of context only compounded the confusion, speculation, and charges of passing that plagued him all the years of his life: "In so far as the old folk-songs, syncopated rhythms, the rich sweet taste of dark skinned life, in so far as these are Negro, I am, body and soul, Negroid." Taking this sentence out of context, as McKay and others have done, it is not difficult to understand why so many have accused Toomer, to embroider upon McKay's language, of racial ambivalence, of passing. Toomer, however, is guilty of neither. If he is guilty of anything at all it is what I would call a sympathetic identification with African-American history—"I have 'peeped behind the veil' "—an identification derived in part from his respect for African-American culture—"old folk-songs"—and in part from a knowledge of "dark skinned life" based upon his exposure to and experiences of African-American life in Washington, D.C., and Sparta, Georgia, where *Cane* was conceived. Plainly, the Negro strain in Toomer's ancestry made him sympathetic to the culture and historical experience of African-Americans. This he freely admitted. But bearing in mind the complexity of his ancestry and his own precise definition of race, it does not make him African-American.

The last two sentences of the paragraph, however, only underscore the fact that Toomer's identification with African-American life was, for most of his life, more cultural than racial and finally only aesthetic: "I see no reason why my style and finish could not have come from an *American* [italics mine] with Negro blood in his veins. The pure fact is that they have, and hence your friends' contentions are thrown out of court." Although Barnett and others may have missed the subtlety of these last two sentences, their important, implicit meanings are now hopefully much clearer. McKay correctly writes that Toomer offered to write for Barnett essays on African-American culture, but he offered to do so not as an African-American but as an "American with Negro blood in his veins." From first to last Toomer remained, in his own words, "neither white nor black" but American. Toomer refrained from identifying himself as white—"your friends' contentions are thrown out of court"—and, equally important, he refrained from identifying himself as African-American, since he had only "peeped behind the veil."

Barnett was not the only admirer of Toomer to raise questions about his racial composition. Horace Liveright also had such questions about the young writer who had recently joined his family of authors. Like Barnett, Liveright assumed that Toomer was African-American, and the proof of this assumption is revealed in Liveright's insistence that Toomer feature his "colored blood" in the publicity for *Cane*. Liveright's attitude deeply angered Toomer, since he had gone to great pains, in letters and discussions, to explain his racial background as well as his relationship to African-American life. But since Toomer had not challenged Frank's identification of him as an African-American poet in the foreword to *Cane*—Toomer remained silent on this point not only because of his admiration for Frank but also because of what he regarded as the ambiguity of Frank's statements about his racial background—Liveright saw no reason why Toomer's Negro ancestry could not be exploited in the expensive campaign to promote *Cane*. In a letter of 29 August 1923, only one month before *Cane*'s publication, Liveright wrote to Toomer with suggestions to improve the biographical sketch Toomer had submitted to the publisher's publicity department. In this letter Liveright revealed himself as not only determined to exploit Toomer's Negro ancestry for commercial gain but also doubtful of the sincerity and legitimacy of Toomer's racial views and position:

> Mr. Schneider gave me today the sketch of your life that you did. I'm returning this to you because I want to make a few suggestions. In the first place, I think that it is at least one page too long. Second, I feel that right at the very start there should be a definite note sounded about your colored blood. To my mind this is the real human interest value of your story and I don't see why you should dodge it. Of course, it is difficult to say where this would be published. My own idea would be to have a

little pamphlet made of it right away and inserted in the review books as they go out. Will you let me know what you think of this plan?[16]

In a matter of days Liveright knew exactly what Toomer thought of his plan. Liveright's insistence upon featuring Toomer's "colored blood" in the advertisements for *Cane* and his admonition that Toomer should not "dodge it" outraged Toomer. Toomer's reply to Liveright bristled with anger and sarcasm. Because of my desire to reveal the consistency of Toomer's enunciation of his racial position, I have reproduced the rather long paragraph from Toomer's reply to Liveright:

> Your letter of August 29th on hand. First, I want to make a general statement from which detailed statements will follow. My racial composition and my position in the world are realities which I alone may determine. Just what these are, I sketched in for you the day I had lunch with you. As a unit in the social milieu, I expect and demand acceptance of myself on their basis. I do not expect to be told what I should consider myself to be. Nor do I expect you as my publisher, and I hope as my friend, to either directly or indirectly state that this basis contains any element of dodging. In fact, if my relationship to you is to be what I'd like it to be, I must insist that you never use such [a] word, such a thought, again. As a B and L [Boni and Liveright] author, I make the distinction between my fundamental position and the position which your publicity department may wish to establish for me in order that *Cane* reach as large a public as possible. In this connection I have told you, I have told Messrs. Tobey and Schneider to make use of whatever racial factors you wish. Feature Negro if you wish, but do not expect me to feature it in advertisements for you. For myself, I have sufficiently featured Negro in *Cane*. Whatever statements I give will inevitably come from a synthetic human and art point of view; not from a racial one. As regards my sketch-life it was not my intention or promise to give a completed statement of my life. It was my intention to give briefly those facts which I consider to be of importance, and then to allow your publicity department or the writers on the various papers and magazines to build up whatever copy seemed most suited to their purposes. I expect, therefore, that you so use it. With this reservation: that in any copy not used for specific advertisement purposes the essentials of my sketch be adhered to. I mean, for instance, that in copies of *Cane* sent out to reviewers (these are not advertisements) that any pamphlets included in these copies should follow the essential lines of my sketch. All of this may seem over-subtle and over-refined to you, but I assure you that it isn't.[17]

In this clear, angry, and defiant reply, Toomer reminds Liveright that his "racial composition and . . . position in the world are realities which [he] alone may determine." Toomer rejects as impertinent the assumption that he can "be told what [he] should consider [himself] to be," asserts that he is not guilty of "dodging," and warns Liveright "never to use such [a] word . . . again." When we recall what is at stake here, namely a young author's self-respect and his first book with a reputable publishing house, Toomer's refusal to be manipulated in so calculated a manner inspires our respect. Toomer advised Liveright that he could "feature Negro" in advertisements for *Cane* if he wished, but that Toomer himself would not, since he had "sufficiently featured Negro in *Cane*." Keenly aware of how the facts of his racial background and position might be misinterpreted or manipulated by reviewers, Toomer insisted that "in any copy not used for specific advertisement purposes the essentials of [his] sketch be adhered to." That Toomer, after his strong beginning, would weaken here is disappointing, since a publicity department's power to shape and influence the reading public's perception of an author is well known. The fact remains, however, that Toomer did insist upon, at the very least, a certain autonomy and precision in his exchanges with Liveright on this important matter of race and self-definition. Therefore he is not, as McKay insists, guilty of a "complete turnabout" regarding the facts of his racial background.[18] On the contrary, in its essentials the complexity of Toomer's reply to Barnett's inquiries matches that of his angry letter to Liveright.

The implications of Toomer's racial position for African-American letters cannot be ignored. We have an author who, because of the facts of his ancestry, determined that he was "neither white nor black" but American. The same author, and herein lies the rub, wrote a work that is one of the most important and seminal works in the African-Amerian canon. It is so because of Toomer's calculated use of African-American art forms, the context for thought and action, the careful evocation of other African-American works, and the intense level of identification that pervades his extremely sympathetic portrayal of particular aspects of African-American history and experience. But just as Toomer rejected traditional racial classifications and created his own, so he also rejected—and calls upon us to do the same— the unexamined assumption that race alone determines the placement of works, as well as the absurd inversion employed by Barnett and Liveright that a work's characteristics determine the race of an author.

Since Toomer did not define himself as an African-American, his stance is an invitation for us to reexamine the importance we attach to race in our effort to place a work. If we were to take the implications of Toomer's racial position as far as he believed we should, then we would reach one extremely fascinating and far-reaching conclusion: that a literary tradition cannot be based solely on race. Having come this far, critics would have to do what Alice Walker has suggested we do in her essay "The Divided Life of Jean Toomer," to "keep *Cane*'s beauty but let Toomer go."[19] In other words, appropriate the work, but exclude the author, who in this case has excluded himself, from the great circle that is the tradition of African-American letters. Actually, in view of the logic and complexity of Toomer's racial position, we are given no other choice and can only conclude that Toomer is not an African-American author but that *Cane*, for the reasons I have given already, is an African-American work. Certainly Toomer was not unaware of the implications of his racial position for African-American letters. Although some—Liveright is an excellent example—may have regarded his racial and by extension his literary distinctions as "oversubtle and over-refined," Toomer did not. The fact that he did not helps to explain his crisis of confidence weeks before the publication of his first book.

Toomer also regarded the act and process of writing as a means to a larger end. Ever in search of what he termed an "intelligible scheme," that is to say, an enlightened system or process that would advance his own spiritual and psychological development, Toomer turned to writing. But since writing had not advanced this search, Toomer began to question not only his decision to become a writer but also the capability of the writing process to produce in him that desirable state of spiritual and psychological wholeness. The following passage from one of his autobiographies reveals his attitude toward writing at this time:

> Writing? Writing was out. I had given it a trial. It wouldn't and couldn't meet what I now realized to be my needs as of this time. From one point of view, writing had failed me. It, alone, evidently was not a conscious means to the goal of consciousness. It was excellent as one

practice, as one way of working; but more was necessary if one was really to go from here to there. From another point of view, I had failed writing. In my present condition I simply wasn't up to writing. Writing, real writing, it now seemed to me, presupposed the possession of the very thing I knew I lacked, namely, self-purity, self-unification, self-development. I wasn't fit to write. I felt and felt strongly that one ought to *be* something before one essayed to say something. I felt and felt deeply that a man ought to be a Man before he elected to write.[20]

Toomer's thoughts during this difficult period in his career seemed to revolve around two fine, slippery distinctions. The young author of *Cane* did not bemoan his lack of talent and ability, only the absence of that state of "self-purity, self-unification, self-development" in which, he believed, the best writing is produced. Toomer felt he needed to be a "Man" before he could express in language the peculiar trials and challenges of his era. But not a man after the fashion of a Hemingway, whose fiction transformed violence and toughness into a kind of brutish religion, but a man in the Gurdjieffian sense, a man whose three centers of being—emotional, physical, and intellectual—were not in conflict but in accord with each other and moving in concert toward the one supreme goal: higher consciousness.

Fortunately, during this painful, deeply perplexing period of self-assessment, Alfred Orage, editor of the *New Age* and Gurdjieff's principal representative in England, arrived in New York City to make final arrangements for Gurdjieff's first American tour. Having read and discussed with Margaret Naumburg, Frank, Munson, and Crane *Tertium Organum* by P. D. Ouspensky, Toomer knew of Gurdjieff as the teacher of Ouspensky. Doubtless, Toomer learned of Gurdjieff's forthcoming visit through Naumburg and Munson, who later became practitioners of the Gurdjieff system, and through his own efforts he acquired a pamphlet describing the history and mission of Gurdjieff's Institute for the Harmonious Development of Man. Thus, as a consequence of Toomer's mood and condition at the time along with his well-developed interest in esotericism, he was more than favorably disposed toward the theories outlined in the institute's pamphlet. Toomer wrote that he "read it eagerly, making happy exclamations as I came upon passage after passage that said just what I wanted said."[21] He further wrote:

In it I found expressed, more completely and with more authority than with anything possible from me, just the conditions of man which I myself had realized. Moreover, a method, a means of doing something about it was promised. Here was work that gave man direction and helped him move on the way out of the chaos of modern civilization. Here was a work that indicated what must be done in order to achieve a balanced development. Here was a work whose scope was greater and more complete than anything I had dreamed of. Here, in fine, was truth.[22]

Plainly, Toomer believed that the search for an "intelligible scheme" was at an end. It seems that in Gurdjieff Toomer had found everything he had been searching for and more.

But who was Gurdjieff? Toomer wrote that, when he was a member of the Gurdjieff groups conducted by Orage in New York City and later when he conducted his own groups in New York City and Chicago, he was frequently asked factual, biographical questions about Gurdjieff but he could not, because of his ignorance of such facts, answer these questions. Gurdjieff was certainly a mysterious figure, but it is possible to move beyond the folklore that has sprung up around Gurdjieff the public figure to a place where Gurdjieff the man assumes less exalted proportions.

Of Gurdjieff's parents we know that his mother was Armenian and that his father, John Georgiades, was a Greek herdsman from Byzantium. According to the information on his passport, Gurdjieff was born on 28 December 1877. Gurdjieff himself disputed this date, much to the consternation of those who prize order and precision in factual information of all kinds, and stated that he was born in 1866. An amusing story has come down from the New York Department of Immigration that Gurdjieff was born in the distant future. The immigration official, confronted with the task of solving this conundrum, did not receive help from the sometimes ironic, sardonic Gurdjieff. Indeed, the Greek-Armenian sage only compounded the difficulty and absurdity of this error by stating in his faltering English: "No mistake. You go arrange."[23] Alexandropol, renamed Leninakan after the Bolshevik revolution, was the city in which Gurdjieff was born. Gurdjieff died of old age and exhaustion on 29 October 1949 in the American Hospital in Paris, and concerning this fact there appears to be universal agreement.

Although Gurdjieff was born in Alexandropol, he grew up in Kars, a town located in northeastern Turkey, where he attended the Kars Municipal School. Gurdjieff was not a student at the school for long. He soon withdrew, but not because he was a troublesome, benighted student incapable of learning. On the contrary, it seems that better things were in store for the young Gurdjieff. As a chorister in the Kars Military Cathedral Choir, Gurdjieff was singled out for special consideration by Father Borsh, dean of the Cathedral School. Father Borsh, "the highest spiritual authority for the whole . . . region," recommended to Gurdjieff's parents that their son, because of his great intellectual promise, be taken out of school and placed in the hands of tutors.[24] He promised to assume responsibility for certain subjects himself. Flattered by the sincerity of Father Borsh's proposal and wishing his son to have every advantage, Georgiades happily agreed to its terms.

Since Gurdjieff's tutors were Roman Catholic priests, it is not at all surprising that he developed at an early age a predisposition for argument and abstract thinking and a deep interest in spiritual and philosophical matters. Listening to his tutors discuss issues in religion, science, or philosophy, Gurdjieff heard many things that aroused his curiosity. Questions leaped into his head but found no resting place. Did man possess a soul? What is the nature of the supernatural? What is man's potential? These and other questions of similar force and character weighed heavily upon the mind of the young Gurdjieff. He began reading more, but reading only increased the number and complexity of his questions. As he had been trained to employ his mind in the same manner that a warrior would his sword, the explanations and arguments advanced by the leading intellectuals of the day were sliced up and discarded like so many bits of useless meat. Gurdjieff's appetite for spiritual matters, particularly the occult, was boundless, and it was fed not only by what he heard and read but also by what he saw.

The town of Kars contained much to delight the imagination and to baffle the intellect. The Kars of Gurdjieff's boyhood was populated by Greeks, Armenians, Jews, Kurds, Tartars, Yesidis, and other tribes that escaped or defied classification. In fine, Kars was a panoply of languages, cultures, and religions that coexisted peacefully under the terms of some ancient, inviolable truce. Gurdjieff interacted freely and confidently with members of these tribes and in the process witnessed a great many things that fall easily under the rubric of the supernatural.

Gurdjieff told a story of a young Tartar who, twenty-four hours after his burial, was seen walking the streets of Kars, his body inhabited by an evil spirit. He also told stories of the paralytic whose powers of motion were restored after praying at the shrine of a saint; of the archimandrite who prayed for rain during a drought and whose prayers were answered with a downpour; and of the consumptive who was healed after a visit from the Virgin Mary. Needless to say, Gurdjieff was confounded by these events and was unable to reconcile all that he had learned from his rational, skeptical tutors with all that he had seen with such disturbing frequency in his own neighborhood. Recalling the terrific impact of these events, Gurdjieff wrote:

> These indubitable facts, which I had seen with my own eyes, as well as many others I had heard about during my searchings—all of them pointing to the presence of something supernatural—could not in any way be reconciled with what common sense told me or with what was clearly proved already by my already extensive knowledge of the exact sciences which excluded the very idea of supernatural phenomena.
>
> This contradiction in my consciousness gave me no peace, and was all the more irreconcilable because the facts and proofs on both sides were equally convincing. I continued my searchings, however, in the hope that sometime, somewhere, I would at last find the real answer to the questions constantly tormenting me.[25]

It is impossible to know if Gurdjieff found the answers to the many questions that were "tormenting" him, but continue in his search he did.

When Gurdjieff left Kars as a young man to begin his worldwide search for knowledge, he could not have been better prepared. Fluent in several languages and having received an excellent education from his tutors in a variety of subjects, he was easily the intellectual superior of any individual who crossed his path. Gurdjieff's odyssey took him through much of Asia and parts of Africa, and throughout the journey he held to two objectives. The first was to visit the libraries, temples, and monasteries of any country in which he might find himself. The second was to meet with the holy men and teachers of all faiths, as they were often living reliquaries of much of the world's esotericism.

After five years of "feverish activity," Gurdjieff, having studied with holy men in the Himalayas and participated in archaeological digs in the Gobi Desert, arrived in Moscow. The year was 1913, and Gurdjieff took up residence in Moscow in order "to actualize in practice what I had taken upon myself as a sacred task." [26] Gurdjieff now believed that he was ready to teach all that he had learned during his travels, and it was not long before he gathered around him a band of individuals with similar interests and sensibilities.

Gurdjieff lectured and established discussion groups not only in Moscow but in St. Petersburg as well. Gurdjieff's lectures in St. Petersburg attracted some of the city's most distinguished residents, including P. D. Ouspensky, who was later the author of *Tertium Organum* and the leading and best-known interpreter of the Gurdjieff system. Thomas de Hartman, a lifelong practitioner of the Gurdjieff system and a distinguished musician whose circle of admirers included Czar Nicholas himself, also attended these lectures. Gurdjieff was encouraged by the popularity of his lectures and discussion groups and looked forward to establishing an institute for the study and diffusion of his ideas in Moscow.

For a short while Gurdjieff's plan to establish such an institute seemed within his reach, but the Great War and the Bolshevik revolution changed everything. As a consequence of these two momentous events in modern Russian history, Gurdjieff became a gypsy. After living with his students in such cities as Essentuki, Tiflis, Istanbul, Berlin, and London, Gurdjieff, Toomer wrote, created a permanent home for his institute when he purchased a "large estate known as *le Prieuré*, on the outskirts of Fontainebleau." Toomer remembered Le Prieuré as "a handsome château, with extensive grounds and woods, all surrounded by a high stone wall in the French style." [27]

The institute, contrary to gossip, was neither a fashionable retreat for the rich and the cognoscenti nor a sanctuary for those seeking protection from the law. It was rather an institution in which individuals interested in their spiritual and psychological development were given the tools with which to build a foundation for growth. "The Institute offered," wrote Toomer, "an over-all system of training and reeducation to promote, in its words, the harmonious development of

man."[28] Students did not come to the institute to luxuriate or to posture, but to think and to work. "Whoever," warned Gurdjieff, "does
not make use of the conditions here for the work on himself and does
not see them—this is no place for him. He is wasting his time by re-
maining here, hindering others and taking someone else's place. . . .
You must either make use of this place or go away."[29]

Gurdjieff took his job as custodian of a new and revolutionary
psychological system extremely seriously. He had not hiked across
some of the most forbidding terrain of Turkestan in search of particular monasteries out of ennui. He had not participated in an archaeological expedition that took him to the center of the Gobi Desert for
his own amusement. Gurdjieff expected his students to approach his
psychological system with a high seriousness and to establish within
themselves an attitude corresponding to the importance of the enormous personal challenge that lay before them.

Of course, the institute had its critics. When Beatrice Hastings described the institute as a "mystical fish-shop," she was displaying to
the world not only her own deep cynicism but also her considerable
ignorance of the mission and character of the work done there. W. B.
Yeats was far more diplomatic than the blunt Hastings, but his pronouncements were also intended to alienate anyone who might be
interested in visiting the institute. "I have had a lot of experience of
that sort of thing in my time, and my advice to you," adjured the
husband of the medium Georgie Lees and the devotee of Madame Bla-
vatsky, "is—leave it alone."[30] D. H. Lawrence, however, in his charac-
teristically passionate and impulsive manner, went much further than
Hastings and Yeats would have dared.

It is important to remember that Lawrence neither saw nor met
Gurdjieff. He visited the institute only once, but at the time of his
visit Gurdjieff was away on his first American tour. Although Lawrence lacked firsthand knowledge of the life at the institute, he was
shamelessly subjective in his assessment to Mabel Luhan, who contributed fifteen thousand dollars to Gurdjieff's treasury and offered
her ranch in Taos, New Mexico, for another branch of the institute.
Orage dispatched Toomer to Taos in order to investigate this astound-
ing offer. Of course, Gurdjieff accepted the money but politely refused
the offer of a ranch. Lawrence was so outraged and threatened by
his benefactress's flirtation with the Gurdjieff work (he had dreams of

establishing his own institute with himself at its head) that he wrote "Mother and Daughter," an amusing, sardonic short story in which Gurdjieff is portrayed as a lecherous old Turk whose mission in life is the seduction and exploitation of young English girls. Accustomed to controversy and perhaps even enjoying it, Gurdjieff ignored his many critics. In the self-assured manner of one who never questions the rightness of his actions, he remained unaffected by the fury raging just above his head. Ironically, the unfavorable publicity the institute received did not mar in the least the success of Gurdjieff's two-week American tour. Indeed, when "that Russian," as Lawrence so contemptuously labeled Gurdjieff, arrived in New York City in January 1924, Toomer was only one of many waiting to see him.

Accompanied by Margaret Naumburg, Frank's estranged wife and Toomer's lover at the time, Toomer first saw Gurdjieff and his students perform at Manhattan's Leslie Hall and then later at the Neighborhood Playhouse. Neither the pamphlet describing the work and mission of the institute nor the many discussions with Orage earlier in the year were sufficient to prepare Toomer for the spectacle and appeal of Gurdjieff's dances, exercises, and music. In his recollection of this decisive experience, Toomer conveyed the full effect of the event in all its varied particulars:

> There was no printed program. You were not given through the mind in advance the slightest idea of what to expect. You did not know what to call the various exercises and dances. You were in no way helped to label and classify. Not until I had seen several demonstrations did I learn that the group of exercises with which the demonstrations invariably began were called "The Obligations," and that another exercise was called "The Stop" exercise, and that one of the dances had the title "The Initiation of the Priestess.". . . The movements . . . [of] the dancers caught hold of me, fascinated me, spoke to me in a language strange to my experience but not unknown to a deeper center of my being. . . . Though I could have listened to it again and again, I had a sense from the very first that the music had not been composed to be listened to, but to be enacted. It was a call to action in those very moments that were being performed on the stage, or in a march of men and women towards a destiny not even foreshadowed in the ordinary world. And so it moved me.[31]

The dances Toomer witnessed were not fanciful movements designed solely for entertainment, but, as his recollection of them reveals, they were choreographed philosophical discourse framed by music essential to its meaning. "The Obligations" and "The Initiation of the Priestess" were elaborate, ritualistic stage pieces that represented the marriage of movement with esotericism. In both pieces, positions assumed by performers were the equivalent of letters in an ancient alphabet. The cryptic messages and lessons of each piece could only be understood if the observer could accurately interpret the gestures and postures of the performers. But even without a precise knowledge of the signs and symbols of these coded movements, the overall effect, as Toomer's recollection makes plain, was quite extraordinary. The music that accompanied these demonstrations of meaning was composed by Gurdjieff in collaboration with Thomas de Hartman, an accomplished composer who had been a practitioner of the Gurdjieff methods since the early days of the Gurdjieff groups in St. Petersburg.

"The Stop Exercise" that Toomer witnessed is one of the most famous of Gurdjieff's methods. Simultaneously an exercise of the will, attention, thinking, feeling, and motion, "The Stop Exercise," according to Toomer, "enables us to see and feel our body in postures and positions totally . . . unnatural to it." At the command *stop*, Toomer explained, a student "must not merely suspend all movement, but also maintain the tension of his muscles, his facial expression . . . in the same state as it was at the word of command, keeping his gaze fixed at the point at which it is directed when the command is uttered." [32] The essential aim of this exercise was to break up what Toomer called our "circle of automaticity," for by holding postures that are not habitual we experience new ways of thinking and seeing and invite new mental associations.

For Toomer, the overall impression of the dances, exercises, and music was electrifying. On the stage of Leslie Hall he had witnessed, to his amazement and satisfaction, the choreographed expression of a philosophical and psychological system that he had despaired of finding, a system whose theories and methods would extend, clarify, and give greater authority to the themes and concerns first propounded in *Cane*. Recalling the power and significance of the performances, Toomer expressed not only a sense of relief at having found the Gurdjieff system but also a sense of expectancy of how it would enrich and alter his life:

Each thing that was done was part of a whole. The exercises, the dances, the music, the ideas, each in their different ways said essentially the same thing. Each through different approaches, impressed the same message on the heart. All together they evoked a life and a world that seemed utterly native to me. Here, without doubt, was a religion of training. Here was a discipline, an invitation to conscious experiment, a flexible and complete system, a life and a way to which I felt I could dedicate my whole mind and heart and body and strength.[33]

For the remainder of his life and particularly during the ten-year period following the publication of *Cane*, Toomer completely dedicated himself to Gurdjieff and his methods. Although there was an observable decline in the level of his participation in the Gurdjieff work following his marriage to Marjorie Content in 1934 and also during his long membership in the religious Society of Friends which began formally in 1940, as Kerman and Eldridge have documented in their important biography of Toomer, even in the last years of his life, even after Jungian analysis and a brief involvement with dianetics, Toomer returned with renewed passion to the teachings of Gurdjieff. As this lifelong preoccupation with the teachings of Gurdjieff makes plain, the major figure in Toomer's full and complex life was neither P. B. S. Pinchback nor Waldo Frank, but Gurdjieff. As we shall see in the pages that follow, the teachings of Gurdjieff had a profound impact upon the content and themes of Toomer's fiction, drama, and poetry. Toomer's belief in the usefulness and value of Gurdjieff's methods and theories remained throughout his life as strong and as keen as it was in 1924.

But Toomer, even under the spell of Gurdjieff, did not immediately set out for France; for a period he held back. Having had an opportunity to observe Gurdjieff during the demonstrations at Leslie Hall and the Neighborhood Playhouse, Toomer wrote that he was disturbed by Gurdjieff's power. Recalling the disconcerting effects of these early glimpses of a man whom he would later call without fear or qualifiers "the master," Toomer wrote: "Power—something more than strength of body, something in addition and other than strength of mind. Though he contained it, it came out of him, this deep, pervasive, unfathomable power. I soon became sure that I had never seen any other man with power of this kind. But how was he using it? For good, for evil? How would he use it on me should I become one of his pupils? From this time on I had no peace until I had finally settled this question so far as I was concerned."[34]

Nothing short of a full and active involvement in the Gurdjieff work would yield satisfactory answers to Toomer's questions. Toomer's skepticism was reasonable, his concerns understandable, but he later confessed that it was not so much Gurdjieff's power that made him hesitate as "a deep-seated unwillingness to put my life under the direction of anyone other than myself, and a stubborn belief that I could make my own way, unaided by such help as I would receive in the course of ordinary life."[35] A proud, critical, and independent thinker all his life, Toomer, much to his credit, paused to consider the possible dangers and difficulties, some posed by Gurdjieff himself and others by his own egotism and vanity, that promised to obstruct the new path that unfurled before him. Considering the many sacrifices he would have to endure in order to study with Gurdjieff, Toomer's reservations were certainly valid. But he overcame them, and in July 1924 he sailed from New York City for Paris.

When Toomer emerged from the omnibus at the country station in Fontainebleau-Avon, he was, so he wrote in an unpublished memoir of this event, "nervous" and "keyed up." After an exhausting and uncomfortable transatlantic crossing, Toomer found himself, for the first time in his life, out of the United States and in a country whose native language he only mangled. Without much money (a recurring affliction at this time) and in a deserted and wholly unfamiliar train station, Toomer realized that he did not have the slightest idea of how to get to the institute. In spite of the newness of his surroundings and the misgivings and confusion they inspired, Toomer managed to summon a fateful certitude. "In short order," he wrote, "I would be within the place towards which I had been moving, inwardly and outwardly, for months, perhaps for my entire lifetime."[36]

Toomer did not, as he had so confidently prophesied, arrive at the institute in "short order." Not having directions to the institute, he was delayed, in fact lost, and the confident, graceful author of *Cane* was suddenly diffident and awkward. Of course, Toomer did everything in his power to appear otherwise, but the driver who would eventually deposit Toomer and his bags at the threshold of the institute saw through his contrived composure. The encounter between Toomer and the driver of the open, horse-drawn carriage was a classic confrontation between an alleged erudite urbanite and a so-called country bumpkin. Perhaps if Toomer had spent more time reading Mark Twain and other American humorists, then he at least would have been prepared for his first "ride" through the French countryside.

Although this was plainly a situation in which he would not, could not, win, Toomer adopted a kingly attitude toward an individual whom he foolishly regarded as a subject:

> It is quite probable that I tried to look calm and collected and in control of the situation. It is certain that I spoke in a peculiarly faulty French, telling the man where I wanted to go. First I said—"To the Gurdjieff Institute, if you please." The driver looked blank; or rather, did not change expression. Somehow I got the impression that he knew nothing about any Gurdjieff Institute, and, not knowing, had no interest in bestirring himself in the least. So I tried again—"To the Château du Prieuré, if you please." No response. So I simply got into the cab and waited to see what would happen. Presently he gave the horse a tap with the reins and off we went. Just where we were going I had not the faintest notion.[37]

The driver made two stops on his circuitous route to the institute. The first was at Toomer's request. Seeing individuals who seemed to be and in fact were Americans, Toomer instructed the driver to stop so that he might ask the Americans for directions to the institute. Having heard neither of Gurdjieff nor of his institute, these American tourists were of no help to a very lost Jean Toomer. The second stop, however, was designed to teach a courtly American an important lesson about the etiquette of French country life. Without warning, the driver pulled into the entrance of a gate house and, much to Toomer's amazement, exchanged pleasantries with a man who appeared to be living there and who seemed only too anxious to put his work aside to converse with a friend. Unable to endure this impertinence, Toomer, in a "burst of impatience," shouted to the driver: "Is this the Château du Prieuré? Is this the Gurdjieff Institute?" After he was told that it was neither, the driver and his companion resumed their conversation. With expressionless faces, they doubtless spoke of supercilious Americans who insisted upon being rude even when lost. This exchange concluded, the driver turned his horse around, continued down the road a bit, deposited an angry and confused Toomer at the entrance of the institute (it seems the driver knew of its exact location all along), collected his fare, and drove away in silence.

If Toomer regarded the behavior of his driver as strange, then stranger discoveries were to be made at the institute. Toomer soon learned that he could not have arrived at a worse time. A few weeks earlier Gurdjieff had been injured in an automobile accident and had suffered a concussion. Toomer was told these facts the morning of his arrival. Needless to say, this was disappointing news for Toomer and for the many students who remained at the institute to watch over Gurdjieff during his convalescence. During these weeks of waiting, Toomer remembered he "was not permitted to see Gurdjieff," a gloom "hung over the place," and little "or no work was going on, and that half-heartedly." [38]

Bernard Metz, a student at the institute, took Toomer under his wing. Metz introduced Toomer to other students at the institute as well as to the routine of exercise and work. As a result of his sessions with Orage in New York City, Toomer was aware of the aim of manual labor at the institute. Toomer recalled that students selected certain projects or were assigned to them according to their individual needs. There were heavy and light tasks: felling trees, uprooting stumps, sawing logs, making roads, and working in the vegetable garden and around the buildings and grounds. According to Toomer, the work-day was from about "eight in the morning to six in the evening" and "if you were dead tired, or thought you were, Gurdjieff would call for volunteers to work after dinner until nine or ten at night." [39]

Students worked either alone or in groups. The work assignments, Toomer explained, served a dual purpose. The fulfillment of each task contributed directly to the support and maintenance of the institute and advanced the work on oneself:

> Manual work is usually done for the sake of the outward results, for the products, that is a farmer works to grow crops, a carpenter to build a house. Here [at the institute] . . . we were to work chiefly for the sake of purification, growth, increased ability and consciousness. Each job, to be sure, was to be done as well as we could do it. Work standards were anything but lax. Each of us was to improve as a workman, acquiring competence and skill. Tools and materials were to be cared for as real craftsmen care for them. But we were not to be attached to

the fruits of our labor. The aim was the same as that expressed in the Bhavagadgita [sic], "Be free from attachment to results." People who became overly egotistical about their accomplishments were likely to find their pet projects mysteriously disrupted.[40]

The highly structured, enervating regimen of the institute was not designed for the lazy, the frail, or the short-winded, and the rich, the distinguished, and the famous did not receive special consideration. When in residence, Orage rose at dawn to milk goats and to dig ditches. The tuberculous Katherine Mansfield, who arrived at the institute only a few weeks before her death and was buried on its grounds, worked in the kitchen. And the celebrated author of *Cane* worked in the institute's large vegetable garden and on road projects. Unaccustomed to "strenuous labor," Toomer found the first few days at the institute extremely taxing. His body "protested" and "rebelled." He remembers that sometimes he "completely lost contact with my purpose for coming to the institute, and could only think of leaving." At such dark times, Toomer would remember the ideas passed on to him by Orage, who contended that the work done after desire ends produces the best internal results, for at these times "automatic activity slows down" and the opportunity for "voluntary, non-habitual action" increases.[41]

Within a few weeks after Toomer's arrival Gurdjieff recovered enough to direct the outdoor projects from an armchair. Deeply concerned about the future of the institute, Toomer remembered that Gurdjieff's improved condition galvanized everyone: "Things began to hum. . . . It was perfectly amazing what his presence did. Extra life, extra zest, extra power, extra will sprang up in us. Everybody worked hard all day long and sometimes into the night."[42] Feeling more and more like himself, Gurdjieff in the evenings would oversee refinements of "The Obligations" and other demonstrations or would gather students around him to explain his theories as well as to answer questions regarding their application. In fine, each day at the institute began early and ended late, and each one, as Toomer wrote, produced not only physical challenges but psychological ones as well: "Each day was a full day. Indeed, more effort and more experience were packed into a day at the institute than in an ordinary month. It gave you a measure of man's reserve power, a standard of human capacity."[43]

After two months at the institute, Toomer was radiant and had dedicated himself completely to every aspect of institute life. "By fall," he wrote, "I was in simply wonderful shape, feeling that I could continue on and on, wanting no other life than this. All other life seemed, by contrast, flat, undynamic, unstretching, ungrowing and, above all, unreal, a mere dream-life of vague surfaces and a stir of words." Plainly, life could not have been much better. Toomer was now in almost daily contact with the master and every day growing in knowledge of his theories on human development. These exchanges with Gurdjieff together with the institute's regimen of manual labor completely transformed Toomer. He felt that each of his three centers of being—in the Gurdjieff system these are the emotional, intellectual, and physical centers—was not wrongfully doing the work of the others, thereby creating disharmony, but was fulfilling its own particular and prescribed functions. The overall effect of this much-desired harmony of body and mind was "a body purified, energized, strengthened, a mind able, lucid, with greatly increased power to grasp and comprehend. Freed of many a constricting habit," explained Toomer, "you are ready for new experience. You feel and in some [sense] are a new man." [44]

At the moment when all the forces touching Toomer's life were in accord with each other, Gurdjieff introduced a note of discord. One day without warning, Gurdjieff "called every person at the institute to gather around him and simply announced," remembered a stunned Toomer, "that he would close the institute—'liquidate' it was his word." As far as Gurdjieff was concerned, the institute "was finished" and it was to be known now only as Le Prieuré, "his home where he would invite those sympathetic to him personally." [45] Why did Gurdjieff dissolve the formal structure of the institute? Although a modified version of the institute existed until 1939, what motivated Gurdjieff to make such a decision in 1924?

It seems that Gurdjieff's decision was based neither on financial concerns, since there was now more than enough money to support the institute's programs, nor on dwindling interest in his ideas, since enrollment was never higher. In all likelihood Gurdjieff was weary of overseeing the institute's activities, not to mention the administrative details of its various branches in England and the United States. Moreover, the automobile accident doubtless instilled in Gurdjieff a profound sense of his own mortality; consequently, he felt a greater sense of urgency to assemble his theories in books, the more well known of which are *Beelzebub's Tales to His Grandson, The Herald of the Coming Good, Meetings with Remarkable Men,* and *Views from the Real World*. Gurdjieff, however, did not explain his decision to close down the institute but without ceremony announced to the dazed group of students and staff assembled before him that all "my life I have lived for others . . . now I will live for myself for awhile." [46] Nothing could have prepared Toomer and his fellow students for the shock of this announcement or the loss of an important and, for some, life-giving base. Recalling the mood of the time and the results of his own ruminations once he had collected himself, Toomer wrote:

> Most of us were shot straight into the air, and stayed there, sus-pended, an uncomfortable length of time. Day after day you would see people, sometimes in twos or threes, sometimes alone, in conference with [Gurdjieff], talking over their future course of life, where they would go, what they would do. I had such a conference. Gurdjieff said I might stay on, if I wished. I thought it over. Not much work would go on. But had I come here only to go away in a few months? Where would I go? What would I do? Finally, after quite a struggle, something clicked in me and I decided to return to New York. . . . I returned there and became a member of one of Orage's by now growing number of groups.[47]

Toomer did indeed return to New York City and join Orage's widening circle of practitioners of the Gurdjieff system. In view of the upheaval occurring at the institute, now known simply as Le Prieuré, he could not have acted more wisely.

Toomer returned to New York City in October 1924. How he sup-ported himself during this period is not known. It is possible that Toomer received some support from relatives, but this cannot be veri-fied. He seems not to have had even a part-time job. Until Toomer married the extremely wealthy Marjorie Content in 1934, it seems that his income was derived in part from a modest stipend he doubtless received from Orage for his fine efforts to promote the Gurdjieff work in the United States, as well as from his honoraria as a Gurdjieff lec-turer. The order and structure Toomer enjoyed at this point in his life were solely a function of his sessions with his students and Orage, and that was precisely as he wished it.

Owing to his literary background, his skill at public speaking, and his quick mastery of Gurdjieff's methods and theories, Toomer soon assumed an important leadership role in the Gurdjieff hierarchy in the United States. So great was Orage's faith in Toomer's abilities that not only was Toomer dispatched to Taos, New Mexico, to investigate Mabel Luhan's extravagant proposition, but he was also given permission to establish his own study groups.

Between three other subsequent, extended visits to Le Prieuré, Toomer, during the ten-year period he was most active in the Gurdjieff work, established study groups in Chicago, Illinois; Portage, Wisconsin; and Doylestown, Pennsylvania. Of course, Toomer established his first study groups in New York City, where he attracted such luminaries as Hart Crane and Gorham Munson, a fellow Gurdjieff practitioner and friend. For nearly one year Toomer lectured on Gurdjieff's methods in Harlem, and his lectures attracted many of the bright stars of the New Negro movement, including Langston Hughes, Zora Neale Hurston, Wallace Thurman, Nella Larsen and Aaron Douglass.[48] Hughes, Hurston, and Thurman attended these lectures not because they were interested in Gurdjieff's theories but because they wanted to meet the author of *Cane*. Aside from Douglass, who remained interested in Gurdjieff's theories for many years, Hughes remembered that Toomer did not win many converts in Harlem, since few people there had the leisure and resources for such activities. Although Toomer would lecture wherever he was invited or wherever he perceived real opportunities to advance Gurdjieff's theories, he remained chiefly, as he had when he first arrived in New York City, in Greenwich Village, where such ideas would find a larger, paying audience.

The psychological system about which Toomer lectured enthusiastically for over a decade and of which he was an important representative and practitioner is a system of considerable complexity. As part of his opening remarks before one of many lecture series he inaugurated in Chicago, Toomer described the Gurdjieff work as a "thing that will enable a person to understand life and himself and then be able to move according to that understanding."[49] Further, the Gurdjieff theories, explained Toomer, "offer an amazingly ordered and detailed conception of the cosmos, its chief laws and substances, its bodies great and small."[50]

The Gurdjieff system does not enjoy membership in that exclusive club of psychological systems that study man as they find him or as they suppose him to be. On the contrary, Gurdjieff would regard much modern scientific psychology, including many of the theories advanced by Freud and Jung, as fixed and limited. Gurdjieff went one step further than most modern psychological theorists. He proposed that man should be studied not only from the point of view of what he is or what he seems to be but also from the point of view of what he may become, that is, from the point of view of his possible evolution.[51]

Gurdjieff argued that man as he is is not a complete being. Nature is responsible for only so much of man's development. If we wish to develop further we must do so by our own efforts. The evolution about which Gurdjieff was principally concerned was the development of certain inner qualities and features that frequently remain undeveloped and that cannot develop by themselves.[52] But the psychological evolution of which Gurdjieff spoke is not for everyone, for the simple reason that not everyone is interested. Those people who shun the burden of development—Gurdjieff called them tramps and lunatics—are essentially lazy. They are content to remain as they are or, as Gurdjieff was quick to point out, as nature has left them.

One of the most important laws of the Gurdjieff system is that man is a mechanical being; man lacks anything resembling independence of will. He is at the mercy of all the influences in his environment. We have the image of man as a weathervane, moving in one direction and then suddenly in another, helpless before the currents of the wind. Because man is a passive instrument, he cannot, so Gurdjieff believed, "do." Everything he thinks he does only happens. Gurdjieff made this point simply and clearly when he wrote: "A man is not free either in his manifestations or in his life. He cannot be what he wishes to be and what he thinks he is. He is not like the picture of himself and the words 'man, crown of creation,' do not apply to him."[53] This is devastating news for those of us who have come to believe through time and experience that we are, without question, the undisputed masters of our fate. Gurdjieff plainly had a different opinion, but his view of man was not entirely dim. Although man is a mechanical being, he can, under the right circumstances and with the right instructions, find a way to alter his behavior.[54]

Gurdjieff argued that if an individual wished to put an end to his mechanical behavior he first had to realize that his life lacked unity, that there was not one permanent, unchanging "I" but a multitude of "I"s struggling for dominance. "Man," wrote Gurdjieff, "is a plural being. When we speak of ourselves ordinarily, we speak of 'I.' We say, 'I did this,' 'I think that,' 'I want to do this'—but this is a mistake. There is no such 'I,' or rather there are hundreds, thousands of little 'I's' in every one of us."[55] As he is, explained Gurdjieff, man suffers from the illusion of unity, and this illusion is created and nurtured by the possession of one physical body, the possession of one name, and mechanical behavior and inclinations that have become habitual.[56]

Since man is a mechanical being, not only does he lack unity, but he lacks consciousness as well. Gurdjieff defined consciousness as a "state in which man knows all at once everything that he in general knows and in which he can see how little he does know and how many contradictions there are in what he knows." Moreover, consciousness, according to Gurdjieff, is "a property which is continually changing. Now it is present, now it is not present. And there are different degrees and levels of consciousness."[57] In his current state, man possesses only the possibility of consciousness, but the illusion of consciousness is created by our thought processes and by memory, which is the product of the highest moments of consciousness.

As Toomer explained to the earnest group of Gurdjieff practitioners in Chicago, there are within the Gurdjieff system four states of consciousness possible for man. These states are the sleeping state, the waking state, self-consciousness, and cosmic consciousness. According to Toomer, "something has happened on earth and in human circumstances so that Mankind is arrested in this waking state. He alternates mechanically between sleep and waking."[58] To illustrate this point, Toomer doubtless used Gurdjieff's metaphor of a man living in a four-story house who spends his entire life on only the two lower levels, never imagining that he could move, if he wished, upward to the third and even the fourth level.

Of the various states of consciousness possible for man, the first and most primitive is the sleeping state. In this state we are immersed totally in our dreams. Sensations, sights, and sounds may enter the mind, but in the sleeping state we cannot determine their origin and significance, and upon waking we may not even remember them. In this passive, subjective state we cannot be logical or exercise judgment. Thoughts move helter-skelter through the mind. In this state of consciousness, intellectual activity of any kind is impossible, because we lack the ability to structure and organize our thoughts.

The second state of consciousness is waking consciousness. This is the state in which we work, interact, and exercise. In fine, this is the state in which we fulfill all of our obligations. But it is important to remember that the effects of sleep remain with us even after we are awake. Plainly, a critical attitude is present in the second state, for our sensory capabilities are fully operable and we are able to engage in complex physical and psychological activities. But the dreams of the night before are still with us, so argued Gurdjieff and Toomer, and they continue to influence our thoughts, feelings, and actions.

The third state of consciousness in the Gurdjieff system is self-consciousness. Self-consciousness is the state in which we become objective toward ourselves. In this third state of consciousness (we have now moved upward to the third level of Gurdjieff's metaphoric house), we possess will, that is, the ability to do. We also possess individuality or a permanent, unchangeable "I." Gurdjieff's theories tell us, and this is a point Toomer emphasized with considerable force in his lectures and study groups, that the primary obstacle to the attainment of self-consciousness is the belief that we already possess it.[59] In Gurdjieff's opinion, to believe we possess self-consciousness is a grave error and accounts for much of the disorder in modern life.

The fourth state of consciousness is objective consciousness or, as Toomer termed it, "cosmic consciousness." In this exalted state we can know the full truth about everything. We can study "things in themselves," asserted Gurdjieff, and "see the world as it is."[60] This level of consciousness is often called enlightenment, but, according to Gurdjieff, it cannot be described in words.

As we may pass most of our lives on only the first two levels—sleeping and waking consciousness—it follows that most of what we do occurs in sleep. We lead governments, participate in sporting events, preside over costly, far-reaching commercial ventures, declare wars, and sign peace treaties, and we do all these things and more with our eyes closed. But how can we escape this dangerous sleep? How can we learn to separate dreams from reality? The Gurdjieff system insists that only through the practice of self-observation and nonidentification can we escape the life of sleep.[61]

To practice self-observation or "self-remembering," as it is also called, is tantamount to being awake in a world that is largely asleep. During self-remembering we realize the extent to which we are controlled by external forces. Further, when we practice self-remembering we do not function mechanically but consciously, for we have marshaled all our critical abilities in the performance of a particular task. In one of his many lectures written for his study groups in Chicago, Toomer explained self-observation in the following manner:

> On first hearing the words, "self-observation," one might think that he is to observe himself, that is, his inner processes, as by introspection. Not at all. One is to try to be aware of his bodily behavior. At first and for some time thereafter, bodily behavior is all that one is to try to observe. Self-observation . . . [means] that one is to be aware of one's own behavior, not the behavior of others. . . . [Self-observation] is not introspection or anything like it, but is a kind of observation, a watching, an awareness of what your body does, as though your body were an object moving just in front of you.[62]

Toomer was careful to emphasize that the aim of self-observation is not to observe our internal behavior, our interior life, but only our external behavior, our exterior activities. Toomer explained that it was possible to practice self-observation by singling out "one aspect of bodily behavior," such as posture, and trying to be aware of it as often as we could and for as long a time as possible. While practicing self-observation, Toomer advised his students to "begin simply, and gradually increase." Students were to begin "by remembering to try to be aware only twice in the course of a day" but then to increase the number of times this exercise would be practiced to three, four, and then five times each day. Students were also to begin self-observation by observing one form of behavior at a time, such as posture, gesture, or tone of voice, and then trying to increase the forms observed to two or three. For example, a student observing his tone of voice would after a period of time observe his posture and gestures while also observing his tone of voice. "This aim is eventually," explained Toomer, "to be able to sustain awareness of all bodily behavior throughout the waking hours. Not for the sake of knowing what the body does, but for the sake of developing pure awareness, sheer consciousness."[63]

The second Gurdjieff method that promises higher levels of consciousness if practiced regularly is nonidentification. According to Toomer, self-observation should be practiced before nonidentification, but over time, in view of their complementary elements, these methods should be practiced concurrently. In the following excerpt from a lecture, Toomer explained the aim of nonidentification as well as the kind of attitude students had to create within themselves to attain favorable results:

> Nonidentification . . . is the effort to break one's identification with the body and, indeed, with the personal self too. It is the attempt to withdraw from the body-bound conditions and attain something of the attitude and feeling had by those who are body-free. It is the endeavor to know and feel, at least in attitude, that I am I, body is body, I am not my body, I have a body but it is not me. It is the striving similarly to know and feel that the real *I am* is not this limited, separatistic self.
>
> There are a number of ways by which this effort may be aided. One is to sort of see the body walking just ahead, that is, to objectify the body. Another is to try to regard one's body as if it were not one's own, but were as removed as another person's body.[64]

Plainly, self-observation feeds upon nonidentification and vice versa. "In other words," Toomer explained, "if we really do the one we do or [are] likely to do the other: the two are no longer two but one." These exercises are not to be practiced in secret or in isolation but as we engage in our regular daily occupations. "They are," stressed Toomer, "to be *added* to what we ordinarily do. It is neither necessary nor desirable that we take time out for them or try to place ourselves in situations removed from the distractions of the everyday world."[65]

Toomer lectured on these and other methods of the Gurdjieff work, and his lectures, if their frequency in Chicago is an adequate measure, were popular and well attended. Toomer usually lectured for an hour one evening each week for eight to ten weeks and then began another lecture series, with adjustments in material, a month later. These lectures were held in the homes of individuals interested in Gurdjieff's methods or in lecture halls in and around Chicago. Toomer was committed totally to Gurdjieff's psychological methods and theories and never doubted their applicability to the principal forms of literature. Toomer's discovery of and full involvement in the Gurdjieff work represented the end of his search for an "intelligible scheme," a search that began years before *Cane*. McKay gives Toomer's absorption with the Gurdjieff work just the right historical emphasis. She writes that Toomer "had read Eastern writings, including some about Theosophy, before he went to Georgia in 1921, and his excursion into the works of Ouspensky and Alexander . . . demonstrate an already-serious interest in Eastern thought and the occult." [66] As mentioned already, then and in later years Toomer was not content to read and practice privately the ancient theories of the East that had come at last in the person of Gurdjieff. Toomer himself dreamed of establishing his own institute in which he would instruct his students in the methods of the Gurdjieff system.

Toomer's first effort to replicate the life of Gurdjieff's Institute for the Harmonious Development of Man is described in almost excessive detail in "Portage Potential" (1931), a rambling unpublished account of the activities and mission of Witt Cottage, located near Briggsville, Wisconsin. Witt Cottage was an experiment in communal living that lasted during the months of July and August 1931. Many of the participants had attended Toomer's lectures in Chicago; others, hearing about the event from friends or reading about it in newspapers, had not had any previous contact with Gurdjieff's methods but desired to achieve the states they promised. An exact number cannot be ascertained, but there seems to have been a core of eight to twelve students who lived at the cottage, while many others came up from Chicago on weekends.

Through a combination of work assignments (kitchen work and cleaning), exercises (hiking and swimming), games (croquet and deck tennis), and discussion, Toomer imparted to his students what he regarded as the essential principles of the Gurdjieff system. Toomer was proud of his achievement at Witt Cottage, and the experience reinforced previously held conclusions: "That it is possible to change. That supposedly set and rigid adults, if they have desire and will, if they are provided with corresponding tools and instruments, can be changed and they can change themselves in most respects as regards eliminating obstacles to functioning, as regards increasing and perfecting their mental, emotional and physical functions." [67]

For all its merits, the Witt Cottage experiment ended in scandal. Reports in local newspapers dismissed the well-intentioned, highly structured psychological experiment as a "love cult." Much was made of Toomer's African ancestry as well as the fact that many of his students were white women. Much to his credit, Toomer did not dignify these racist, sensational attacks with responses. In spite of these setbacks, several fine developments came out of the cottage experiment, not the least of which was Toomer's marriage to the novelist Margery Latimer. Latimer, however, died in childbirth only weeks before the couple's first wedding anniversary.

Toomer was anxious to extend the Witt Cottage experiment, but a lack of money and the inflexible work schedule of participants militated against such a possibility. In the weeks following the end of this experiment in communal living, Toomer drew up plans and a five-thousand-dollar budget for a house in Chicago where the routine and methods at the cottage might be continued, but these plans were never actualized. It was not until 1934 when Toomer married Marjorie Content that he came closest to re-creating an environment that approximated the life of Gurdjieff's institute. With the considerable wealth she inherited from her stockbroker father, Marjorie Content purchased a large farm in Doylestown, Pennsylvania, where she and Toomer, joined by Toomer's daughter from his first marriage, lived together until his death in 1967.

In 1936, just two years after the move to Doylestown, Toomer established the Mill House Experiment, another experiment in communal living. With Gurdjieff's psychological theories as its framework, the Mill House Experiment lasted with varying degrees of success and interest until 1940. Under Toomer's direction, students performed the manual labor so essential to attaining the desirable results promised by the Gurdjieff methods. Working in groups and individually, students restored an abandoned grist mill and also farmed the large tracts of land on the Toomer estate. In spite of his training in agriculture at the University of Wisconsin and the Massachusetts College of Agriculture, Toomer's attempts at farming came to little. Although Toomer enjoyed some successes during this four-year effort to live and practice the Gurdjieff methods, his weakening health due to deteriorating kidneys together with Marjorie Content's growing opposition to the investment of time and money in a venture that was not paying for itself, forced him to end what would be his last attempt to replicate the life of Gurdjieff's institute.

Toomer now believed more than ever before that life was to "be lived as a religious process wherein we work consciously to face our-selves [and] promote purity, unification and development." As the teachings of Gurdjieff radicalized Toomer the man, so they also radi-calized Toomer the artist. Although Toomer would write, at the apex of his involvement with the Gurdjieff work, that "human beings, not books, are of paramount importance," he nonetheless continued to write.[68] It is not a well-known fact, but during the ten years that Toomer was most active in the Gurdjieff work, he wrote more novels, plays, poems, sketches, and essays than at any other period in his life. This was an enormously productive period for Toomer. Although there is not much published evidence of his efforts, we need only visit the Special Collections Library at Fisk University or Yale Univer-sity's Beinecke Rare Book and Manuscript Library for confirmation of this fact.

Toomer never supported the view of art for art's sake, and his ex-periences during the Gurdjieff period only reinforced his opposition to what he perceived as narrow, self-indulgent, self-centered aesthet-ics. Having passed through the fire of the Gurdjieff teachings whole and purified, or so he thought, Toomer believed now more than ever before that art possessed a specific use and function. "If art," he asked, "does not promote human development in those who produce it and in those who receive it, of what use art?"[69] In Toomer's view, art was a grand and in some ways holy mechanism for engendering growth and development. Art was a means to larger being and higher con-sciousness for the artist and for society. Toomer's conception of art differs, in part, from the one held by the principal cultural theorists of his day: W. E. B. Du Bois and Alain Locke. For both Du Bois and Locke art was a means of advancing the political, social, and eco-nomic interests of African-Americans, of demonstrating to a skeptical European-American readership that African-Americans were a people of culture, intelligence, and ability. This is the spirit that pervades all of Du Bois's work, and it is certainly at the core of Locke's *The New Negro* (1925). In his meditations on the value and function of art, however, Toomer went one step further than Locke and Du Bois. For Toomer, a writer for whom race was always a secondary matter, art would not only demonstrate that African-Americans possessed a re-fined sensibility, but it would also inspire and advance the spiritual and psychological development of all people—black and white—and bring them to, in the Gurdjieffian sense, higher levels of consciousness. The two views are not necessarily in opposition to one another, but the scope of Toomer's view of art, one which bears the unmistakable imprint of Gurdjieff's psychological system, is broader and perhaps even more ambitious.

The most outstanding feature of Toomer's writings between 1924 and 1936 is his self-conscious use of literary forms—the novel, drama, and poetry—to promote and inspire human development, but, more particularly, the kind of development set forth in the Gurdjieff system. Toomer would go much further in the later works than he would have thought necessary in *Cane*, his most successful attempt to give artistic significance to his great theme of human development. But of course much had transpired since his first visit to Sparta, Georgia, in the summer of 1922. Completely convinced of the redemptive, transformational powers of the Gurdjieff system, Toomer assumed the role of poet, psychologist, social critic, and spiritual reformer. As we shall discover, Toomer believed absolutely in the promise and applicability of the Gurdjieff system. With Gurdjieff's theories as his platform for personal and social change, Toomer became a spokesman and an advocate for a psychological system whose expression through the forms of literature would lift man out of the misery of the modern age into a state of "purity, unification and development."

3

I Would Rather Form a Man
Than Form a Book

❧

ALMOST IMMEDIATELY AFTER returning to New York City from
Gurdjieff's institute in the fall of 1924, Toomer began writing. Although a significant amount of his time was spent lecturing about
and promoting the Gurdjieff system, writing by now had become a
preoccupation with Toomer, and it was not long before he began ar-
ranging his thoughts on paper. Intellectually, this was probably the
most exciting, productive, and challenging period in Toomer's life.
Completely committed to the Gurdjieff work, Toomer seemed to appreciate fully the implications that this commitment would have for
his writing. "I knew very well," he wrote, "I'd have to serve a long
apprenticeship to manhood before I'd write another book."[1]

This "long apprenticeship" refers to Toomer's own belief that an
individual must master the private failings that hinder his personal development before undertaking any public responsibilities. Toomer believed that it was every individual's duty, but particularly the artist's,
to cast off the false features of the self in order to attain what he called
"self-purity, self-unification, and self-development."[2] "An artist is he
who can balance," wrote Toomer in *Essentials*, "strong contrasts, who
can combine opposing forms and forces in significant unity" (xliv).
Because the artist has gifted sight, because he is the vessel through
which the multitudes find their voices, Toomer believed it was incum-
bent upon the artist to become an example for the multitudes and to
assume the burden of development. It was the duty of the artist to
purge himself of all psychological and spiritual impurities before he
could address the problems of his age.

Just as Toomer predicted this long and arduous "apprenticeship" that altered radically all aspects of his life, so he also predicted significant changes in the fiction, drama, and verse he would eventually and inevitably write. The "next work of mine," prophesied Toomer, "would have but faint resemblance to the writing on which my reputation was being built up."[3] As we shall see, Toomer surpassed the terms of this ominous prophecy and in the process produced materials that were unlike anything his contemporaries ever wrote.

When the story "Easter" appeared in *Little Review* in 1925, it scarcely elicited the praise and critical attention that attended the publication of *Cane*. Although Gorham Munson lavished excessive praise upon the story, asserting that it surpassed "any achievement in *Cane*," it did not inspire wide interest.[4] Actually this is true for all Toomer's fiction, drama, and verse published after 1923. The unhappy fact that his new work was going largely unnoticed did not disappoint Toomer nearly as much as the expectation, which by 1925 had assumed the character of a demand, that he would one day write another *Cane*. To the disappointment of many, Toomer had no intention of repeating an experience in art he had already placed far behind him. In Toomer's view, *Cane* was "a song of an end," and, as he said again and again, "why no one has seen and felt that, why people have expected me to write a second and a third and a fourth book like *Cane*, is one of the queer misunderstandings of my life."[5]

As we have seen, Toomer's life and interests changed dramatically after 1923, but the reading public, unaware of these realignments, persisted in its demands. Toomer had accepted the Gurdjieff system as the nostrum that would save man from himself, and the influence of jazz, the blues, and other regenerative African-American art forms could not be found in his writing. Nor could one find even an honorable mention of race or the glamorous, often exaggerated portraits of Harlem life so common in the fiction of black and white writers of the day. Toomer had put aside forever many of the concerns that constituted the core of the work by such writers as Sherwood Anderson, Langston Hughes, Waldo Frank, and Claude McKay. The author of *Cane* ignored the demands and expectations of the public and chose to keep faith with himself.

Toomer began to write a new kind of fiction that reflected his deepening spiritual and psychological concerns. Toomer hoped that this kind of fiction would not only furnish his readers with provocative and novel perspectives on the nature of human existence but also with believable, inspirational models for higher development. Although Toomer once said that he "would rather form a man than form a book," it was through his books that he expected to form and to influence the lives of others.[6] Toomer wrote three novels after *Cane*: "Caromb," "The Gallonwerps," and "Transatlantic."[7] All three novels remain unpublished. The first is largely a retelling of the public outcry that followed his marriage to the white novelist Margery Latimer and will not, given its narrow autobiographical focus, receive attention within this study.[8] The other two, however, because of their thematic resemblance to *Cane* and Toomer's self-conscious use of Gurdjieff's theories, are the subject of this chapter.

The setting and characters, as well as Toomer's attempt to join the disparate elements of several discrete genres in one work, make "The Gallonwerps" a very interesting novel. Written during Toomer's early years in Chicago and completed around 1927, it is a lengthy and unusual work that possesses the characteristics of both fiction and drama. "The Gallonwerps" is faithful to the requirements of the novel, but because of its dramatic content, it also resembles a work written for the stage. Indeed, in earlier drafts it was a three-act play. Toomer believed "The Gallonwerps" capable of fulfilling this dual role, but it is more successful as a work of satiric fiction. Because of Toomer's didactic and clumsy application of Gurdjieff's theories, however, it remains deeply flawed satire. In a preface to the novel, Toomer describes briefly the influences of other genres that affected the work and attempts to set the proper mood for a meaningful reading of the work: "An unusual book, to be featured as such, and the warning given that it is a deliberate burlesque or satire of the suspense-novel, that most of the happenings are aslant, cockeyed, or distorted to the point of ridiculousness, that it contains a sense of humor based on a perception of the grotesque, that, in fine, it is a twister."[9] "The Gallonwerps" is indeed a "twister," and given the many verbal contrivances and turns in the plot, it is evident that Toomer takes great pleasure in confounding and testing the patience of the reader.

"The Gallonwerps" is written in the third person, and the action takes place in a single evening. The setting is the imaginary city of Billboa, capital of Baaleria. Billboa, a poorly disguised Chicago, is the invention of "neurotics." Its "outward forms," proclaims the narrator, "are nothing more than attempts to compensate for inner emptiness and boredom." Billboa, vast, imposing, and fantastic, is a metaphor for the "cultural and spiritual dry-rot" of the modern age (179). It is in the lives of Wisthold and Wimepime Gallonwerp, the novel's protagonists and Billboa's most distinguished residents, that this spiritual malaise assumes human form.

Wimepime is a woman of great physical beauty. Albeit middle-aged, she could still, exults the narrator, "have any man she wished." But the physical near-perfection of Wimepime belies her spiritual deterioration. Toomer writes that various "aspects of the modern experience . . . had somewhat twisted her and made her doubt herself" (8). Wimepime has suffered certain "spiritual failures," the causes of which are buried in a difficult adolescence. These "spiritual failures" have increased her feelings of emptiness and diminished her feelings of self-confidence and self-worth. Wimepime's marriage to Wisthold, doubtless an important factor in her spiritual decline, is a dreary affair with decreasing rewards and benefits. Although unfulfilled, Wimepime remains with Wisthold, for she seems to have found a modicum of satisfaction in the order and security of their marriage.

She possesses neither a career nor personal ambition, and Wimepime's sole mission in life is the promotion of Wisthold's career and his professional interests. In the novel's opening scene, we learn that Wisthold, a middle-aged man with the habits and bearing of a pundit, has just completed an essay on the Pure Manhood movement. Convinced of the importance of Wisthold's essay, Wimepime suggests that he deliver a public lecture on the subject in their home. Flattered by Wimepime's interest in his work, Wisthold happily agrees to deliver the lecture, on the condition that he not be responsible for the planning and organization of the event.

Bored with her chores as a housewife, Wimepime is only too glad to take charge. She enthusiastically begins making all the necessary preparations, but in the midst of them she begins to have doubts about the broad appeal of Wisthold's topic. In fact, she fears that the lecture will not attract the number and class of people she is so anxious to impress. Determined to please her husband and to spare him any possible embarrassment or disappointment, Wimepime decides instead to host a reception for the visiting Prince Klondike of Olderope. She had been planning to do this for some time anyway and concludes, in view of her present difficulties, that it is time she welcomed the prince into her home. Wimepime will of course make certain that at some point during the reception Wisthold will deliver his lecture.

What was previously to have been a public lecture on a subject of interest to only a few is now being falsely presented as a formal reception honoring a visiting dignitary. Wimepime is confident that she will succeed in this deception and goes forward with her plans. Wisthold remains completely ignorant of Wimepime's machinations. During the reception, hearing much talk of the imminent arrival of a Prince Klondike, he expresses surprise at the interest generated by his topic.

As we might expect, Wimepime is looking forward to an interesting evening, but there are some unexpected, indeed startling, developments. Somehow Prince Klondike learns that he is really only a decoy whose purpose is to attract larger prey. Refusing to be exploited by a housewife obsessed with her husband's obscure intellectual pursuits, he disguises himself as a butler. But as the novel unfolds, we learn that Prince Klondike is more than just Wimepime's lure—he is Toomer's prophet, the mouthpiece through which he delivers the gospel according to Gurdjieff.

Prince Klondike sees the spiritual desolation evident in all aspects of Wimepime's life and through discussion seeks to help her. He informs Wimepime that the race of man is divided into three classes: the first class possesses individuality; the second class has not developed individuality but senses that potential; and the third class is unaware of its possibilities for higher development and is content to "eat, reproduce, and participate in collective experience" (77). Prince Klondike believes that Wimepime is floundering in the second class. He tells her that life is difficult for individuals of her class, "for they suffer between two cross-pulls, one drawing them towards the mass . . . the other drawing them towards an individualization which they often fear to strive for" (77). Prince Klondike urges Wimepime to take the path leading to individuality but warns her of the difficulties she will encounter along the way.

Wimepime is inspired by the prince's remarks. She senses the sincerity of the prince's interest in her psychological and spiritual well-being as well as his confidence in her ability to transcend the banality and triteness of her circumstances. Wimepime also senses that the prince has given her exactly what she had hoped to find in her marriage—"the key to her entire life." Wimepime is fully aware of the challenge and importance of the prince's message, but she doubts her ability to "grasp" and "apply it" (77). Having revealed himself to Wimepime as the bearer of light and truth, Prince Klondike again assumes his butler's disguise. As he attends to the needs of the guests, he is amused by their impatience over trifles like cocktails and their contempt for what appears to be his inferior social status.

At this point in Toomer's novel, the action becomes jumbled and chaotic. Wisthold, in spite of Wimepime's manipulations, is prevented from delivering his lecture. This development is not fully explained, but it seems that a small number of the guests resent Wisthold's interest in the Pure Manhood movement and have decided that he should not be permitted to speak. Just moments after this rebellion, the Gallonwerps learn that Gasstar, their son, has been kidnapped.

The sudden and mysterious disappearance of Gasstar is upsetting to everyone. The guests, who earlier prevented Wisthold from speaking, are now full of sympathy and concern. The police are called in to investigate. Everyone is interrogated except Prince Klondike, who seems to have vanished. The atmosphere becomes tense. At the moment when things begin to collapse, Prince Klondike reappears with Gasstar and reveals his true identity to all present. The Gallonwerps are of course grateful for the safe return of Gasstar, but their guests are horrified that they had mistaken a prince for a butler. There are, happily, no ill feelings. Wisthold forgives Wimepime for her plots, and Prince Klondike makes a joke out of his kidnapping of Gasstar.

Prince Klondike, having set everything right, announces his departure. Although the prince's destination is unknown, his journey possesses the character of a pilgrimage. The prince is eager to have the Gallonwerps accompany him and extends to them a warm invitation to come along. It is clear that the journey, should the Gallonwerps decide to join the prince, is intended to reveal to them the shallow nature of their existence and to aid them in a search for more satisfying alternatives. The novel closes on a suspenseful note, with Prince Klondike waiting for the Gallonwerps to reply to his invitation.

When Toomer stated that his later works would have "but faint resemblance to the writing" for which he had become famous and admired, he kept his word. The world of "The Gallonwerps" is alien to the world of *Cane*. We search for the land and the people of Toomer's first and only masterpiece in the pages of this later novel but do not find them. We miss the canefields, the pine trees, and Georgia's red, magical clay. We miss most of all the beauty of black people and the complexity of their experiences as shaped by Sempter, Washington, and Chicago. The extreme contrasts between *Cane* and "The Gallonwerps," the absence of even a trace of the life discovered in Sparta and the disappearance of what I would call a racial consciousness, are largely results of Toomer's surrender to and complete acceptance of the Gurdjieff system.

Because the Gurdjieff system did not emphasize race, Toomer avoided racial themes in his fiction after 1923. As a consequence, the experience of African-Americans, so central to *Cane*, is not even a peripheral concern in "The Gallonwerps" or, as we shall see, in "Transatlantic." It seems that in the quest for higher consciousness—the promise and reward of the Gurdjieff system—one loses one's racial consciousness. But this was by no means the expected outcome of an application of Gurdjieff's theories. Those who studied at the institute were not required to renounce their ancestry, and I do not mean to imply that Toomer, by avoiding racial themes, committed such an act. I suspect that Toomer's enthusiasm for the Gurdjieff system and the confusion caused by his own racial position forced him to reexamine his position and responsibilities as a writer. As a result, he wrote fiction that ironically did not reflect the complexity of his own racial background or of American society.

Toomer had always believed that race was a secondary matter, and the Gurdjieff system reinforced this belief. According to Gurdjieff, man's problems were not external but internal. Accepting this belief as the guiding principle for his writing, Toomer, it seems, decided that the best face for his literary experiments with Gurdjieff's theories was white, or American, as Toomer would have it, because any other might distort, dilute, or, worst of all, obscure his spiritual and psychological objectives. Toomer never explained his reasons for this striking change in content, but it was doubtless linked not only to his own decision to de-emphasize race but also to the spiritual, raceless temper of the Gurdjieff system itself. But there is, I believe, another reason that might help to explain why Toomer in his writing after 1923 intentionally avoided portraying the experiences of African-Americans.

This reason is grounded in a misunderstanding about Toomer's racial position. Because of its personal, social, and, most important of all, aesthetic ramifications, Toomer's racial position deserves further clarification.

"In my body," wrote Toomer, "were many bloods, some dark blood, all blended in the fire of six or more generations." The blending of these various "bloods" formed the basis of Toomer's racial position. Viewed cartographically, Toomer's ancestry would comprise much of Europe, parts of Africa, and America before the arrival of the settlers: his ancestors were Scotch, Welsh, German, English, French, Dutch, Spanish, Negro, and Native American.[10] The notion of declaring allegiance to one particular strain was repugnant to Toomer, and he decided that he would "rise above the divisions, be neither white nor colored, be both white and colored, achieve a synthesis in something new." In Toomer's opinion, the constant mixing that had taken place between races in this country had produced a new race. He called it the American race: this was his "synthesis." Toomer proclaimed himself a member of this new race and announced that the "old divisions into white, black, brown, red are outworn" and that it is "time for a new order."[11] Toomer concluded then that he was "neither white nor black" but an American and a member of this new order.[12] A few years later, in *Essentials*, Toomer assumed an even more abstract position on race, but it was a position consistent with his Gurdjieffian role of spiritual reformer: "I am of no particular race. I am of the human race, a man at large in the human world, preparing a new race."

This is a radical conception of race even today, and we can well imagine its reception in the 1920s. This is the racial position Toomer presented to and discussed with Waldo Frank before Frank wrote the foreword to *Cane*. For all its sensitivity and verbal ingenuity, however, Frank's document does not contain the depth and scope of Toomer's racial stance. The absence of it posed serious problems for Toomer, and he asserted that the omission started a "misunderstanding in the very world, namely the literary art world, in which [I] expected to be really understood."[13]

Toomer was ambivalent about Frank's foreword from the beginning, and the sentence that filled him with apprehension was perhaps the following one: "A poet has arisen in that land [the South] who writes, not as a Southerner, not as a rebel against Southerners, not as a Negro, not as an apologist or priest or critic: who writes as a poet." [14] Although Toomer was concerned about the impact that this mention of race would have upon the public's perception of him as a writer, he consented nonetheless to the inclusion of the foreword because of his admiration for Frank, his wish to have a book published, and his naive belief that no one would fasten upon what he called the "minor point" of race. [15]

While Toomer admired and respected Frank, he firmly believed that through Frank "an erroneous picture of me was put in the minds of certain people in New York before my book came out." [16] Toomer found Frank's apparent blindness extremely disturbing:

> How explain Frank's behavior? . . . I cannot credit that he failed to understand me, my words were clear, my meaning definite. No doubt it was an unusual stand, demanding a clear reception and an accurate retention; but Frank, the champion of new and original art-expression, was surely not blind to original life. Nor can I believe that, in face of the facts, he deliberately misrepresented me. Then what? It wasn't necessary that he mention race at all—I mean, theoretically, it wasn't. If he felt compelled to, then certainly he could have told the truth—and this truth would have been far more interesting than the fiction. Some motive was at work. I have my guesses. Perhaps he himself will one day tell us what it was. [17]

I cannot say that Frank had a "motive," as Toomer seemed to think, for emphasizing race in his foreword. What is obvious, however, is that Frank could not embrace the racial complexity that Toomer represented and espoused. In spite of the admiration he felt for Toomer's gifts, Frank "limited him," like Sherwood Anderson and many critics and writers since, "to Negro." [18] It seems that Frank never accepted Toomer's racial position, for years later he wrote that Toomer's need to "forget he was a Negro" led to his immersion in the Gurdjieff work. [19] On this point, Frank was mistaken. As I have shown, Toomer became active in the Gurdjieff work for very different reasons. Frank's insistence that Toomer used Gurdjieff's theories as a means of avoiding what Frank and others perceived as Toomer's racial dilemma reveals a narrowness in thinking on Frank's part that is consistent with his exclusion of African-Americans in *Our America.*

The success of *Cane* and Alain Locke's linking of Toomer to the new generation of African-American writers in *The New Negro* only embellished the image of Toomer that Frank had placed in the mind of the public. (Toomer claimed that he never gave Locke permission to reprint his stories and poems.)[20] Although Toomer later rejected Frank's foreword and repudiated Locke for the liberties he took in his anthology, he never escaped the label of Negro or African-American writer, and we might argue that he sought to avoid the possibility of future mislabeling not only by clarifying and refining his racial position but also by excluding African-Americans from his books.

Throughout his life, Toomer found himself explaining and defending his racial stance as well as his uncodified, unarticulated, but fully operational, aesthetic position. Toomer's reply to a request by Nancy Cunard for contributions to her anthology *The Negro* typifies his attempts to explain his racial stance and his aesthetic concerns: "Though I am interested in and deeply value the Negro, I am not a Negro. And though I have written about the Negro, and value the material and the art that is Negro, all my writings during the past seven years have been on other subjects. In America I am working for a vision of this country as composed of people who are Americans first, and only of certain descents as secondary matters."[21] Although Toomer had voiced such views as early as 1917, his involvement in the Gurdjieff work crystallized them.[22] In this letter to Cunard, Toomer underscores his Americanness, he reaffirms his stance as an American, as an individual who, because of the complexity of his ancestry, is "neither black nor white." It seems then that after *Cane* Toomer was not writing about blacks or whites but about "people who are Americans first." But there is an absurdity here that Toomer doubtless did not miss. We could accept his new vision of a unified America if it reflected America's cultural and racial complexity. But Toomer's method of de-emphasizing race—the total exclusion of nonwhites—ironically calls more attention to the subject than he intended it to receive. Toomer's idealistic aim would have been better served if his fiction had corresponded more to the features of the American landscape, if he had endeavored to portray America as a land of diverse racial types all working together toward higher development. Aside from *Cane*, "The Blue Meridian" is the only work in which Toomer recognized and celebrated America's racial diversity. The several works written in the interim between these two do not contain the range of physical types so common in America or even the mention of the conflict this range has engendered in our national life and history.

It is patent that the theories of the Gurdjieff system were an important element in determining Toomer's aesthetic choices, but it seems that in making choices he wished also to increase the distance between himself and his public image as an African-American writer. We would be naive not to consider this possibility, but we must understand why Toomer rejected the label Negro or African-American writer. It was not, as Alice Walker has argued, because he wished to pass for white—Toomer never denied his Negro ancestry—but because to accept any racial classification would be inconsistent with his identity as an American.[23]

Further, Toomer believed that the problems of man were not racial but spiritual and psychological. By writing only about Americans, that is, by avoiding racial themes, Toomer sought to remain faithful to his own self-conception and also to what he believed were the central concerns of the Gurdjieff system. Although some may argue, as Frank did, that Toomer embraced the Gurdjieff system in order to bury his racial past and that his decision to exclude African-Americans from his writing is an extension of that effort in art, it is my conviction that he did neither. Toomer believed deeply and sincerely in the Gurdjieff system, and his aesthetic choices, although they may raise other questions for us, reflect the depth of his commitment. But the most important issue is not that Toomer in the fiction after *Cane* chose only to write about individuals who are, it seems, white. Ultimately, the issue is *how* he wrote about them and whether or not the effort meets certain artistic standards. As we shall see, the rich potential of *Cane* was not realized in the later works.

As we read "The Gallonwerps," we do not sense that the novel was the product of a great cosmic upheaval but that it was simply concocted. "The Gallonwerps" is not a book with a vision, as *Cane* surely is, but one with a thesis. The thesis is that modern man is fragmented and that our lives lack unity, purpose, and direction. Man is out of harmony with the ancient and true forces of the earth and lives instead by a code that hinders psychological and spiritual growth, a code that will eventually make growth or change of any kind impossible. In man's movement away from the land toward a dehumanizing technology, in our abandonment of traditional values for the self-serving commitment to luxury, prestige, and profit, something vital has been lost. This is the message, the theme, of "The Gallonwerps." Toomer was obsessed by this theme and its Gurdjieffian explication, and his obsession weakened and then wasted his great talent.

Toomer was not the only writer who came to maturity during the 1920s who was preoccupied with the destructive, corrosive nature of modern civilization. He shared these fears and concerns with such writers as Anderson, Frank, and Munson, and also with Fitzgerald and Hemingway. The important difference, however, between Toomer and these other writers is that Toomer believed he had discovered a way for men and women to cope with the dehumanizing aspects of modern living. For Toomer the way out of the madness and the turbulence of the twentieth century was through Gurdjieff. Toomer's belief in the great redemptive powers of the Gurdjieff system imbued him with a confidence and sense of mission few writers of his generation enjoyed. But Toomer's newly found confidence, his sense of himself as the bearer of a fabulous and powerful message, did not bode well for his writing. We have only to glance at the pages of "The Gallonwerps" to appreciate fully the ill effects of Toomer's conversion to the Gurdjieff system.

An example is in order, and Prince Klondike's attempt to reveal to Wimepime what he perceives as the general condition of man illustrates the didacticism and theorizing that plague the novel. The setting for Prince Klondike's remarks is Wimepime's drawing room. Having just arrived, Prince Klondike seizes an opportunity to share privately with Wimepime his views on the nature and order of human existence:

> The mass of people do not have the task of becoming individualized. Their role in life has to do with mass functions. They eat, reproduce, and participate in the collective experience—and, for them, that is enough. There are, to be sure, many misfits, many maladjusted members of this class. But they should not be confused with those who belong to one of the other two classes. All who are of the mass of people, whether they fit or misfit—this constitutes one class. A second class is made up of those who are already individualized. Then, third, there is an in-between class—people who do not belong to the mass class but who have not yet developed individuality. Life is very difficult for people of this kind, as you yourself know. They suffer, sometimes helplessly, between two cross-pulls, one drawing them towards the mass, to which

they can never really belong, the other drawing them towards an individualization which they often fear to strive for. Life rides them on a rail.
They can fall and break themselves. They cannot dismount and walk
the earth until they have learned to make courageous efforts to create in
themselves a natural individual centre of functioning. (77)

This passage begins with one of the fundamental laws of the Gurdjieff system, which is that the "mass of people" are not the least
bit interested in assuming the burden of higher development.[24] That
Toomer's most important character articulates such a belief reminds
us of his literary purpose and objective: to inspire higher development in those who wish it by providing the equivalent in fiction.
Although Toomer uses the word "individualized" to suggest the presence of a more sophisticated consciousness, his meaning is the same.[25]
In this passage, Toomer uses the various states of consciousness in
the Gurdjieff system as a framework through which Prince Klondike
isolates and describes the different characteristics of the three classes
of man. Although Toomer changes the order, excludes objective consciousness (the fourth state of consciousness in the Gurdjieff system),
and substitutes "class" for "consciousness," he does little more than
repeat Gurdjieff.

According to Prince Klondike, those who are content to participate in "collective experience" occupy the first class. The psychological state of individuals in this class corresponds to Gurdjieff's clear,
waking consciousness, a state that is second in his psychological system, preceding self-consciousness. The second class of which the
Prince speaks is comprised of individuals who have attained what
Gurdjieff called self-consciousness, but in his cosmology they would
occupy the third state of consciousness and not, as Prince Klondike
argues, the second. The third class of which the Prince speaks exhibits
traits that are characteristic of individuals who possess what Gurdjieff
termed clear consciousness, which is the state after sleep.

This exegesis indicates the extent to which the specialized and technical language of Gurdjieff's psychological system dominates "The
Gallonwerps." We see this plainly in the repeated use of such words
and phrases as "individualized," "mass function," "collective experience," and "centre of functioning," which is a rephrasing of Gurdjieff's
"magnetic center."[26] While such language may be consistent with

Toomer's objectives as a spiritual reformer and social critic, it is at odds with the expectations we have of him as a poet and fiction writer. Such language is clearly out of place in a novel and would be better confined to an essay or tract. But Toomer employs such language throughout his novel, and his continued use of it suggests not only a failure to recognize its inappropriateness but also an inability to transform the theories of the Gurdjieff system into materials suitable for fiction. By themselves, these theories are no better or worse than any that a writer might use in order to create a literary text. As demonstrated by the passage under review, however, theories do not necessarily lead to novels.

What is striking about this passage is Toomer's stubborn adherence to technical language and his unfortunate avoidance of the usual, effective tools of the poet. Here and in other passages, Toomer ignores the possibilities of the beautiful language of metaphors and symbols. We remember his remarkable exploitation of such tropes in "Calling Jesus," in which man's spiritual fragmentation is presented as a whimpering dog that follows its unconscious owner. "The Gallonwerps" is not distinguished by this kind of verbal inventiveness. An undisguised, forthright statement of theme is, unfortunately, preferred.

The passage under review also reveals the extent to which lyricism, a much celebrated feature of *Cane*, has been supplanted by a precise, logical, didactic prose. The rhythm, imagery, and tone of the line "They cannot dismount and walk the earth until they have learned to make courageous efforts to create in themselves a natural individual centre of functioning" (77), differs radically from those features of the line from *Cane* "Her skin is like dusk on the eastern horizon, / O cant you see it, O cant you see it."[27] In abandoning lyricism, incantation, ambiguity, and rich, sensual imagery for an anesthetized, highly rational, coercive prose, Toomer apparently believed that he had to create a new language, as Whitman believed he had to do in *Leaves of Grass*, to frame his psychological precepts and concerns. We can only conclude then that Toomer regarded the language of *Cane* as inadequate, perhaps even inimical, to his new role as spiritual reformer and social critic. In view of Toomer's outstanding achievement in *Cane*, his use of this unpoetic language represents an unfortunate step backward from art to a curious, occasionally insightful, but frequently tiresome and predictable propaganda for the Gurdjieff system.

In *Cane* Toomer is content, after the fashion of an artist, to suggest the dangers and effects of a particular disorder, whether it is sexual, racial, or economic, and to permit the reader to formulate his or her own conclusions. We remember with pleasure and sadness such stories as "Karintha," "Blood-Burning Moon," and "Theatre." We suffer with Karintha, Louisa, and Dorris, and we suffer deeply, because their pain is revealed to us incrementally through metaphor, through the haze of an evil mist. These women, and the others in *Cane*, are deeply ensconced in mystery, and it is through mystery that we comprehend their terrible disfigurement. In "The Gallonwerps" Toomer seems to have lost completely his gift for mystery. He boldly, even sometimes crudely, identifies the causes as well as the effects of our fall from grace and leaves no doubt about the solution. The marked differences in the tone and in the alteration of the mood and intent of this novel from those of *Cane* are measures of the depth of Toomer's faith in the power of Gurdjieff's teachings.

It should be remembered that when Toomer wrote *Cane*, he was still searching for the answers to some rather important questions. What is the nature of man? What is the purpose of existence? What is honorable and meaningful in life? These are some of the questions that Toomer strained to address as he wrote his first book. But when Toomer came upon what he thought were the answers to these questions, that is, when he accepted Gurdjieff as the most potent force of his generation, indeed of the century, we lost one of the most promising writers of our time.

The beginning of Toomer's Gurdjieffian discipleship marked the end of his career as a creative writer. In "The Gallonwerps," the philosopher-poet we know from *Cane* has become a social critic and spiritual reformer. The search for meaning is over. The seeker has found the truth, and the truth is in Gurdjieff. Now that Toomer's search for meaning is behind him, we are told in the confident, arrogant, and condescending manner of the anointed how, where, and why we have failed. We are given, much to our supposed relief, a formula for our liberation. In "The Gallonwerps" and in the novels that follow it Toomer has forsaken the subtlety, mystery, and majesty of art for cant, contrivance, and didacticism. We witness this regression in almost every scene of the novel. The spokesman for this new system and the representative of this new way of being is Prince Klondike.

Prince Klondike is easily the most important character in the novel. He is important not only because he is Toomer's mouthpiece but also because he is the linchpin around which all the other characters revolve. It is through Prince Klondike that Wimepime sees herself as a foolish, frightened, lost woman. It is also through Prince Klondike that Wimepime's guests discover the depth of their stupidity and blindness. Moreover, it is through Prince Klondike that we discover the whereabouts of Gasstar, the kidnapped son of the Gallonwerps. And finally, through Prince Klondike the Gallonwerps are offered a means of escaping their vacuous, stultifying existence.

But for all his importance to the novel's action and development, Prince Klondike is not a character but a concept. In writing this novel, Toomer was not interested in portraying one individual's attempt to influence others in their effort to cope with some of the more crippling features of their personalities and environment but in providing a perfect example. Prince Klondike has achieved a level of development that few people achieve even after a lifetime of self-examination and self-study. He is obviously a member of that first class of humanity, the class of individualization, which he goes to great lengths to describe to the baffled Wimepime. Although Prince Klondike has seemingly reached the apex of human development, we are told nothing of his personal struggle to lift himself out of the mire and up to the first class. This omission heightens the difficulty of Wimepime's struggle and makes Prince Klondike less believable as a character.

In his apparent perfection, Prince Klondike reminds us of the brilliant, almost flawless characters that appear so frequently in the novels of Hermann Hesse. Prince Klondike is essentially Toomer's Gurdjieffian counterpart of Max Demian, Brother Narcissus, and Siddhartha—characters whose profound knowledge of human nature and human experience make them the superiors of their companions, lovers, and detractors. Prince Klondike functions in much the same manner as Demian, Narcissus, and Siddhartha: he is a catalyst for higher development, the means through which the other characters realize both the limitations of their actual state and the vastness of their potential state. Although there are some similarities between Toomer's and Hesse's characters, there are also many differences. The chief difference lies in Toomer's failure to give his characters life, to make them real, to make them more than just abstractions. Hesse's characters, although highly advanced, do not hold themselves back from the drama of human experience, as Prince Klondike frequently does, but recognize their part in it. Nor do they address the issues and problems of human development in language that is riddled with jargon, road maps, and categories. At times Prince Klondike's remarks and observations are nothing more than restatements of fundamental beliefs within the Gurdjieff system. We recall that Prince Klondike's division of mankind into three classes is a none-too-artful variation of Gurdjieff's own arrangement of consciousness into four discrete groupings.

Although Prince Klondike is Toomer's principal spokesman, it is clear that Wisthold is a character of some importance as well. For example, Wisthold shares Toomer's fascination for the occult, his respect for scholarship, and, most important of all, his lack of racial definition. The following excerpt suggests the complexity of Wisthold's racial makeup and the scrutiny to which he is subjected as a consequence: "He told them he was a Baalerian. But he looked too unusual to be a Baalerian. Surely he had a little Pinglish blood? A little Guope? A little Bench blood? A little dash of Astian? A drop of Sagarsalt? A pinch of Pluff? A pint of Bedoobian? A quart of Cuff? Wisthold thumbed his nose at them, but they pestered him all the same" (24). Toomer is obviously retelling his own story. We are reminded here of his now-famous letter to Claude McKay and Max Eastman, then editors of the *Liberator*, describing his own extremely complex racial makeup.[28]

Wisthold's interest in esotericism keeps him in the public eye, as Toomer's interest in such matters kept him. In newspapers Wisthold is frequently described as a cultist and as a leader of cults, but again this is a recasting of Toomer's early involvement in the Gurdjieff work and the scandal that followed the founding of study groups in Chicago and Portage, Wisconsin.[29] Toomer treated these incidents extensively in "Caromb," an unpublished novel that rehashes the public outcry caused by his marriage to the writer Margery Latimer. These autobiographical sprinklings are placed throughout "The Gallonwerps" not just for effect but for a reason. In assigning Wisthold traits that he himself possessed while at the same time assigning Prince Klondike traits that he obviously found desirable, Toomer provides us with a record, however incomplete, questionable, and inaccurate, of his own odyssey toward truth, of his own transformation from man of letters into spiritual reformer.

Toomer was quite comfortable in his role as spiritual reformer. In fact, he regarded it with a high degree of seriousness and filled his novels with characters who possess what he believed were his own great spiritual and psychological powers. Prince Klondike is quite obviously one of these characters, a fact that reveals fascinating but troubling patterns in Toomer's depiction of relationships between men and women. In most of Toomer's writings the highly developed characters are always male, and the object of their attentions is always a weak, confused female. Needless to say, this sexism is inconsistent with the Gurdjieff system's objective of higher consciousness. We find early examples of this sexist pattern of the male savior come down to rescue and to lead a helpless female in the story "Box Seat" and in the play *Natalie Mann*.

In both these works, the male protagonists intend to give comfort and direction to the women whose love they yearn for but whose fears muffle the expression of love. Dan Moore seeks to release the embattled Muriel from the prison of conventions, and Nathan Merilh succeeds in bringing Natalie Mann to a new knowledge of herself. These are examples of the subtle sexism that showed itself in bud form in Toomer's pre-Gurdjieffian period but was in full bloom by the time he wrote "The Gallonwerps." Prince Klondike possesses powers that Dan Moore and Nathan Merilh never dreamed of, and he succeeds in working changes in the dreamy Wimepime even without her knowing it, only by the touch of his hand: "Unknown to her, beneath the level of her consciousness, there was taking place a transformation. It had begun when the Prince first really touched her, when he opened to her a world she had always wished to enter but had never known how to, when something long buried in her had begun stirring and moved to the fringe of birth. And, once started, this activity of her essence had continued its parallel movement during all subsequent events, even while on the surface she disported herself" (115). As Prince Klondike assists Wimepime in her movement toward self-knowledge, Toomer is guilty of the most offensive sexism. The pattern of the bright and handsome young man who rescues the benighted, but beautiful, young woman is one that appears only faintly in Toomer's early works, but after 1923 it becomes, as is seen here in "The Gallonwerps," a deeply entrenched convention.

Sensitive readers will be dismayed and disappointed as they read "The Gallonwerps" and the other novels written during this period and will wonder whatever became of the perceptive, sensitive poet of *Cane*. The answer is obvious. As Toomer more deeply immersed himself in the Gurdjieff teachings, he accepted the traditional view set forth and defended in the Gurdjieff system of women as essentially emotional and men as essentially intellectual. Having accepted this construct as true and constant, Toomer used it not only in "The Gallonwerps" and in other novels but most notably, as we shall see, in the play *The Sacred Factory*.

Although "The Gallonwerps" is on one level an entertaining work of satire, it remains an abysmal failure. Toomer, however, seemed to anticipate criticism of the novel by stating in his preface that the events portrayed were purposefully "aslant, cockeyed, or distorted to the point of ridiculousness." We appreciate Toomer's candid, truthful warning, but it does not relieve him of his responsibility to create a unified and intelligible work of art. The warning is accepted gladly, even cheerfully, but we would have been grateful for an integrated, structured novel.

After reading more than five hundred pages, we still have no inkling of the purpose and goal of the Pure Manhood movement, unless of course we are to take Wisthold's interest in the movement as an ironic comment upon his own condition. We also do not know the reasons why Wisthold's guests are so violently opposed, to the point of a rude and open rebellion, to his even lecturing on the subject. There are also many questions about Prince Klondike's kidnapping of Gasstar for which Toomer fails to provide even a single clue. But these breaks in meaning are small when compared to the huge problems of didacticism, incomplete character development, and sexism. Worst of all, Toomer fails to meet the terms that he himself set forth in the novel's preface.

Toomer intended "The Gallonwerps" to be a "deliberate burlesque or satire of the suspense-novel," but it lacks most of the properties associated with these genres. Although the novel contains the critical attitude of satire—Toomer goes to great pains to demonstrate the utter superficiality and vacuousness of Baalerian existence—it is sadly bereft of wit and humor, two important characteristics of satire. There is not one comic scene in the novel, and wit seems to have taken a back seat to Toomer's incessant sermonizing.

But like other satirists such as Mark Twain, James Thurber, and, most important of all, George Bernard Shaw (Toomer's model and chief inspiration as a young playwright), Toomer is not afraid to deliver a clear, even sometimes harsh, judgment. Through Huck Finn's brave decision to manumit Jim, Twain expresses his disdain for the values of the American slaveholder. Likewise Toomer, through Wimepime and Wisthold Gallonwerp, expresses his contempt for the values of the American middle class.

But Toomer is not content merely to judge and to criticize. In his role as social critic and spiritual reformer, Toomer, like other satirists, seeks to make improvements. It is not enough to list the faults of a society. A spiritual reformer must somehow devise a means for society's redemption. Unfortunately, in this particular novel the means are not fully articulated, although it is understood that redemption would follow a kind of grueling and interminable self-examination and self-study—hallmarks of the Gurdjieff system.

In "The Gallonwerps," Toomer is interested more in propounding the means of our redemption than in creating a great and masterful novel. He is more concerned with the existence of his message than with the manner of its execution. This accounts for the great unevenness of "The Gallonwerps," the disappointment we feel after reading it, and its failure to meet the high standards of art. "The Gallonwerps" is not, however, the only novel in which Toomer placed his objectives as a spiritual reformer and social critic ahead of the requirements of art. "Transatlantic," or "Eight Day World," as it was later retitled, is another such novel.

As in the case of "The Gallonwerps," Toomer did not leave behind much background information on "Transatlantic." This is rather surprising considering the scale of this work, not to mention the importance Toomer attached to it. Admirers of Toomer are more than grateful for the many notes on *Cane*'s meaning scattered throughout his correspondence, but they would search in vain for such clues to the meaning and structure of the later fiction.

There is a handful of notes that we might find useful in examining "Caromb," the least compelling of the novels written during this period, but there is even less information that we might use in making sense of "The Gallonwerps." Without Toomer's brief preface, I would hazard that most readers would be lost completely. As far as "Transatlantic" is concerned, there is more, though not much more, background information. According to Kerman and Eldridge, Toomer wrote "Transatlantic" in seventeen days while he was at Fontaine-bleau. The first draft of the novel was completed in 1927; the final draft was completed in 1933. There is an occasional mention of this novel in Toomer's correspondence. In a letter to the publisher Harrison Smith, Toomer admitted the flawed nature of "Transatlantic" but emphasized his belief in the importance of his new work: "Despite the defects I am satisfied that it is my best work thus far, and I have a feeling that my future is linked with what happens to it." [30]

"Transatlantic" was Toomer's last and most ambitious novel; in-deed, it was his magnum opus. It was the novel in which he at-tempted to give the most extensive treatment of his theme of human development, and it represents his most self-conscious rendering of Gurdjieff's teachings. As we read "Transatlantic," we clearly see that Toomer labored over this novel and that he gave to it only the best parts of himself. In a second letter to Smith, a letter in which Toomer asked Smith to reconsider his decision not to publish "Transatlantic," we are given a poignant sense of the work's importance to him: "The publication of this book means everything to me. I've got to know that the materials and the forms of this book are in the world, available to, and known by some number of readers." [31] Although "Transatlantic" was never published, it was plainly the novel for which Toomer most wanted to be remembered.

The title of the novel suggests something about the nature of its setting. Toomer takes us aboard the cruise ship *Burgundy,* also known as the *Plantarion,* for a transatlantic crossing that will take eight days. The action of the novel takes place within this eight-day period, hence the change of the title years later to "Eight Day World." The year is 1930, and the novel begins essentially with the boarding of passengers in New York City and ends with their disembarking in France.

During the eight-day passage the *Burgundy* becomes the only world the passengers know. It becomes their base, their backdrop, their earth. Marsh Tilden, an automobile executive and a minor character in the novel, describes the *Burgundy* as a kind of miniature America containing the diversity that is America's strength and hope: "Here we have America. She's all here. All the types, all the classes, all the nationalities. Look at the names on the passenger list. Names from every country on earth. Here you have us in a nut-shell and if you and I weren't so hide-bound we'd go around and have a look and get into things and we'd experience the whole globe in these eight days."[32] The range of types reflected in the passenger list is not reflected in the novel's action. As in "The Gallonwerps," African-Americans and other nonwhites are not part of the fabric of this novel. They do not appear in Toomer's white world, not even on its fringes, Tilden's claims of racial and ethnic pluralism notwithstanding. Tilden and the other passengers on board the *Burgundy* remain "hide-bound" to the end. They do not "experience the whole globe," which would have been impossible to do in eight days anyway, even aboard the *Burgundy*, but they socialize exclusively within their own racial and class groups.

Ironically, the *Burgundy* resembles more the America we all know rather than the raceless, classless America that Toomer envisioned. But in drawing this fantastic analogy, Toomer wishes to make the simple point that we are all, as trite as it sounds, in the same boat. Because we are, we should work fiercely and tirelessly for the same goal: higher development. Toomer offers the *Burgundy* and its inhabitants as a metaphor for all humankind and asks us, although it is sometimes difficult, to view the action of the novel in these terms. "Transatlantic" opens with a passage from the notebook of Hugh Langley, Toomer's principal spokesman. This passage, alternately pessimistic and optimistic, sets the tone and indicates the theme of the novel:

> The world in chaos is collapsing. Human life is in transition from an unknown past to an unknown future. Now we move. No more than this do we know, no less than this can we do. We who are shaken, insecure, bewildered, paralyzed—move.
>
> We might do more, we might build, if it were not for backward glances that turn us into pillars of stone that crash when pushed.
>
> We might build if it were not for selfishness and fear, if it were not for blindness which hides our vision of what can be built.
>
> If it were not for dread.
>
> Our dread is the dread of giving birth. There is something in the race, a deep-seated reluctance, a profound intelligence which knows that he who gives birth risks death. . . .
>
> This is the human crisis—that the birth is not yet accomplished; that we who are in the midst of it may die; that only great wisdom and heroism can bring mother and child through the ordeal—and both alive. (1)

When Langley writes that the world is "collapsing," and that human life is in "transition from an unknown past to an unknown future," he is actually describing his own psychological and spiritual condition, as well as the condition of the other passengers on board the *Burgundy*. Hod and Barbara Lorimer, Sid and Betty Chase, and the other passengers on board the eight-day cruise have all reached a point in their lives at which they can no longer escape the pressure of some of life's most irksome questions. How can I live better with others? What am I most afraid of? How do I change the worst parts of myself? What is my potential? Each passenger must find a means to address, without further delay and subterfuge, these and other important questions.

Curiously, each character feels that in boarding the *Burgundy* he or she has taken the first step in addressing these questions. Toomer writes that a "day or two on the *Burgundy* would liberate this life and return it to a sense of its own possibilities" (74). Langley himself, so the narrator tells us, also senses the significance of this particular voyage, not only for himself but for the other passengers as well: "This one held out the hope of fulfilling the marvels of life and adventure which the sea and ship to a foreign port are forever promising. There were unmistakable signs that this time he would find and be swept along by swift experiences which would run, the entire scale— perhaps to end abruptly, leaving an aching emptiness, when the *Burgundy*, a finished dream, reached France" (110). Of course the novel does not end on such a solemn note. In his role as catalyst and spiritual reformer, Langley brings the "shaken, insecure, bewildered [and] paralyzed" passengers of the *Burgundy* to stability, security, knowledge, and action. Langley helps Hod and Barbara Lorimer, as well as the others on board, to see themselves dispassionately. Through discussion, he brings them to a keen awareness of their strengths. He helps them to identify and cope with their vulnerabilities, their secret hidden selves. Initially they are in "dread of giving birth," that is, they are fearful of stripping away their public and private disguises, but through Langley they somehow find the courage to do so.

Langley, as mentioned earlier, acts as Toomer's spokesman throughout the novel. Like Prince Klondike, he is of mysterious origins. We know nothing about his childhood, education, or profession, but he is unequivocally a man of wide and complex experiences, handsome, youthful, fiercely articulate, and unusually perceptive. Langley's most distinctive feature is his hands. Toomer writes that "they had a life, a restlessness, a tireless nervous energy that made them seem like separate things which had nothing to do with the rest of him" (110). Langley is far from being another Wing Biddlebaum, of Anderson's *Winesburg, Ohio,* although he is as profound and as enigmatic. Langley's hands do not, as in Biddlebaum's case, speak of a tragic misunderstanding with crippling effects but are the physical counterpart of his intensely cerebral nature.

We know little about Langley's past, and we do not know why he is on board the *Burgundy.* There is a brief mention of unfinished business in the south of France, but Langley seems to be traveling for his own amusement. Again, Toomer sees fit to drape the novel's most important character in yards and yards of mystery. Although Langley is not unlike his antecedent and counterpart Prince Klondike, he is a more fully developed character. Engaging and charismatic, Langley is the object of unconcealed scrutiny within hours of his arrival on deck: "All the while . . . they were curiously aware of Langley, the new man in their midst, a fine-looking, strangely impressive, enigmatic presence. Who was he? What was he? He made them want to know. At the same time he gave them a feeling they would never know" (65).

The women find Langley particularly attractive, and he has affairs with the married and the single women on the *Burgundy.* He takes all of this as a matter of course. In this regard, Langley represents a side of Toomer not generally known to his readers. Like Langley, Toomer enjoyed the company of beautiful, talented, wealthy women. He was the lover of Margaret Naumburg, Waldo Frank's former wife.[33] After his brief, but much publicized, marriage to the novelist Margery Latimer, a descendant of Anne Bradstreet, Toomer was the paramour and confidant of Georgia O'Keeffe during some of the lonely periods of her marriage to Alfred Stieglitz.[34] The number of love letters in the Toomer collections at Fisk and Yale universities tells part of the story, for as a teacher of the Gurdjieff system Toomer won the hearts of many young women. Toomer settled down, it seems, when he married Marjorie Content, a wealthy photographer and a former student of Stieglitz.

Although Langley's interest in the women who flock to him is more than intellectual, like Toomer he does not permit his amorous entanglements to impede his work as a spiritual reformer. He plants the seed for change in each character and through discussion, observation, and manipulation, nurtures it and charts its growth. We observe

Langley at his best in his exchanges with Hod and Barbara Lorimer, whose personal transformations are due in large part to his constant promptings.

Hod is a tall, muscular, blond, thirty-nine-year-old entrepreneur with a "flare for the artistic and intellectual." His lips, writes Toomer, "though red, full, and generous were cruel and sensual. A hero yes; but a villain too" (5). As this sketchy description suggests, Hod is a man of opposites, a man balancing extremes inside himself. It is Hod's task to merge these opposing forces into one force, to achieve an inner unity through the tempering of the diverse range of impulses and drives vying for dominance.

We first meet Hod in his hotel room on the morning of his departure for France on the *Burgundy*. We do not know exactly why Hod is leaving New York City, but it seems that he is following his wife Barbara. Fed up with the turbulence of their marriage, Barbara has decided to divorce Hod and is traveling to France to complete the arrangements. Presumably Hod is following Barbara, for it is no coincidence that they are on the same ship.

Hod is shaken deeply by the dissolution of his marriage. Barbara's decision to leave him has forced him to take a long, hard look at himself, and he finds no comfort in what he sees: "You are homeless and without goals; but you are goaded on and on in blindness, with no rest, no peace, no happiness, on and on in a futile search for glory" (7). Although Hod's view of his situation is a little melodramatic, it is clear that Barbara's decision to end the marriage has hurt him deeply. He feels dislocated and orphaned, but the marriage, as we learn, could not have possibly succeeded.

A man of great physical appetites, Hod was only stifled and frustrated by the demure and very tame Barbara. Hod, who hunted wild game in Africa and who made a fortune before the collapse of the stock market, could only be satisfied with a woman equal to him in arrogance and daring. In his rambling, masculine robustness, Hod reminds us of the men who live and die so valiantly in the fiction of Hemingway. He possesses the aplomb and resourcefulness of Robert Wilson and, like Francis Macomber, he has known failure. For a brief while Hod is able to escape his marital difficulties in the arms of Andra Feala, an old lover from years back who, by coincidence, is also traveling on the *Burgundy*. Andra, so the narrator tells us, is a "man's

woman" (130). Beside Andra, Barbara is a "timorous, defensive infant" (133). For all Andra's beauty, magnetism, and sexual appeal,
however, Hod fears her. Like Margaret Macomber, Andra is manipu-
lative and destructive, but Hod, unlike Francis Macomber, escapes
death at the hands of a bitter and controlling woman.

Although Toomer describes Hod as "one of countless members of a
lost generation, broken, burnt-out, a hulk, a derelict destined to drift
aimlessly over four waters" (11), he is far from being J. Alfred Prufrock or another Jake Barnes. Although one may question Toomer's
intentions in this novel and label them contrived, derivative, and
heavy-handed, Hod is clearly his reply to Eliot's ritualized lamenta-
tion and to Gertrude Stein's melancholy pronouncement, You are all
a lost generation. Because Toomer rejected Stein's assessment of his
own generation, because he believed in change and transformation,
because he defied the vision of American life typified by Barnes and
Prufrock, and because he was hopeful, we observe in Hod a slow but
certain transformation.

Although Hod feels the despair and the alienation of his generation, these feelings do not dominate him. Unlike Jake Barnes, he is
not afflicted with impotence. Although weak, he has the necessary
strength to move forward. In a troubled but strong voice, Hod shouts,
"I want to be a part of things" (118). But before this fellowship is possible, before he can become a part of the life around him, he must
confess to Barbara his culpability in the failure of their marriage.

As Hod goes to Barbara, he is remorseful, beleaguered, and peni-
tent. He is not seeking a reconciliation. He realizes that this is impossible, for the distance that separates him from Barbara can never
be bridged, not even by explanations, sincerity, or, best of all, truth.
Having accepted the futility of marriage with Barbara, Hod seeks instead to build with her a peace born of their regard for one another's
needs and desires. The man called Bull Lorimer has come down a peg
or two, and his capacity to feel remorse is convincing evidence of a
willingness and desire for personal change.

In a simple, straightforward manner, Hod tells Barbara what he
has learned since accepting the finality of their divorce and where he
failed during their marriage: "I've realized that we human beings are
awfully much alone, and awfully afraid of being alone. That's why
we want so desperately to possess and be possessed. That's why we

make drives for love and companionship. I grant that when we get it we don't know what to do with it; but, as the old saying goes, one must live and learn. I've learned a bit, and simply want you to know it" (168). Buried beneath the surface of this sparse, tough, Hemingwayesque confession is an apology. Although we would have been more pleased with an apology, not to mention the avoidance of a much over-used cliché, it would be unrealistic to expect more from Hod at this point. Needless to say, Barbara is shocked by Hod's sudden impulse to reflect upon the past, and his awkward but sincere attempt to place the mistakes of their marriage in a larger, broader context pleases her. Hod was neither philosophical nor reflective during their marriage, and inwardly Barbara strains to know the source and cause of this puzzling alteration in his behavior. Although Hod is still devoted to Barbara, he has decided not to interfere in her life or to make the process of divorce more painful and complicated than it need be. From now on, writes Toomer, Hod's "joy would not be in his own selfish desires, but in seeing [Barbara] made happy the way she wanted to be" (174).

The changes set off in Hod by the dissolution of his marriage and his contact with Langley are dramatic and irreversible. Hod struggles to master the powerful emotions that the loss of a base and the intrusion of new influences have induced, but he remains moody, introspective, and intensely "critical and bitter with himself." At certain moments, Hod is the epitome of aplomb, formality, and grace, but frequently he resembles the other passengers, who are "will-less" and "full of backward glances, waiting, wondering, worrying, as though they had a suspicion something was being done to them—but what?" (192). Like the other passengers, Hod senses that something is being done to him, and like them he is unable to identify or determine the source of his uneasiness. At this point in the novel, Hod is far from stable, but with the clear-sighted support of Langley, he is able to achieve a certain balance between these extreme emotional states.

As Hod's reflective state deepens and expands, he comes to certain realizations. One of the most illuminating occurs during the afternoon before the *Burgundy*'s masquerade. During the crew's frantic preparations and the arguments between passengers over the appropriateness of this or that costume, Hod, for the first time it seems, recognizes the extent to which people assume and play roles—not just for moments, but throughout their lives. "We don't do a thing," Hod observes to Langley, "but enact our ideas or pictures of ourselves—or someone else's ideas or pictures of us" (426). Rejecting the falseness of such behavior, Hod declares that he has had enough of acting:

> I don't want to pretend I'm it. . . . I want to be it completely. . . . I want to be an artist. Not one of those fellows who spends all his days fiddling with paints or words but an artist in life. I want to find out how life, my life and all the lives I come in contact with, from the point of view of balance, of contrasts, of right beginnings and fine progressions and perfect ends, can be lived. . . . I've had enough of bungling and living as uglily as possible. I want to live skillfully and as beautifully as possible. . . . It may be an impossible order now that the world is in chaos and is plunging down the shute to a bigger and better world war. What of it? One is living. Let's live nobly while we do live. (426)

Although the language is forced and contrived, these are nonetheless worthy sentiments, and they indicate Hod's changing values, the radical shift in his mood and consciousness.

Hod makes a sincere attempt to integrate these noble sentiments into the changing pattern of his life. The former big game hunter and rake now eschews the ship's bar and represses his sybaritic impulses. Finding himself alone with an eager and desirable woman during the evening of the masquerade, Hod is not, as he otherwise would be, contemplating his next move in a masterful seduction, but he is primarily concerned about the chilliness of the night air and its effect upon his thin-skinned companion. Such gallant behavior until this evening was completely foreign to Hod. Meditating upon the strangeness of these new feelings, he is surprised at how much the voyage has changed him: "He, Hod Lorimer, concerned about a girl's health. What was coming over him? Who or what was working the miracle that he should care for another's welfare? . . . . It was too much for him" (448).

But Hod's exemplary behavior does not last long. When on the sixth day of the voyage he discovers that Langley, his spiritual adviser, fast friend, and confidant, is in love with Barbara, Hod is understandably angry. In fact, Hod is more than angry; he is outraged. Lacking the necessary equipment for a duel or any other gentlemanly means of settling a dispute of this kind, Hod challenges Langley to a silly, arduous, and dangerous test. Both men are to ascend to the top of one of the ship's masts and then descend by a rope to which will be attached a handkerchief belonging to Barbara. The one who successfully completes this test without injury to himself will be the victor and may keep, so it seems, Barbara as the prize. By the morning of this "duel" Hod has come to his senses. The fact that he has done so prior to the contest is significant, since it is generally his pattern to see the foolishness of his behavior only after he has jeopardized someone else's life and his own.

For the first time Hod has prevented the eruption of his most negative and destructive tendency by checking his behavior, or, to use a Gurdjieffian term, by remembering himself. Hod is fully aware of the significance of this psychological development and shares with Langley the special meaning it has for him:

> All my life I've been doing simply godawful things and persuading myself I would make up and atone for them by saying I'm sorry. . . . I'd never check myself in advance. Hell no. I'd never check myself midway. . . . I'd crash through with the awful thing—and feel powerful doing it—and when, later on, my conscience would begin working. . . . I'd rush to the person and beg pardon. . . . And I'd give myself hell . . . do anything to atone and square myself with myself and with the world . . . but all of it afterwards.
>
> Right now, just in this thing with you, this is the first time ever that I've ever caught myself in advance. . . . I don't guess you can see what this bit of realization means to me. You don't do asinine things. You consider yourself and others before you leap. It means life to me, Hugh. Just life, and nothing less. (495–96)

All of the action of the novel has brought us to this moment. Hod is now changed. He is no longer, like the other passengers on board the *Burgundy*, only "partially awake." Hod has presumably learned the importance of what Gurdjieff called being awake. He sees the advantages of being conscious of his behavior and actions, and he will presumably continue to exercise similar levels of awareness, restraint, and discretion in all the activities of his life.

Hod's recognition of his chief feature, to use a Gurdjieffian term, is proof of his transformation as well as the apex of Toomer's novel. All other such transformations, if they can be called that, are as a consequence of their timing plainly secondary. Toomer obviously attaches the most importance to Hod's elevation in consciousness. He offers it as a symbol of similar changes occurring concurrently within the lives of other characters. For example, just minutes before Hod's poignant confession to Langley, Barbara, who, like Muriel of "Box Seat," has been struggling to free herself of her "zookeeper restrictions," is virtually swept away by the intensity of the feelings rocking the *Burgundy*. Toomer writes: "After a time the ship's intoxication caught her, made her thrilled and heady as though she were walking amid adventure and danger. Never before had she seen such doings, this pagan reckless mingling of the sexes, this feeling of having the lid pulled off, this utter disregard for convention and other people's opinions" (456). Barbara is slowly showing a new side of herself. Under the able stewardship of Langley, she is emerging from her protective covering to participate fully in the life beyond her cabin door.

In the process of taking this giant step forward, Barbara falls in love with Langley—"she had a sly, secret thought Hugh and herself might slyly taste of the forbidden fruit" (456)—and the depth of feeling is mutual. Although frightened and insecure, Barbara has taken risks by revealing the dark side of her nature to a stranger, and these risks have had their rewards and benefits. She is now stronger and more confident than she has been in her entire life:

> And she suddenly realized that ever since she could remember she had wanted just this, this feeling that the world was hers, that she belonged to it, that she was free and unafraid to mix and mingle and participate.
> Truly it was an achievement, an unexpected miraculous achievement right in the midst of a situation she had feared would pain and defeat her. Thanks to Hugh . . . to Hugh who had come for her and drawn her out, out of herself. (514)

Just as Langley freed Hod from the stranglehold of his destructive, tempestuous tendencies, so he also released Barbara from the cage of her fears and inhibitions. For a moment Langley believes he has failed with Barbara—"I gave her philosophy, not myself. . . . She gave me nice feelings, not herself"—but this feeling, the product of a momentary lapse of confidence, passes (518).

During the last evening on the *Burgundy* Hod, Barbara, and Langley find themselves on the deck at the same time. They are joined by Vera, who has also, thanks to the impressive psychological powers of Langley, come to a new knowledge of herself and of the complex forces stifling her personal development. The four of them, fortified and strangely altered by their transatlantic crossing, assemble on deck for a kind of "silent ritual of quickened life": "All of them were together, interwoven, blended, electrically awake, silent, gazing out, communicating subtly, filled and substantiated, moving on, lifting, lifting" (611). In this Whitmanesque passage, Toomer suggests the depth and breadth of the transformations that have occurred in each of the characters and also suggests that this shared experience of growth and regeneration, this kinship of higher consciousness, will nourish and sustain them as they strive to deepen their knowledge of themselves and their place in the world.

The same sentiments are expressed moments later: "A mystery held them, and they were still and they were seeing—as if, just behind the covering of night were a world unfolding in brightness and swift beauty" (612). This passage, containing the belief in human possibility Toomer affirmed throughout his life, is followed by a poem that embodies both a wish and a prophecy:

> Stretch sea
> Stretch away sea and land
> We are following thee
> Thy lead is dangerous
> And glorious
> Stretch thyself and us
> And make us live
> To mount the ladder of horizons
> Until we step upon the radiant plateau.
>
> (612)

This poem, this silent prayer, is the mystery that holds and binds them together. Although the "lead" of the sea, a metaphor for life's estrangements, defeats, and imponderables, is dangerous, life itself is glorious. This fact is confirmed by the "radiant plateau," a metaphor for the transcendent knowledge of human life and human experience, what Gurdjieff called "objective consciousness," toward which Hod, Barbara, Hugh, and Vera seem to be progressing.

As this prayer/poem is uttered, the sun breaks through the night's darkness, bringing with it the bright and glorious promise of a new day. As the sun rises, it dispels the clouds and ascends into a clear, blue sky. The sun becomes a sign, a harbinger of a hopeful and harmonious future. We are reminded of the sunrise, the "birth-song" that is the closing scene of "Kabnis," and we feel that, like that drama's tortured and beleaguered protagonist, Hod and Barbara have come through their personal ordeal whole, changed, and renewed.

As we know from our study of *Cane* and "The Gallonwerps," Toomer, in writing these books, boldly struck out in new directions. In "Transatlantic" he continued to play the part of the experimentalist, but this time his experiments centered more upon the tricks of narration than upon the possibilities of form and content.

The events of "Transatlantic" represent the fictional outpourings of an anonymous, omniscient narrator of divine origins who relates the events in his novel to two other divine beings. Although the narrator remains nameless, he does identify the two gods who are his captive audience. They are called Sboots and Droofle. Sboots and Droofle do not criticize, nor do they interrupt the narrator with questions or observations. It seems that their role is to listen—in this regard they are as helpless as the reader—and that is all they do.

Judging by the narrator's patronizing manner, Sboots and Droofle do not share his high station. It seems that they are being given instruction on the habits and conditions of lower forms of life by someone far more exalted than they. This convention of superior beings observing and commenting upon the activities of inferior life forms is a common feature of science fiction writing. An example of this form of narration can be found in the fiction of a writer who is relatively new to the genre. I am thinking of Doris Lessing and her new series of science fiction novels entitled *The Marriages Between Zones Three, Four and Five, Shikasta,* and *The Sirian Experiments,* novels which represent a dramatic departure from the concerns expressed in *The Golden Notebook* or the *Martha Quest* series. Toomer obviously made use of this narrative technique years before Lessing discovered it, and no doubt he turned to it for vastly different reasons. The technique itself is an extremely interesting one, and Toomer was, I believe, attracted to it for at least two reasons.

First, by creating this anonymous, superior being with literary pretensions, Toomer was able to sermonize, psychologize, and criticize as loudly and as long as he pleased. It is, of course, unproductive to do this in a concentrated and integrated work of fiction, but "Transatlantic" is none of these things. The unfortunate cracks in the dam appear in "Wag-hint," the novel's first chapter. Here the narrator states his intentions and in the process forecasts action: "I'll scamp a bunch of egos on board an outbound transatlantic liner and let them swagger and bang until their ribs stick" (1). After this rather crude statement of purpose, the narrator briefly introduces each character and casts them as representatives of particular psychological types.

He describes Hod as the "puritanical sensualist." Barbara is dubbed "Frigid-Fair," and Langley is introduced as the "suspicious philosopher." The predictions and pronouncements posited in this chapter are, as we discover, fully developed in subsequent chapters. To be certain that the reader perceives the action in the manner intended, the narrator frequently stops all action and analyzes each significant development. There are several chapters within the novel that contain only the observations and reflections of the narrator, not to mention his detailed predictions of future developments, and the fact that they exist at all is an indication of the difficulties Toomer encountered in composing "Transatlantic." Such road maps and guideposts are unnecessary, and they attest to Toomer's failure in a long, rambling work like "Transatlantic" to sustain a complex narrative.

By creating this supernatural, omniscient narrator, Toomer not only gave himself the freedom to comment on and interpret the action for the reader, but he also invested a relatively flat, uninteresting novel with new levels of meaning. As Hod and Barbara struggle to overcome the evil within themselves, we discover that the gods who inhabit the narrator's universe are engaged in a similar battle against evil, but the evil that threatens them is external. Razzgold and Plassoval, the gods of "life and construction," are pursued and challenged by Maramon and Drackas, the gods of "destruction and ravage." The battle of battles is protracted, bloody, and violent. At the moment when Razzgold and Plassoval seem close to defeat, Oster-Rey, the god of the "Beyond and the Unattainable," intercedes, and the forces of Maramon and Drackas are vanquished.

Toomer obviously intended to raise the psychological and spiritual transformations of Hod and Barbara to the level of allegory. Drackas embodies the evil in Hod and in all mankind, and Plassoval embodies the good that is also in Hod and in each one of us. There are several confrontations between Drackas and Plassoval, and each one corresponds to the personal efforts made by the human characters to identify and to master their most disagreeable features. Plassoval's victory over Drackas occurs after Hod's and Barbara's transformations, and thus it seems to confirm their expansion and growth of consciousness.

Although Toomer took great pains to make "Transatlantic" interesting and compelling, the result is not art. Indeed, it is much less than that. "Transatlantic" is marred by the theorizing, didacticism, and jargon that are the bane of "The Gallonwerps." References to the theories of the Gurdjieff system appear frequently in Langley's speeches. As he holds forth in typical fashion before Hod and Barbara, his points are colored by the language and ideas of Gurdjieff. In describing the causes and effects of man's limited intellectual abilities, Langley states: "We've been so misimpressed and misprinted that all or most of our impressions are distorted as they pass through various receiving-apparatuses distorted by us as we register and recollect them" (224). The phrase of interest to us is "receiving apparatuses." This is a thinly disguised version of "formatory apparatus," which, according to Gurdjieff, inhibits complex intellectual processes.[35] In the same conversation, Langley suggests that "human beings in particular and all beings in general may be what we may call the breathing-lines of the cosmos, that through and by means of us the cosmos breathes" (225). This is another one of Gurdjieff's ideas that Toomer brought out for our consideration. Gurdjieff argued that all "organic life on earth" was little more than a "highly sensitive mass for the reception of planetary influences."[36] This is essentially Langley's point. Here again, Toomer did little more than weave Gurdjieff's theories into the pattern of his narrative.

This occurs again when Langley, addressing his remarks to Vera, describes the manner in which she and all human beings cope with stress and criticism: "How is she going to escape the common fate? As she grows she will develop a buffer. We who sit here do not have one, and when life hurt us we threw up defenses which, in time, formed into a protective mechanism. A protective mechanism is a makeshift and rather unfortunate substitute for a buffer" (226). The key word in this passage is "buffer," which Gurdjieff defined as an artificial "appliance" involuntarily created by man to neutralize the impact of contradictory views, emotions, and words.[37] That Toomer would write such gibberish and later refer to it as his "best work" illustrates not only the great importance he attached to Gurdjieff's theories but also his failure to recognize how his obsession with them destroyed the fertile imagination that produced *Cane*. [38]

Although we welcome the impulse and admire the attempt to introduce to American literature new interpretations of the nature and aim of human existence, Toomer fell short of the high standards to which he aspired and established in *Cane*. "Transatlantic" shares the same fate as "The Gallonwerps." These are not novels in the sense that we would like them to be; they are not masterful prose works in which an author seeks to reorder reality through the filter of his own inspired imagination. These works do not come close to this definition but are, to borrow a damning phrase that Flannery O'Connor employed to describe the work of inexperienced writers, "essays with sketches woven through them, or sketches with essays woven through them." In O'Connor's meditations on the regrettable tendencies of beginning fiction writers, she touched upon several points that illustrate the mistakes Toomer made again and again in his fiction after 1923: Beginning fiction writers "are concerned primarily with unfleshed ideas and emotions. They are apt to be reformers and to want to write because they are possessed not by a story but by the bare bones of some abstract notion. They are conscious of problems, not people, of questions and issues, not of the texture of existence, of case histories and of everything that has a sociological smack, instead of with all those concrete details of life that make actual the mystery of our position on earth." [39]

Toomer was far from being a beginning fiction writer—his first book was proof of that—but in his role as social critic and spiritual reformer, Toomer was guilty of all the indiscretions O'Connor identified as the most offensive and the most unfortunate in a young writer. The abstract notions by which Toomer was possessed were the theories and practices of the Gurdjieff system. As we read the "The Gallonwerps" and "Transatlantic" or any of the fiction after *Cane*, it becomes painfully evident that Toomer was far more interested in ideas and problems than in character development, or in what O'Connor called the "texture of existence."

Toomer's literary objective, the elevation of mankind to a higher level of being and awareness, doubtless would have been better served if he had confined himself to writing essays or, still better, if he had continued to write books like *Cane*. Toomer's purpose in writing "The Gallonwerps" and "Transatlantic" was to promote higher development, but the works themselves do not inspire it. Since publishers refused to publish these works, describing them as overly specialized, repetitious, and of limited appeal, only Toomer's great belief in their importance could have provided him with the necessary confidence to continue to write such fiction. Like Walt Whitman, who despaired at the initial reception of *Leaves of Grass*, Toomer believed in the value of his work. He doubtless took courage from the example of the "good gray poet" and shook off the disappointment of so many rejection slips.

But a writer needs more than just courage and confidence to produce a good novel. An appreciation for mystery, as O'Connor would be quick to assert, a knack for telling a story, a gift for constructing believable situations, and the ability to educate and to inspire interest without condescending also help. We might add to this long list a gift or an appreciation for lyricism. *Cane* is intensely lyrical, and one can point to almost any story or poem within the work for examples of Toomer's great gift for song. John McClure, editor of *Double Dealer*, believed that lyricism was Toomer's greatest strength and warned that this strength would be weakened if Toomer strayed too far from his muse: "[Toomer's] finest work so far is lyrical and . . . if he ever does supreme work it must be in a lyrical manner. . . . He should mold his stories into lyrical rhapsodies rather than attempt to present them realistically. I am sure if Toomer attempts realistic fiction as his life-work he will be merely one of a number of men." [40]

McClure could not have been more correct in assessing Toomer's strengths or more accurate in prophesying the fall he would take as a consequence of his experiments with realistic fiction after his discovery of the Gurdjieff system. After *Cane*, lyricism was largely replaced by didacticism, for when Toomer accepted Gurdjieff he placed his creative abilities in service to a philosophical and psychological system that stripped them of their enormous power. Toomer himself realized the deficiencies in "The Gallonwerps" and "Transatlantic" as well as in the other works written during the Gurdjieff period. Doubtless it was difficult for a writer of Toomer's talent and prominence to accept the judgments and implications of the increasing number of rejection notices, but eventually he did and in the process recognized his own part in his literary decline. In an unpublished memoir, Toomer wrote frankly and sincerely of the reasons for his failure to secure publishing contracts:

> But, by and large, the chief reason why my writings were rejected was because they did not strike the publishers as being authentic. Nor were they.
>
> They were imperfect projections from a half-world. I had gone off, far off into a world beyond literature. I resumed writing before I had completely come back. I used writing as a means of return, as a means of full return and connection. The reader would have had to be in a condition similar to mine, with a similar need, in order to have had the books perform a similar function for him. As the condition was not a usual one, rarely did my writings mean to others what they meant to me. To most people and indeed in fact, my novels were not novels, my expositions were unfinished, my articles did not connect in a vital way with the lives of the contemporary world.[41]

Without exaggeration and distortion, without shifting the blame to the shoulders of others, without even the protection of weak excuses, Toomer gave the correct timbre and accent to his disappointments with publishers. Although Toomer wrote that the writings of the Gurdjieff period were not "authentic," the plain fact is that they are, for no other writer then or since has employed the theories of the Gurdjieff system as his point of departure, as his ultimate frame of reference. In their purity, "The Gallonwerps" and "Transatlantic" are as authentic as *Cane*, authentic in the sense that they are without literary antecedents. The problem lies not in their authenticity, that is, in their originality, but in their execution.

"The Gallonwerps" and "Transatlantic" remain, as Toomer so honestly and correctly characterized them, "imperfect projections from a half-world." Over time Toomer not only realized that the reader would have to have been in a "condition similar to" his own to enjoy the relief, pleasure, and direction these works were intended to provide, but he also realized the difficulty of and his failure in joining Gurdjieff's ideology with art. But the poet who gave us *Cane* had not disappeared completely. Not everything Toomer wrote during the years he was most active in the Gurdjieff work was flawed or "imperfect." The same poet would emerge again and in certain moments approach and perhaps even match the beauty and power of the single work for which he is remembered.

4

The Sacred Factory:

Drama as Development

@

"I AM NOTHING if not a dramatist," proclaimed Toomer, "and, together with everyone, I make drama of even the minutest features and behaviors of myself and others."[1] A critic is wise to be suspicious of what a writer asserts about himself or herself, especially when a writer's statements, like the one above, contain contradictions. But such seemingly misleading statements are, as many have discovered, more revealing than they appear and possess truths not found in the sincerest pronouncements. On first reading, we may find Toomer's rather bold, romantic statement contradictory for the simple reason that he did not, in spite of his rhetorical flourishes, write many plays. Toomer was mainly a poet and fiction writer, but as we know from reading "Kabnis," he was keenly aware of the possibilities of the dramatic form. But the fact that Toomer was not a prolific playwright makes him no less a pioneer in drama than Eugene O'Neill, Ridgely Torrence, and Elmer Rice. Like these writers, Toomer recognized the deficiencies of the American theater and sought to bring to it more relevant, believable, and inspirational images. Although Toomer's statement suggests a connection with a literary tradition that is, considering his modest contribution to it, a bit spurious, his words are more an expression of an attitude toward drama and its relationship to life than a promise to participate fully in the making and remaking of the customs of the American theater.

In Toomer's view, drama was not a creature of the theater, something separate and apart from the everyday occurrences of life but was everywhere and in everything. "For every play," wrote Toomer, "that appears in the theatre there are millions enacted in bedrooms, and kitchens, along the streets, in all conceivable places from privies to sanctuaries. . . . Life is far greater and more prolific than any score of writers. Indeed, it may in truth be said," and at this point Toomer expressed the sentiments of the Greeks, the Elizabethans, and the great playwrights of the modern era, "that life writes the dramas, while man but plays them."[2]

Like Shaw and Ibsen, Toomer believed that drama should be thoughtful and provocative, that it should correspond in a truthful and meaningful way to the best and worst parts of human existence. He insisted that the "more serious among us demand that the theatre be serious . . . that it convey in contemporary terms about contemporary life a reality and a meaning comparable to the reality and the meaning that the drama had in the days of Shakespeare and Ben Johnson [*sic*]."[3] Toomer's expectations of the American theater were great, and, as we shall see, the handful of plays he wrote all conformed to his belief that the theater should be more than just a procession of masterful illusions devised for an evening's entertainment. For drama to be meaningful and of lasting value it had to contain, Toomer wrote, a message:

> The vital drama of today, is of necessity, drama with a point. The vital theatre is the theatre with a message. Amusement has never made great plays, so we need not consider it here. . . . The great things of today are not those that please man but those that help man in his struggle to keep his head above water, to arise from the water and place new buildings upon a new earth. . . . If art is to be not the indulgence of personality but the contribution of a human being to the human beings of his time, art too must come within and be of the contemporary spirit in that it is first useful to man and only secondarily a thing of beauty or a thing of pleasure.[4]

For Toomer, then, drama had to first be useful, a tool for the elevation and renewal of the spirit, and secondly a distraction or a thing of beauty. Toomer expressed this sentiment in *Essentials:* "A symbol is as useful to the spirit as a tool is to the hand" (v). This functional view of drama is wholly consistent with Toomer's general position on art—

"If art does not promote human development . . . of what use art?"—
that he adopted shortly after his immersion in the Gurdjieff work.[5]

Since Toomer believed that the mission of the American theater
was more glorious and exalted than that suggested by its box office
successes, it is probable that he, a serious dramatist with a reformist
agenda, was not altogether impressed with what he found on and
off Broadway. Toomer was doubtless repelled by the legacy of the
minstrel tradition. Although he may have appreciated the inventiveness of Egbert Williams and George Walker, whose *In Dahomey* (1902)
and *Bandana Land* (1908) represented the beginning of a break from
the minstrel tradition, it is clear, as we know from our examination
of "Kabnis," that he aspired to more.[6] Likewise, Toomer may have
thoroughly enjoyed such musical successes as *Shuffle Along* (1921),
a work that suggested all the vitality, bravado, and abandon of the
Jazz Age, but he was not the least bit interested in writing musical
reviews.[7] Toomer was interested in drama—serious, relevant, and inspirational drama—and it is conceivable that by the time he wrote his
first play in 1922 he had read or seen O'Neill's *The Emperor Jones* (1921)
and *The Hairy Ape* (1922), plays that contained the range of thought,
action, and complexity Toomer was determined should characterize
his own work.

But in 1922 the American theater, as far as drama was concerned,
was still in its embryonic stage. Although O'Neill had by this time
been honored with a Pulitzer Prize for *Beyond the Horizon* (1920), he
had yet to write such masterpieces as *Desire Under the Elms* (1924),
Mourning Becomes Electra (1931), and *The Iceman Cometh* (1946). The
work of Elmer Rice, an acquaintance of Toomer, was largely unknown.[8] Rice's *The Adding Machine* (1923) had not yet gone into production, and it would be years before the public could pay to see
the experimental drama of George Kaufman, Marc Connelly, Sophie
Treadwell, and Channing Pollock. Plainly, the experimentation in fiction and verse inaugurated by Stein, Eliot, Anderson, and Pound did
not as yet have a counterpart in drama, and Toomer, hungry for novel
and stimulating perspectives, turned to the great dramatists of Europe
for nourishment.

Of all the European dramatists writing before and around 1922, including Ibsen, Strindberg, Maeterlinck, and Hauptmann, the dramatist who had the most profound influence upon Toomer was Shaw.

Toomer discovered the works of Shaw in 1917 while still a student at the City College of New York, and the event possessed all the significance of Alice Walker's discovery of Zora Neale Hurston or of James Baldwin's discovery of Richard Wright. In his recollection of this event, it is apparent that the reading of Shaw was a revelation for Toomer that had literary and nonliterary effects: "Shaw's independence and candor showed me to myself. He as a person struck deep into me, convincing me that it was valuable to be as he was. I felt I could be and should be independent and candid. I experienced a sudden turnover—a spiritual bath, a complete cleansing. I became candid. And the minute I did so, I felt myself, for the first time in years, standing squarely and frankly on my own feet. I was what I was. The world could take me or leave me." [9]

The reading of Shaw engendered a defiant, almost militant response in Toomer, but it should be remembered that Toomer first encountered the works of the Irish playwright during one of the most confusing and turbulent periods in his long life. Toomer began reading Shaw in 1917, near the climax of his six-year period of wandering. He had not yet settled upon a profession and had changed disciplines several times, as easily and as quickly as he had changed schools. The young Toomer was just beginning to experiment with writing, but his family had expected greater things from him and so displayed only a polite interest in his dreams of a literary career. Thus, it is not surprising that with only the tepid support of his family, Toomer found in Shaw a bold, courageous example, and he gained the necessary confidence to endure the criticisms of his grandfather, the imperious Pinchback, who did not conceal his displeasure at what he regarded as his grandson's aimless and self-indulgent course.

But the romantic figure of Shaw imbued Toomer with more than just the pith to withstand Pinchback's fulminations. For Toomer, Shaw was a masterful playwright whose verbal dexterity imparted to him a keen appreciation for the force and beauty of language. In his raptures over the Irish playwright, Toomer wrote that "ever since discovering Shaw my taste for the written word had increased." [10] If Shaw, as Toomer asserted, sensitized him to the magical properties of the written word, then it is conceivable that Shaw's popular *Pygmalion* (1912), a play about, among other things, the sacredness of language and its transformational powers, must have possessed special significance for Toomer. In act 1 of this romantic comedy, Henry Higgins, "an energetic phonetic enthusiast," encounters Eliza Doolittle, an uneducated flower girl, on the street. Doolittle's speech patterns are so primitive and appalling that Higgins is moved to exclaim: "A woman who utters such depressing and disgusting sounds has no right to be anywhere—no right to live. Remember that you are a human being with a soul and the divine gift of articulate speech: that your native language is the language of Shakespeare and Milton and the Bible: and don't sit there crooning like a bilious pigeon." [11] Higgins's caustic pronouncement must have made quite an impression upon the young Toomer, but the principal objective of the intelligence behind this most well-known of Shaw's plays perhaps made an even deeper one.

Clever and amusing from beginning to end, *Pygmalion* was more than just the means by which Shaw purged himself of the hostility he felt for the public's contempt for elevated language. As in all his plays, Shaw's objective was not only to criticize but also to teach his audience an important lesson about itself, to provide its members with an opportunity to see themselves as they sometimes were—foolish, pompous, and gullible. The use of the stage as a vehicle for instruction struck a deep chord in Toomer. Prone to didacticism himself, he admired Shaw's skillful and ironic manipulation of his characters and audience.

Higgins's transformation of Eliza from an ungrammatical street urchin into a graceful, relatively articulate parlor ornament—a feat achieved as a consequence of Eliza's determination to master the intricacies of polite discourse in spite of the abusive, tyrannical nature of her instructor—dramatizes the working class's unwavering belief that the tempering of certain personal shortcomings assures one's social mobility. Eliza is a welcomed guest in the homes of middle-class matrons with nothing better to do than pour tea (it would have been unladylike for them to expect or demand more) because she is attractive and seems to be, through the power of speech, cultivated. Because Eliza appears refined, she is accepted as such: perception becomes the truth. Of course, Eliza, if we take the larger view, is no better or worse than her hostesses before she begins instruction with Higgins, but her lessons in grammar and elocution magically make her a member of a group that is disdainful of anyone outside of it.

In *Pygmalion*, it is evident that Shaw despised this middle-class preoccupation with exclusiveness and appearances, but his impatience with such shallowness was exceeded only by his wish to make the middle class, by means of his wit and insight, aware of its foolish pretensions. As we know from reading *Cane*, Toomer was as anxious to employ his talents in a similar service for a similar good. It is quite clear that reading Shaw not only increased Toomer's regard for language but also influenced Toomer in determining his views on the function and purpose of art, which, he believed, should be both critical and didactic, inspirational and reformist.

Coincidentally, Shaw held a similar view of art. In his opinion, art was of little use unless it was didactic. Indeed, he asserted that it "should never be anything else." For art's sake alone," wrote Shaw, "I would not face the toil of writing a single sentence."[12] Such a statement is entirely consistent with Toomer's own conception of art. Since Toomer regarded himself as a "Shaw enthusiast," it is reasonable to assume that his opinions were shaped by, if not borrowed from, his reading of Shaw's provocative prefaces.[13] Clearly, Toomer strove to imitate Shaw's inimitable manner of dramatic instruction. *Natalie Mann* (c. 1922), Toomer's first play, contains that element of didacticism and critical reflection that is not only at the core of *Pygmalion* but is also present in *Major Barbara* (1905) and *Man and Superman* (1903). The last-mentioned work was unquestionably a favorite of Toomer, for John Tanner, a central figure in Shaw's fascinating critique of marriage, bears an uncanny resemblance, in temperament and outlook, to Nathan Merilh of *Natalie Mann*.

But Toomer, a daring experimentalist, extended Shaw's contention that a play should be critical and didactic to the frontier of a new genre. Years after his discovery of Shaw, Toomer envisioned writing what he called a "lecture drama." This was a drama in which "prospective theatre goers" would not be entertained, but "talked to by an actor as seriously as if this actor were . . . an agent in life through whom certain ideas and feelings of importance are transmitted."[14] Such a conception of drama is unabashedly Shavian. Plainly, Shaw was an important influence and model for Toomer. We might go as far as to say that with regard to all questions pertaining to drama, Shaw was Toomer's foundation. But if the writings of Shaw served as the basis for Toomer's introduction to drama, Gurdjieff remained, above all others, his intellectual framework—the man from whom his drama, particularly those plays written after 1923, assumed its tone, direction, and theme.

In his role as spiritual reformer and social critic, Toomer doubtless perceived advantages to writing drama that were not to be found in either fiction or verse. Of all the arts, drama, with perhaps the exception of music, is the most seductive and the most powerful because it is the most immediate. Playwrights enjoy a tremendous advantage over poets and novelists, because their works are meant to be performed. Novels and poems, on the other hand, are usually read in solitude with nothing to disturb readers except their own thoughts or the writers' poor mastery of their subjects.

There is a vitality and an excitement about a live theatrical performance that cannot be found in reading. As a former usher at Washington's Howard Theatre, Toomer was aware of the broad appeal of the theater and perceived it as a powerful vehicle through which to propound his cherished theme: human development. Did Toomer not assert that he "would rather form a man than form a book"?[15] Given his great desire to bring his contemporaries to a knowledge of their own spiritual and psychological fragmentation, in fine, given his desire to play the part of Pygmalion, we should not be surprised that Toomer wrote plays but only that he wrote so few. It seems that Toomer wrote only seven plays: *Natalie Mann, Balo,* "Kabnis," *The Sacred Factory,* "Man's Home Companion," "A Drama of the Southwest," and "Pilgrims, Did You Say?" Of all Toomer's dramas, *The Sacred Factory* is the most ambitious and the most deserving of production. It constitutes the central focus of this chapter. The other six are, with the exception of *Balo* and "Kabnis," slight in their achievement, but all deserve commentary.[16]

A drama in three acts, *Natalie Mann* (c. 1922), was Toomer's first play. Set in Washington, D.C., and New York City in the early 1920s, the play dramatizes the successful struggle of Natalie Mann, an attractive, educated black woman, to free herself from the repressive conventions and expectations of Washington's black middle class. Natalie achieves her independence with the assistance and support of Nathan Merilh, a critical, outspoken philosopher with literary pretensions whose background and origins are unknown. The relationship between Natalie and Nathan is extremely symbolic. In his notes on characters and setting, Toomer described Natalie as a "personality who achieves herself"; Nathan was described as an "instrument of achievement." [17] This heavily symbolic male-female relationship, a feature common to much of Toomer's work, provides the framework for thought and action.

In conversation with Tome, one of the play's minor characters, Nathan refers to Natalie as a "girl who's at the cross-roads. Either she breaks her environment," he asserts, "or it'll break her." Natalie is aware that she has reached a point in her life at which she must either go the way of her parents or go her own way. Since her engagement to Nathan, she has become more resistant to her parents' manner of living as well as to the customs and values that inform it. In act 1, Natalie, unable to contain the revulsion she feels for the life of her parents and the life they are planning for her, expresses her contempt for her mother's strict compliance with the standards of her class: "You are a powdered and scented and proper bundle of don'ts and prohibitions. I have never expected that you would understand me. . . . But a daughter's starvation rations should include at least a bare crust of love. All the old hens in this city—and the young ones too, have tried to peck at me and pull me down. I don't complain that you have often believed them—you are more like them than you are like me, but it has nearly crushed my soul to feel not even a spark of blind faith and sympathy." [18] Plainly, Natalie's conflict with her mother foreshadows the struggle of Dorris with Mrs. Pribby in "Box Seat" and Carrie K's submission to the "sin bogies" of the old women of Sempter in "Kabnis." Mrs. Mann is shocked and hurt by Natalie's harsh words, and the attack only widens the gulf between them. Although Natalie, after recovering her temper, makes a sincere effort to see the world from her mother's point of view, the gulf is never bridged. The consequences of the argument are not entirely negative: Natalie realizes that it is now time to leave home. After a period of reflection, Natalie, against the wishes of her parents and friends, moves to New York City with Nathan.

The play's ending is contrived and melodramatic. Nathan and Natalie return to Washington, D.C., to visit their dying friend Mertis Newbolt, who, it seems, is the victim not of an incurable disease but of the city's smugness. After the funeral, Natalie, Nathan, and Therman Law, Mertis's bereaved husband, join friends at a local jazz club. All enjoy the music and the atmosphere of the place. After a few drinks, Nathan joins the club's featured singer, an old friend and former lover, on the dance floor. Their dance is no ordinary two-step, and the music it evokes is "symbolic," as Toomer tells us in his stage notes, "of the dance and triumph of souls."[19] At the climax of this dance, Nathan collapses in the arms of his partner. The men and women in the club, unaware that Nathan has only fainted, panic. Natalie is contemptuous of their confusion and of their failure to grasp the significance of Nathan's dance, a dance that was intended to reveal not only every individual's wish to be free of society's controlling forces but also Nathan's catalytic role in that liberation.

Natalie Mann is plainly the product of a critical and reflective imagination, but there are weaknesses within this work. The dialogue is often forced and pompous. For example, Mary Carson, an overbearing and opinionated matron, vacillates between jargon and a kind of Victorian cant. The following line illustrates her torturous manner of speech: "You are aware, I suppose, that the world is drifting into an almost complete materialization of thought and chaos."[20] The prototype for such characters as Dan Moore, Prince Klondike, and Hugh Langley, Nathan suffers with the same linguistic affliction. Nathan's manner of speech may not be as pretentious as Carson's, but it is in its own way as clotted and as confusing. In conversation with Tome, Nathan spews forth the following verbiage:

> Come old man, I may not have faced all of the experience that you have on your plane, but I've backed it in my own way. Hell, that's not what I want to say to you—it's this, a river, blocked, spreads out over the plain, and if it does no other damage, it wastes and dissipates itself. The thing to do is to dreg the bottom, get it full of melting snows and April rains, and then by the cumulative velocity of its own current there is no such thing as blocking it. That's unnecessarily involved, I admit—I've been beached on some old jargon I thought I was rid of—but anyway, you get what I mean.[21]

We do "get" the meaning, but we would have been grateful if Toomer had created a more lucid, intelligible language to carry it. Toomer learned several lessons from reading Shaw, but it is obvious that he had yet to learn from him or from anyone else how to write realistic dialogue. Though he may have stumbled initially, Toomer kept the brilliant example of Shaw ever before him—at one point in the play Natalie quotes Shaw—and it is obvious that Toomer hoped to replicate the clever, witty dialogue so characteristic of Shaw's own work.

In addition to the horrific problem of language, the play is shamelessly and exceedingly autobiographical. All writers draw on their own experiences, but there is an element of vanity, even narcissism, in *Natalie Mann* that perhaps diminishes the importance of the work. Toomer's unsophisticated exploitation of significant personal and familial events makes *Natalie Mann*, in spite of all Toomer's efforts and planning, the work of a young and inexperienced writer. It is apparent that the struggle of Natalie Mann is the struggle of Nina Toomer, Jean Toomer's mother, who was rescued from the tyranny of Pinchback's household by Nathan Toomer, Toomer's father and probably Merilh's namesake. But the marriage of Nina and Nathan Toomer did not end as happily as the marriage of Natalie and Nathan Merilh. Nathan Toomer abandoned Nina, forcing her to return to her father's home to raise her only child—Jean Toomer—alone.

But actually the situation that unfolds in *Natalie Mann* contains more autobiographical asides and convolutions than the Pinchback family album. Natalie's struggle for independence is also to some extent the struggle of Toomer himself who, like his mother Nina, resisted and resented Pinchback's domination. Toomer described the long contest of wills between him and the redoubtable Pinchback: "Not until I was three could I rule my nurse. Not until I was seven could I rule my mother and grandmother. Not until I was twenty-seven did I finally conquer my grandfather." [22] As Toomer was growing up, there was much shouting between the maverick grandson and the conservative grandfather, and not until the former lieutenant governor of Louisiana was too old and feeble to shout back did Toomer feel bold enough to assert himself in Pinchback's presence. Although Toomer may have identified with the plight of Natalie Mann, it is clear that he aligned himself finally with the character of Nathan Merilh.

Nathan's friendship with Therman Law was doubtless based upon Toomer's friendship with Henry "Son" Kennedy, a high school classmate. Toomer described Kennedy as a "radical and a rebel." [23] We might also add "disciple" to the list of labels, for the young Kennedy looked to Toomer for guidance and support. Both were known not only for their advanced political and social views but also for their rowdiness and hedonism.

As we probe more deeply, we discover other autobiographical parallels. Not only does Nathan Merilh bear a physical resemblance to Toomer, but like his creator he is also a writer. At one point in the play

Nathan, over cocktails with friends in a Manhattan restaurant, reads his newest story. It is none other than "Karintha." Toomer weaves the complete text of this story, which Nathan reads from beginning to end, into the fabric of his play.

It should be apparent by now that Nathan Merilh, the poet, social critic, philosopher, expert on jazz and folklore, reformer, and liberator is most certainly an idealized version of Jean Toomer. Although some may find Toomer's self-analysis a bit self-serving, *Natalie Mann* is an important work precisely because it contains, for those in search of more revealing pictures of Toomer the man, poses that he was careful enough, modest enough, to expunge from his several autobiographies. But more than this, *Natalie Mann*, perhaps the most amateurish of Toomer's dramas, remains an important work because it is the first self-conscious articulation of issues, patterns, and themes to which Toomer returned again and again in his later works. With the aid of the accomplished, highly advanced Nathan Merilh, Natalie Mann achieves a level of personal freedom and development not realized by most of the characters of *Cane* or by most of the characters of "The Gallonwerps." We do not witness again this degree of personal development and fulfillment until "Transatlantic" and "The Blue Meridian." The latter was Toomer's most successful effort to join his great theme of human development with the theories of the Gurdjieff system.

Balo (1922), Toomer's second play, is, as Sterling A. Brown notes, "more incident than play but shows early promise of the power uncovered in 'Kabnis.' " Written for the Howard Players of Howard University, *Balo* is the only play by Toomer ever produced on the stage. Darwin T. Turner describes *Balo* as the "least comprehensible" of Toomer's dramas, but the cause of Turner's mystification is itself a mystery.[24] The play, set in a Georgia town at harvest time, dramatizes the conversion of Balo Lee, the introverted and deeply religious son of Will and Susan Lee. The action of the play takes place in a single day and is probably based on events and people Toomer observed during his sojourn in Sparta, Georgia.

The setting and characters of *Balo* represent a radical departure from those of *Natalie Mann*. In his second drama, Toomer turned his thoughts away from the trials and difficulties of Washington's black middle class in order to give us a vivid, though brief, picture of family life among southern black farmers. The integrity and simplicity of the

lives of the Lee family are plainly a criticism of the artificial, unfulfilled lives of the Manns. Toomer's portrait of rural, southern life does
not contain any of the harshness of "Kabnis" or of the other parts of
Cane. *Balo*'s mood and setting are idyllic. Seated near the fire, Will
and Susan Lee read the Bible while their sons, Balo and Tom, doze at
their feet. The Lee home is modest but comfortable; its occupants live
gracefully and with dignity.

The drama's emphasis is upon agrarian and spiritual values. Toomer
is careful, however, not to romanticize the condition of the Lees. We
do sense that their lives are difficult and proscribed by the customs
that influence the movements and aspirations of people of their class
and race. But the Lees are not paralyzed by these customs; indeed,
their strength and dignity belie their circumstances. Balo's mystical,
emotional conversion, which is the drama's conclusion, is not only the
means by which Toomer suggests the particular nature of the underlying strength of the Lees, but it is also the means by which we witness
the assertion of spiritual values in the face of an encroaching technology. More precisely, Balo's conversion is the means by which we
discover and measure the effects of a godless, alienating technology
upon our own lives. Balo himself seems aware of the importance and
benefits of a spiritual life and spiritual values; such a life and such
values plainly have implications for his personal development. It is
this awareness and these values that Toomer treats and celebrates in
this one-act drama.

Balo represents a self-conscious attempt on Toomer's part to experiment with a relatively new form made popular by some of his contemporaries—African-American folk drama. Ridgely Torrence did much,
in his short but brilliant theatrical career, to increase national interest in the possibilities of African-American folk drama. Toomer was
doubtless aware of the efforts of Torrence, O'Neill, and Paul Green to
introduce the American public to these new dramatic materials. *Balo*
(along with "Kabnis") is plainly Toomer's response to the call of Torrence, O'Neill, and Green, an effort to match the beauty of thought
and expression in Torrence's *Three Plays for the Negro Theatre* (1917),
O'Neill's *The Dreamy Kid* (1919), and Green's *Granny Boling* (1921).

By studying the example of the Irish theater, Torrence, O'Neill,
Green, and many other American playwrights learned that they
needed no longer to confine themselves to traditional subjects, that

is, to the pathologies and conflicts of the American white middle class. They learned that there were fresh possibilities in other groups, namely the African-American folk, whom they had, because of snobbery, custom, and racism, ignored or, worse, treated only as the subject of humor.[25] Although Toomer wrote only two folk dramas, *Balo* and "Kabnis," they are, in their careful rendering of the folk speech and folk customs of African-Americans, exemplary among similar works written and produced during the 1920s and are as worthy of production or, in the case of *Balo*, revival.

"Man's Home Companion" (c. 1933), a drama in one scene, was the second dramatic piece (it followed *The Sacred Factory*) written by Toomer during his involvement in the Gurdjieff work.[26] It bears a close resemblance in theme and content to all the other works Toomer wrote during this period. In this drama of three characters—a husband, a wife, and their robot-maid Argive—we observe the sinister effects of an extremely sophisticated technology on the institution of marriage. In a curious reversal of roles, the wife is the dominant force in this union; the husband, who possesses all the attributes we traditionally associate with women—patience, emotionalism, affection—is domestic to an extreme degree. The wife, who is completely dedicated to her career, has little time for her husband and is contemptuous of his financial dependency as well as of his need for and frequent displays of affection. She is disdainful of kisses (they are described as "historical habits"), and it is obvious, in view of their novel sleeping arrangement (twin test tubes), that she is also disdainful of the intimacy that is customary between spouses.

Since the wife is uninterested in meeting her husband's emotional and physical needs, he finds comfort, or its modern counterpart, in technology. Argive, the technochaser or robot-maid, not only prepares meals and darns socks but also provides the husband with the kind of companionship that his unfeeling wife seems incapable of giving. This machine displays a concern for the husband's welfare that is completely absent in his wife, and evidently it feels pity, not to mention a certain superiority, for the human beings it serves so conscientiously. In his loneliness and isolation, the husband is kept amused and occupied not only by Argive but also by an "aniphograph," or talking photograph. Not surprisingly, this particular aniphograph depicts his neglectful and frequently absent spouse. It is the husband's custom, with Argive seated beside him, to spend hours conversing with the synthetic image, and it is painfully apparent that their exchanges are more fulfilling than any he has ever had with his wife.

"Man's Home Companion" is apparently an offshoot of "Transatlantic," because Hod Lorimer, one of the principal characters in the novel, also owns an aniphograph. Intrigued by such a fanciful invention, Toomer evidently felt compelled to examine its possible uses and implications within a dramatic framework. Like the novel from which it emerges, the theme of "Man's Home Companion" is modern man's lack of and search for wholeness. The husband longs for contact with his ambitious and distant wife, but he is rejected by her. He is a misfit in a society in which such human values as affection, kinship, and love are no longer cherished. In her coldness and preoccupation with externalities, the wife reminds us of the protagonists in "Rhobert" and "Calling Jesus," for she is plainly the product of a society that attaches more importance to things than to people. In his loneliness, the husband stands prepared to receive, like the reaper in "Harvest Song," a response to his call for emotional connection that never comes.

The most salient difference between "Man's Home Companion" and *Natalie Mann* and *Balo* is the absence of black characters and the avoidance of racial themes. We recall that as a consequence of his position on race, his acceptance of Gurdjieff's theories, as well as his desire to avoid any further misunderstanding among critics and readers concerning his racial background, Toomer refrained from treating the experience of African-Americans in his works after *Cane*. (The exception is "The Blue Meridian.") But there is perhaps another reason, one at the core of an avant-garde arts movement, that helps to explain the striking absence of black characters and racial themes in "Man's Home Companion."

When Toomer wrote "Man's Home Companion" in 1933, expressionism had been a dominant force in German culture for nearly seventeen years. Since expressionism, as it manifested itself in literature, sought to inspire a moral regeneration in man by externalizing the essential emotions of a situation, it is not surprising that Toomer, a great experimentalist in search of a method consistent with his own objectives as a spiritual reformer, was interested in the formal application of expressionist theories and methods. "Man's Home Companion" is well within the expressionist tradition, for it possesses many of the features associated with this arts movement.

Shadowy, unidimensional characterization is a hallmark of expressionism, and Toomer adopted this mode of presentation in "Man's Home Companion." The expressionist dramatists, among whom Georg Kaiser was foremost, eschewed what they perceived as the encumbrances of naturalism. They were not interested in fully developed characters or what E. M. Forster called "round characters"; on the contrary, they much preferred types or "flat characters."[27] A character's name, race, gender, and personal history were unimportant to the expressionists; what was important to them was the emotion, attitude, or belief that dominated and motivated a character. In obedience to this expressionist credo, Toomer identified his characters in "Man's Home Companion" as only husband and wife. We do not know their names, their ages, or their personal or racial backgrounds. Since the expressionists stressed only what was essential to the comprehension of theme, it is clear why Toomer, given his passion for fundamentals, found their works so appealing.

The dialogue in "Man's Home Companion" is brisk, clipped, self-revealing, and highly rhetorical—another outstanding characteristic of expressionist drama.[28] The pointed, unfeeling statements made by the wife certainly conform to this pattern. There is also in expressionist drama an affection for weird effects and tricky devices.[29] Argive the robot, the aniphograph, the test-tube beds, and the slick, laboratory-like setting are consistent with the expressionists' predilection for the bizarre and the fantastic. In fine, "Man's Home Companion" is the product of Toomer's flirtation with expressionism, a relationship that achieved its full, mature expression in *The Sacred Factory*. Although "Man's Home Companion" is one of Toomer's minor dramas, it is of particular importance because it reveals his sustained, pronounced interest in certain aspects of modernism and underscores the thematic unity within his canon.

In "A Drama of the Southwest" (c. 1935), Toomer eschewed the expressionist method and returned to what in this instance may be called naturalism.[30] Set in Taos, New Mexico, this drama in one scene is essentially a dialogue between Lewis Bourne, a visitor from the East, and Clifford Genthe, a local resident and artist. We recall that Toomer had intended one day to write what he termed a "lecture drama," and it seems that "A Drama of the Southwest" was his first offering of this kind, for the play is without action or plot. What there is of movement and cohesiveness depends on the sometimes stilted, extremely self-conscious chatter of Lewis and Clifford.

Lewis has come to Taos for the summer with his wife Grace. It seems that the Bournes have spent other summers in Taos, but there will be something different about this particular summer. They have arrived, after an exhausting drive across the country, weighted down by a question that has plagued them for some time: "What is my function in life?"[31] We do not know if Grace and Lewis are successful in devising an answer to this nettlesome Gurdjieffian question, because the drama concludes before they have an opportunity to address it.

It seems that at least Lewis (Grace's plans are unknown) will not be content to pass the summer merely ruminating about this large, troublesome question, but he intends to shape his reply into a book. In his discursive, gossipy conversation with the congenial Clifford, Lewis reveals the theory behind his book:

> The thesis, in brief, is the more or less obvious one that what is automatic takes care of itself unless irregularities occur, that what is conscious is not taken care of by the general processes of the world, and that, therefore, those who are conscious—if they would function—must build their own worlds. As you can see, it's not a new idea: but my understanding of it, and my development and application of it to the modern situation may help clarify the basic needs and desires of many who now see only chaos and a clash of surface phenomena.[32]

Lewis is correct when he states that the theory behind his book is not new, for it is a restatement, in opaque, unintelligible language, of a fundamental law within the Gurdjieff system. The behavior of human beings will remain "automatic" or unconscious and mechanical, as Gurdjieff argued, until certain "irregularities occur." These "irregularities" are "B influences." According to Gurdjieff, in their concrete form these influences are religion, literature, and a sincere dissatisfaction with our present circumstances.[33] Without the presence of these influences, or "irregularities," to return to the language of Toomer's spokesman, growth and development of any kind remain only a remote possibility.

In "A Drama of the Southwest" Toomer returned to a region of the United States that he knew rather well. The Bournes are a thinly disguised version of Jean Toomer and Marjorie Content, who also, like their dramatic counterparts, traveled by car across the country each year to their summer residence in Taos. Toomer and Content were married in Taos, and Georgia O'Keeffe, Toomer's former lover, witnessed their impromptu marriage. We also recall that Toomer, several years before his marriage to Content, had visited Taos on behalf of Gurdjieff in order to investigate a proposal made by Mabel Luhan (another woman smitten permanently by Toomer), who had offered her ranch as another possible branch of Gurdjieff's institute. Luhan makes a cameo appearance in this drama as Hanna Gow. A rich, influential resident of Taos, Gow, who is described by Clifford as a "wild cat," is most certainly, with all her Native American jewelery, shrillness, and force, a caricature of Luhan.[34]

"A Drama of the Southwest" is not an outstanding work. It is not distinguished by the linguistic and formal inventiveness of "Man's Home Companion" or, as we shall see, of *The Sacred Factory*, but it remains a significant work because of Toomer's undisguised exploitation of Gurdjieff's theories for the purposes of art and his continued treatment of his theme of human development. The drama is also important because it contains, like *Natalie Mann*, yet another picture of Toomer the man, a picture not fully set forth in his autobiographies.

"Pilgrims, Did You Say?" (c. 1940) was probably the last drama Toomer ever wrote.[35] Set in an unnamed village in India, the drama chronicles the efforts of John and Mary, two Americans traveling with their daughter Missie, to discover the meaning and purpose of human existence through their study of Eastern philosophies. During their pilgrimage through India, John and Mary are accompanied by Manasingha, their Indian servant. Manasingha is an aging Buddhist who dispenses bits of Eastern wisdom as he goes about his duties of washing the laundry and preparing meals.

Even though he is a servant, Manasingha is clearly superior, like Argive in "Man's Home Companion," to the people he serves, for he has long since found that sense of wholeness for which his employers have traveled so far to find. "Pilgrims, Did You Say?" (in an earlier draft it was called "Tourists in Spite of Themselves and Colombo-Madras Mail"), is essentially a fragment of a larger work that was never completed. It is obviously based upon Toomer's own visit to India with Content and his daughter (by his first wife Margery Latimer) in 1939. Interestingly, the purpose of Toomer's pilgrimage was identical to that of the protagonists in his drama.[36] Since the play is incomplete, we cannot evaluate it in quite the same way that we would a finished work, but it is revealing. It suggests that Toomer, in

1939 a man in his middle forties, was again in search of that sense of completion promised by the application of Gurdjieff's theories and that he had retraced, knowingly or unknowingly, the route of his teacher's celebrated journey to the East. In their detailed and engaging reconstruction of Toomer's six-month sojourn in India, Kerman and Eldridge reveal that this expedition in search of higher knowledge was not only dangerous (the Toomers were traveling at the outbreak of World War II) but also unfulfilling. In his visits to such cities as Agra, New Delhi, Bombay, and Colombo, Toomer did not find the master who possessed the arcane knowledge he was so intent on securing. Indeed, at the end of this journey, which placed a strain not only on his health but also on his marriage, Toomer concluded, in the words of Kerman and Eldridge, "that the Gurdjieff work had taken him farther than any system he had encountered in India." [37]

The Sacred Factory (1927) is Toomer's most important and most complex drama.[38] In an earlier draft it was entitled "Saints of Men" and later "Saint Homo: A Religious Drama of Today." Like "Man's Home Companion," *The Sacred Factory* is an expressionist drama and is as good as any play of its kind by an American playwright written during the 1920s. Unlike the most popular expressionist dramas staged in the United States during this period—the works that come to mind are O'Neill's *The Emperor Jones* and Rice's *The Adding Machine*—*The Sacred Factory* does not contain a clear, definable plot. This omission, for audiences accustomed to a beginning, middle, and end, may explain why the work was never produced for the stage.

But Toomer, more than any of his fellow American playwrights, adhered to the German ideal in expressionism and ruthlessly and consistently subordinated action and plot to theme and theory. Expressionist drama is theme-centered rather than plot- or conflict-centered.[39] The theory behind a play or the concept on which it depends for meaning is far more important than any conflict that can be witnessed with the assistance of actors. In the case of *The Sacred Factory*, the theory or theme that infuses the play is human development, or modern man's lack of and search for wholeness. Thus the intellectual emphasis and the intense preoccupation with theme in *The Sacred Factory* do not point to, as some might suppose, an inability on Toomer's part to construct tight, believable plots. On the contrary, they throw into high relief the purity of his applications of expressionist theories.

The characters in this four-act drama seem doomed, although the ending is somewhat hopeful, to live out the most meaningless of existences because they have glorified the things that are inimicable to a sense of wholeness: violence, war, conformity, materialism, technology, and hedonism. The action of the drama takes place in a three-chambered dwelling place that symbolizes, as Toomer wrote in his notes describing the action and characters, "life in the modern western world."[40]

In its spaciousness and dignity, this dwelling was intended to remind us of a cathedral. The setting may seem strange, but such imaginative props were typical of the expressionists.[41] Since Toomer wished to call attention to modern man's spiritual and psychological fragmentation, the cathedral setting is entirely appropriate to his intent and theme. The central chamber of this faintly Gothic structure is the largest of the three and is painted a pale blue. The three groups that constitute the principal characters in this drama—the Worker Group, the Mass Group, and the Family Group—occupy the two smaller chambers. Only in the final act does this trinity, symbolizing movement toward completion and higher consciousness, become one and converge en masse in the central chamber.

The Worker Group, which consists of a married couple, occupies the right chamber. These characters, in contrast with the others in this expressionist drama of higher development, are without the power of speech. Voiceless and nameless—here again Toomer adheres to the expressionist credo—the man and woman communicate to one another only through gesture. During their elaborate pantomine, they move in circles, one behind the other. Their motion reveals their lives for what they are: a repetitious, mechanistic, unconnected series of days, hours, and minutes without design, grace, or meaning. This anonymous and mute pair produces children, who in turn imitate the behavior of their parents. Of course, we have witnessed the sterility and vacuousness of the life of the Worker Group in other places. We are reminded of the protagonists of "Rhobert" and "Calling Jesus" and the multitude of minor characters who appear in "The Gallonwerps" and in "Transatlantic." All are guided, like the absurd family in Georg Kaiser's *Die Koralle* (1917), not by the light of an exalted purpose but by the fumbling and uncritical thrust of their instincts.

The quality of life of the Family Group occupying the left chamber

is, when compared to their speechless, nameless blue-collar counterpart, significantly better. But there is still, as we shall see, much room
for improvement. In contrast with the Worker and Mass groups, the
characters who make up the Family Group—John, Mary and their
daughter Helen—are given names, but only their Christian names.
Plainly, this is in keeping with the expressionist practice of mini-
malism, of providing the audience with only what is essential to a
dramatic situation in order to imbue each character with a universal
significance that might be lost with studied, detailed portraiture. John
and Mary function on the highest level of symbolism, for Toomer intends us to perceive them as any couple who discover, after years of
marriage, that their relationship is based not on love but on a cluster
of selfish and, in this instance, repressive assumptions.

The atmosphere of *The Sacred Factory* is one of revolt, of the fateful
collision of opposing points of view. Revolt is a favorite theme of the
expressionists, and through it is often embodied a terrible antagonism
between a father and son—the plays that come to mind are *Vatermord*
(1915) by Arnolt Bronnen, *Der Sohn* (1914) by Walter Hasenclever, and
Der Bettler (1912) by Reinhard Sorge.[42] In Toomer's drama, however,
the conflict is between a husband and wife. Although the gender and
relationship of the combatants have changed, the nature of the conflict
has not, for in her own way Mary is as determined to remove herself
from John's perversities as Sorge's poet and Hansclever's son are to
remove themselves from the nefarious influence of their fathers. Unlike his counterparts in *Der Sohn* and *Vatermord*—in the first play the
father dies of heart failure after a violent altercation with his son, and
in the second the son actually murders his father—John emerges alive
from the conflict with Mary. But he is not free, changed, and moving
toward completion at the drama's conclusion, as Mary is.

We meet John and Mary at a critical point in their marriage. For
some time, Mary has been living under "the strain of an interior conflict," which has led her to consider the possibility not only of taking
on lovers but also of initiating a divorce. Mary feels, more deeply
than ever before, the dissatisfaction of her life with John as well as
his unwillingness to even consider an adjustment in his attitude and
behavior. Mary discusses with John the ambivalence she feels for him
and their marriage. With the arrogance of one who boldly thinks and
acts for others, John informs Mary that he will not stand by and watch

"these desires" spoil things, but that he intends to "deliberately up-
root and kill them."[43] John is not the least bit interested in accepting
or even considering his part in Mary's unhappiness and decides instead to purge her of the feelings that threaten the order and security
of what he believes is an ideal marriage.

The pain, hostility, and fruitlessness of the discussion between John
and Mary is acted out by the Mass Group, who occupy the same
chamber. Although sometimes acting independently, the Mass Group
extends and amplifies the conflict between John and Mary. The group
is a kind of Greek chorus, who underscores and develops the specific emotions and complaints that emerge as Mary attempts to evoke
within John such human feelings as compassion and empathy. Mary is
unable to penetrate John's elaborate psychological defenses, for each
represents two very different modes of perceiving and interpreting
experience. Their conflict is actually the ancient conflict between reason and faith, and it is clear, given the outcome of the drama, that
Toomer cast his lot with faith.

At the climax of their discussion, Mary is forced to admit that John,
in all the years of their marriage, has succeeded in modifying her behavior in order to make her more agreeable and pleasing to him. The
significance of John's manipulations fills Mary with an anger so great
that it provides her with the necessary courage to dissolve her marriage. John's actions, although essentially negative, lead to extremely
positive and beneficial effects. Ironically, in his selfishness John has
helped Mary to see their marriage for what it is not—a loving, nur-
turing, supportive union. In her last words to John, Mary outlines,
in that contrived, measured, excessively formal language so beloved
of the expressionists, their fundamental differences and expresses her
appreciation for her new knowledge of them:

> You have wanted me to have your knowledge. I have wanted you to have
> my faith. We have succeeded only in opposing them. It has been knowl-
> edge opposed to faith; faith opposed to knowledge. You and I opposed—
> until now; the struggle is ended. I have gained in understanding, and
> for this I thank you. John, I bless you because you have helped me to
> be as I am. But you are still faithless. I cannot help you. So I, separately,
> must act according to my faith, and now according to my need. So you,
> separately, must act according to your lack of it.[44]

John, like Nathan Merilh, is Mary's "instrument of achievement." He unwittingly provides her with the vision to measure and judge his limitations as well as the strength to cast them off.

In the drama's final act, Mary, after much fumbling, finds her way into the central chamber. This act is proof of her triumph over John and her movement toward wholeness. She is joined in the central chamber not only by her daughter Helen, who is unaware of her parents' separation, but also by the Worker and Mass groups. In his blindness and vanity, John remains in the right chamber and is the only character who does not enter the central chamber. John is content to remain where he is, so much so that he is completely unaware of Mary's absence. He continues to speak to her as if she were still present, all the while pontificating upon the futility of human development, of human progress, or of any other principle that provides man with inspiration and courage. John scorns these principles and in his cynicism states that a "wise man gifted with a bit of force and courage" can only "have the pleasure of being pleased with himself." In other words, a perverse narcissism is all that anyone can achieve in life, and this bitter and pessimistic view is for John "the ultimate good sense." [45]

In the final scene of the drama, all the characters, with the exception of John, congregate in the central chamber. As members of each group enter the chamber, they kneel and form a semicircle around a platform. When all have found their places, the Being enters by a rear door in the central chamber and stands in "firm repose" on the platform. The Being, as Toomer wrote in his stage notes, is male and is "dressed in a rich but simple white garment, on the breast of which, embroidered in gold, there is a triangle surrounded by a circle." [46] As indicated by his manner and dress, the Being possesses special spiritual powers. His white robe and the symbols that adorn it, the triangle and the circle, are proof of his elevated status. Toomer was not unaware of the significance of these symbols, for as a student of Gurdjieff he learned that each had a particular meaning and importance.

For Gurdjieff, the triangle was not only a way of counting and a symbol of the Trinity (this view was doubtless based on his study of the Tarot), but it was also a representation of what he called the Law of Three. In the Gurdjieff system, the Law of Three proposed that three forces enter into every manifestation, into every phenomenon, and into every event. These forces were called positive, negative, and neutralizing; active, passive, and neutralizing; or simply first force, second force, and third force.[47] Gurdjieff argued that man was not usually aware of the presence and role of the third force, and this limitation in our perception was a direct function of our state of being or level of consciousness.

The triangle emblazoned across the robe of the Being is enclosed by a circle—the universal symbol for unity, order, and completion. We recall that Toomer used this symbol in *Cane,* only there the circle was broken and thus symbolized man's spiritual and psychological fragmentation. But it is clear that the Being is not fragmented and that he possesses everything necessary for his existence, that is to say, he has achieved that sense of wholeness that the Worker, Mass, and Family groups have assembled before him to receive.

Of all Toomer's fictional creations, the Being is plainly the most important. Even those characters who are idealizations of Toomer himself—Hugh Langley, Prince Klondike, Nathan Merilh—do not possess the spiritual powers of the Being. Though they are models and catalysts for higher development, Langley, Klondike, and Merilh are, for all their power, mystery, and appeal, plainly of this world. The Being is not of this world but is unquestionably an inhabitant of the next, or rather, he is the promise of higher development incarnate: the word made flesh. In the final moments of the last act, the Being leads those kneeling before him in an incantation that contains all the mystery and power of a prayer:

> I am that I am
> I am that I am
> The Father.
>   I am that I am
> I am that I am
> The Mother.
> I am that I am
>   The Son
> That I am
> I am that I am
>   The Son.[48]

In the words of the Being we hear again the words of God as he revealed himself to Moses: "I *am* the God of thy father, the God of Abraham, the God of Isaac, and the God of Jacob." [49] Just as God revealed himself in his terrifying majesty to the frightened and bewildered Moses, so the Being, without the aid of the burning bush, reveals himself to the confused and anxious group assembled before him in the central chamber. The Being is all things at once: Father, Mother, and Son. This is plainly not the Trinity of the New Testament—the inclusion of a female principle makes that impossible—but of Toomer's new spiritual order of which the Being is representative and head. Through the strange force of his incantation, the Being, divine and messianic, proclaims the arrival and foretells the permanence—"I am that I am"—of this new spiritual order. As he repeats the incantation, the Being seeks to instill in everyone kneeling before him a sense of the unity and wonder of the new order and to dispel forever the memory of the old materialism that has blinded them to the beauty of the life of the spirit.

As this examination of *The Sacred Factory* and the other five plays reveals, although Toomer was not always a dramatist of the first order, he was in many instances a dramatist of brilliant, dazzling effects and one who experimented with all the currents within the genre. Toomer's naturalist dramas, his folk dramas, and his expressionist dramas are all the products of a probing and restless intelligence in search of dramatic forms suitable to his objectives as a spiritual reformer committed to realizing a new spiritual order. It was Toomer's intention to make his audiences as uncomfortable and as insecure as Shaw set out to make his and to force them to come to terms with the questions that he regarded as the most important of his age: What is the purpose and nature of human existence? What are the forces that are inimical to a sense of wholeness, and how can they be controlled? These are the questions that motivated and animated Toomer the dramatist, and their answers, as in Toomer's fiction, were rooted in his unassailable belief in the healing, redemptive powers of the Gurdjieff system.

In the first comprehensive examination of Toomer's drama, Darwin T. Turner argues that Toomer failed as a playwright essentially because he was unable to sell his plays to producers. [50] If the sale and production of a dramatist's work are the only means of measuring his success, then it is arguable that Turner is correct, though plainly there must be other criteria. Of course, not every play by Toomer is worthy of production. *Natalie Mann* is at best amateurish, the early work of a young writer experimenting with a difficult form. "A Drama of the Southwest" and "Pilgrims, Did You Say?" are essentially fragments of dramas that were never completed. "Man's Home Companion," although possessing a certain potential, is, like the two works just mentioned, the beginning of a larger, more complex work. "Kabnis" and *The Sacred Factory* are, as Turner correctly asserts, Toomer's best and strongest plays. I would amend Turner's pronouncement, however, to include *Balo*. Plainly, these three plays are the most deserving of serious study, production, and, in the last instance, revival. All three represent the moment in which philosophy achieves a synthesis with art, the moment in which the agenda of a spiritual reformer is subsumed within the larger vision of a poet.

If only *Balo*, "Kabnis" and *The Sacred Factory* merit staging and scholarly study, what then is the value of the other plays? Plainly, *Natalie Mann*, "Man's Home Companion," "Pilgrims, Did You Say?" and "A Drama of the Southwest" are of special importance for several reasons. First, they are indisputable proof of the thematic unity within Toomer's canon; they belie the general view that his canon is composed of unrelated fragments. Second, these works, with the exception of *Natalie Mann* and *Balo*, underscore the importance and prominence of Gurdjieff's theories in Toomer's development as a dramatist. Finally, these works are important because they were written by the author of *Cane* and because they are a reliable, irreplaceable index of the range and complexity of interests and concerns he selected for treatment throughout his writing career.

Toomer's use of Gurdjieff's theories in his drama is, by and large, more subtle and more sophisticated than the clumsy manipulations in "The Gallowerps" and "Transatlantic." But in both his fiction and his drama, Toomer's purpose was to point us in the direction of something better and larger than ourselves and to stress—without ever losing sight of our many shortcomings and inadequacies—our strengths and possibilities. As a dramatist, Toomer intended, with the confidence and pathological optimism of a visionary, to "place new buildings upon a new earth."[51] In his role as the supreme architect of a new spiritual and psychological order, an order whose foundation was the Gurdjieff system, Toomer sought to dispel the cynicism, chaos, and fragmentation of his age by bringing a new message of hope to the American theater and by infusing it with relevant, inspirational symbols of higher development. The irony is that, with the exception of *Balo*, Toomer's dramas were never performed, and only two, *Balo* and "Kabnis," were published during his lifetime. Although it seemed that publishers and the reading public had abandoned Toomer, he did not, during the thirteen-year period following the publication of *Cane*, abandon his work as a spiritual reformer or his dream of a whole, redeemed, and spiritualized America.

5

"The Blue Meridian":
Poetry as Development

❧

IN THE OUTLINE of a lecture delivered to the Catholic Poetry Society of America on 15 April 1947, Toomer declared that the "writing of poetry, and, to [a] less extent, the reading," leads to "restoration, renewal, rejuvenation, [and] oneness." He asserted that the reading of poetry written by poets who "possess" their "possessions"—that is, verse by poets who, through some sustained, Herculean effort, have achieved a high level of consciousness—is a "means of moving" and bringing others into their "possessions" or higher consciousness. Such poetry, according to Toomer, transmits powerful, inspirational influences, "opening and enlarging" the "heart and consciousness" of all who read it. This species of poetry, whose properties are symbolic, dramatic, and restorative, is the product of the poet's "momentary fusion and wholeness" with himself and the spiritual forces of the universe. During these intense and rare intervals of knowledge and integration, poetry is born, and "for this time," asserted Toomer, "the poet possesses and is possessed by his possessions." Through such inspired verse, the poet, observed Toomer, shares his "possessions" and in so doing brings others to a "similar level" of thought and feeling. Poetry thus becomes a prod, a catalyst for higher development, as well as a record of the effort to achieve it. This particular function of poetry, concluded Toomer, is "more important than aesthetic pleasure."[1]

Although this lecture was delivered nearly twenty-four years after Toomer first visited Gurdjieff's institute in Fontainebleau, it is marvelously consistent with the aesthetic position he formulated in 1924 at the outset of his involvement with the Gurdjieff work. It was then that he asked: "If art does not promote human development in those who produce it and in those who receive it, of what use art?"[2] This rhetorical flourish, one so characteristic of Toomer, reveals his principal mission not only as a Gurdjieff lecturer but also as a poet: to inspire and to promote human development. Toomer was faithful to this mission throughout his writing career. We first glimpse the outline for it in *Cane*, and then watch it assume a more distinct form and greater proportions in the later works, most notably "The Gallonwerps," "Transatlantic," *The Sacred Factory*, *Essentials*, and, finally, as we shall see in this chapter, the poem "The Blue Meridian."

"The Blue Meridian" was published in *The New Caravan* in 1936, but an earlier version of the poem, then entitled "Brown River, Smile," appeared in *Pagany* in 1932. Although the earlier version is much shorter than the final one (the first contains only one hundred twenty-six lines), the theme of both is the same—human development. "The Blue Meridian" is Toomer's last significant work, and if *Cane*, as I have suggested, is the work from which all the others emerge, then "The Blue Meridian," if we extend the broken circle of *Cane* to signify the beginning and completion of a literary canon, is the point at which the arcs meet, the point at which theme pauses and then finds fulfillment. The thematic movement within Toomer's canon has led us to and prepared us for the specific, special moment of "The Blue Meridian," and it is in this moment, a moment that possesses the strains of the "swan-song" first heard in *Cane*, that Toomer came closest to achieving his greatest literary triumph. I say "came closest" because Toomer's most supreme moments as a poet were not in "The Blue Meridian" or in any of the later works, but in *Cane*.

In her intelligent ruminations on the strengths and weaknesses of some of Toomer's most important works, Nellie Y. McKay reaches a similar conclusion regarding the place and importance of "The Blue Meridian." McKay writes that "The Blue Meridian" is "second in significance among [Toomer's] works only to *Cane*." McKay also suggests, and I believe correctly, that "The Blue Meridian" represents the culmination of a developing vision of America, a vision that is passionately optimistic and that has its beginnings in *Cane* but that finds its full, mature expression in this last great work. "In *Cane*," argues McKay,

"Toomer had looked at the past and discovered the tragic consequences of racial distinctions and separations on human relationships; in 'Blue Meridian' he attempted to redeem the past and envision an America that would evolve into the prototype of a society that had achieved universal humanity."[3] This new society, or this "new order" as Bernard Bell describes it, was the product not only of Toomer's controversial racial position, a position formulated as early as 1917 and treated in "The First American," the prototype for "The Blue Meridian," but also of years of immersion in the Gurdjieff system, a philosophical and psychological system that not only de-emphasized race but also promised the much desired sense of wholeness and personal unity that Toomer celebrated in "The Blue Meridian."

Since the first drafts of "The Blue Meridian" date back as early as 1920, it was, as McKay asserts, a "well-considered, carefully reasoned" poem, a poem that represented a dramatic departure from the precise, vivid Imagist poems of *Cane*.[4] In "The Blue Meridian" Toomer's objective was not simply, as in "Reapers," "Nullo," or "Conversion," to preserve a particular moment or act in its grace and purity but to pose a question, to inspire reflection, and to compel movement toward a significant and meaningful end. The verse of the Imagists was not designed for such purposes, and therefore Toomer, wishing to write a poem sturdy enough to support the weight of his Gurdjieffian vision of a whole and spiritualized America, looked backward beyond Ezra Pound and H.D. to Walt Whitman.

Toomer read Whitman during that fecund, formative period before the publication of *Cane* when he was reading everything from Goethe to Bernarr McFadden. The influence of Whitman's verse is negligible in *Cane* (Whitman is mentioned once by name in "Box Seat"), but the unmistakable characteristics of *Leaves of Grass*, the irreverent mixture of prose and verse rhythms, the excessive use of parallelism, the cataloging of emotions, objects, and human types, as well the informal but exalted tone, are all present in "The Blue Meridian." In this work Toomer was greatly indebted to Whitman, indeed more so than to Hart Crane and his visionary poem "The Bridge," which appeared three years before. "The Blue Meridian" contains the sensuality of "Song of Myself," the adventure and the challenge of "The Open Road," and the extreme confidence of "I Hear America Singing." These three poems, and many others by Whitman, doubtless informed the writing of Toomer's last and most passionate call for the rise of America's dormant spiritual powers.

Although Whitman was an important influence on Toomer during the writing of "The Blue Meridian," Crane's influence needs to be clarified since, given the friendship between these poets and the importance of "The Bridge" to the development of modern poetry, it is generally assumed that Crane, not Whitman, exercised the greater influence.

Toomer's friendship with Crane began in the early 1920s. It was during these early, formative years of his literary career that Toomer shared his ideas on writing and the changing direction of American literature not only with Crane but also with such writers as Gorham Munson, Kenneth Burke, Sherwood Anderson, and, most important of all, Waldo Frank. Toomer admired Crane's work, and Crane's poem "The Black Tambourine" (1921), which, as R. W. B. Lewis tells us, is the poet's effort to create a "complex and living image of multiple victimization" for the poet and for African-Americans is evoked in "Kabnis."[5] The blind, aging Father John recalls Crane's nameless black man who, like his double in Crane, is "forlorn in the cellar" and "Wanders in some mid-kingdom."[6] Father John, however, unlike his twin in verse, is more than just a victim of racial oppression—here Toomer enlarged and extended Crane's effort. He is a living, dynamic symbol of the African-American past.

But to return to Crane's influence on "The Blue Meridian," it seems that the Cleveland poet exercised little, if any, influence upon Toomer's impressive effort to convey the cultural complexity and spiritual potential of America. As stated earlier, Toomer did not meet Crane until the summer of 1923, and by then he had already written "The First American," the model and predecessor of "The Blue Meridian." Although the content of the poem would change somewhat, Toomer claimed that into this first version of "The Blue Meridian" he did "put something of [his] actuality, something of [his] vision of America—though it needed explaining."[7] It took Toomer some time to explain, because eleven years passed before "The First American" appeared in a 1932 issue of *Pagany* as "Brown River, Smile." "Brown River, Smile," however, is essentially an excerpt from the completed work that we know as "The Blue Meridian." My own examination of the *Pagany* version and the version published in *The New Caravan* in 1936 reveals more the efforts of an editor to compress a long poem into a few stanzas than evidence of a work in progress. I suspect that even before 1932 "The Blue Meridian" was a finished poem. Owing to the limitations of space in both *Pagany* and *The New Caravan*, only parts of "The Blue Meridian" were published; thus, Toomer was forced to make twenty stanzas perform the work of eighty-five.

But if this poem's early and long gestation period is not enough to persuade any reader of its independence of "The Bridge," then we have only to examine the significant elements of each poem to discover that they are not the products of collaborative, mutually inspired exchanges but of two discrete visions on a parallel course framed and propelled by different motives and purposes.[8] First, the language of both poets reveals debts to Whitman, but Toomer remained closer to the "good gray poet" than did Crane. The language of "The Blue Meridian" is an accessible mixture of unrhymed prose and verse rhythms containing parallelism and the usual cataloging and piling up of emotions, observations, and actions so beloved by Whitman. Crane, on the other hand, consistently employed the elegant, opaque language of modern poetry, a language that frequently obscures meaning and that, in this instance, is governed by a weak, occasional end rhyme. The structures of the poems further underscore their differences. "The Blue Meridian" contains three sections, all of which are held together by the complex relationship between the three meridians. "The Bridge," however, contains seven sections with numerous divisions within each of these, and all are held together and anchored by the recurring image of the bridge itself. While Toomer took human development, the goal of higher consciousness, as his theme, Crane's theme was the unity of human experience, the sense of connectedness between man, the earth, and the universe. These two themes are certainly complementary, but Toomer did not stop here, that is, at the point of Crane's revelation, but went farther. For Toomer and Gurdjieff such a discovery was only a prelude to higher levels of meaning and consciousness. For Toomer such a revelation marked the beginning of our journey through time and history, whereas for Crane it was the journey's end and reward. Finally, while it was Toomer's purpose in "The Blue Meridian" to join his vision of a progessive, democratic America with the promise of Gurdjieff's higher consciousness, thereby promoting movement toward a distant but perhaps obtainable goal, it seems that Crane's sole purpose, for all his movement through history and time, was to celebrate and reflect upon the revelation—the unity of human experience—that imbued his poem with its tremendous power and coherence.

The fact that "The Blue Meridian" went largely unnoticed at the time of its publication does not diminish the importance of this great poem. Like *Leaves of Grass*, "The Blue Meridian" did not hold initially the roving, mercurial attention of the American reading public. Nonetheless, Toomer's great poem remains, like *Leaves of Grass*, nothing less than a national epic, an attempt by an American poet to cast in heroic terms not only the complexity of his own ancestry but also that of his fellow citizens who, together with the poet, realize, through their shared union/communion with the Black, White and Blue meridians, their and the nation's own extraordinary potential for growth and development. The speaker of Toomer's poem possesses the authority and wisdom of the consciousness that stands behind each poem in Whitman's magnum opus, and this speaker, like the one in Whitman, is our guide on a journey through the intricacies of the American landscape with its great rivers and cities and through American history with its mistakes and lessons to that place where the principles of a wild, young nation and the vision of a poetic imagination converge and are transfigured. The dreams of a nation become—are—the dancing, dervishing Blue Meridian.

But that such a vital and hopeful expression of this nation's possibilities went unnoticed and ignored is not only a function of the arbitrary workings of fortune but also evidence of a change in the mood of American poetry. In 1936 the reading public, perhaps still reeling from the effects of Eliot's "The Waste Land," was then in the process of further exploring the work of a cadre of poets who were, in their attitude and approach to poetry, radically different from Toomer. These poets did not write the sometimes didactic, reformist Gurdjieffian verse that Toomer wrote most of his life, and this fact helps to explain their ascendancy at a time when Toomer was falling swiftly downward. The poets of whom I am thinking are Sterling A. Brown, Carl Sandburg and Robert Frost. Like the early Toomer, these poets had an unwavering regard for the folk and for the land on which they toiled and by which they were frequently defined. And like Toomer, these poets wrote in the tradition of Whitman, but they were Whitman without the mysticism and his desire to merge, as D. H. Lawrence scornfully observed, with everything and everybody. The men and women and children about whom Brown wrote with such delicacy, truth, and power in *Southern Road* (1932), that is, the folk with their agrarian-based values and beliefs, were, it seems more than ever, the subject and focus of American poetry, not Toomer's carefully orchestrated meditations on a Gurdjieffian mode of higher consciousness. When "The Blue Meridian" appeared in 1936, the reading public, having grown accustomed to the special diet of Frost, Sandburg, and Brown (and conditioned by the work of Edgar Lee Masters, Vachel Lindsay, and Langston Hughes), did not take to the unusual flavor of Toomer's last great effort. The enthusiastic reception of Sandburg's *The People, Yes* (1936) and Frost's *A Further Range* (1936) seemed only to compound Toomer's obscurity. Moreover, in the years preceding and at the time of the publication of "The Blue Meridian," the reading public was distracted further by the musings of another extremely talented and enormously important literary triumvirate: Ezra Pound, T. S. Eliot, and William Carlos Williams. Caught between these two extremely powerful and influential cross-currents in American poetry —ironically Toomer was to a certain degree a force in both—Toomer and "The Blue Meridian" were, not surprisingly, eclipsed.

Containing over eight hundred lines, "The Blue Meridian" is divided into three sections.[9] Each section is introduced by an italicized stanza that evokes and establishes the tone and mood for the action that follows it. The first stanza reads as follows:

> Black Meridian, black light
> Dynamic atom-aggregate
> Lay sleeping on an inland lake.
>   (214).

The second is

> White Meridian, white light
> Dynamic atom-aggregate,
> Lay waking on an inland lake.
>   (223).

And finally the third is

Blue Meridian, banded-light,
Dynamic atom-aggregate,
Awakes upon the earth;
In his left hand he holds elevated rock,
In his right hand he holds lifted branches,
He dances the dance of the Blue Meridian
And dervishes with the seven regions
of America, and all the world.

(233–34)

The key words in these stanzas are "sleeping," "waking," and "awakes." As we recall from our examination of the Gurdjieff system in an earlier chapter, these words denote the first three levels of consciousness possible for man: sleeping, waking, and self-consciousness. The attitude and activities of the figure in each stanza—the Black, White, and Blue meridians—correspond to the mental properties and capabilities of these three levels of consciousness. But these metaphors do more than just signify the stages of consciousness that Gurdjieff and Toomer believed possible for man; they also provide the poem with direction and an internal order that are consistent with the poet's vision of a spiritualized America.

The poem opens with lines that are hopeful and confident, lines that affirm the poet's vision of his homeland: "It is a new America, / To be spiritualized by each new American" (214). As we ruminate about the implications of this pronouncement and prophecy, we wonder what the poet means by "new," since America is far from being new, and we also wonder what he means by "spiritualized," since the spirit or spiritual matters have played paradoxically a regrettably small part in the drama of American life. The poet is, I believe, rooted in the vision of the historical America we know, that is, the America of the Puritans, of slavery, and of war. But he is also rooted in yet another vision of America, a "new" America, an America mercifully free of the rigid, corrosive divisions of race, gender, and class, an America in which spiritual matters—the workings of the heart and soul—predominate. Over time, this second extraordinary vision, which is the inspiration and subject of the poem, not only imparts to the poet an oppressive knowledge of certain facts and events in American history, but through the sheer accumulation and repetition of these facts and events the poet also realizes that the "new" America of his vision is also the America of his birth or, rather, that this land and its people possess the potential realized in the vision by which he is captivated and enthralled.

This is the "new" America, but this America will become real, concrete, only when the people "spiritualize." But to spiritualize, that is, to reject violence and materialism and to give ourselves over completely to the life of the spirit; to examine and reexamine our laws and belief systems; to purge ourselves and our institutions of immoral, discriminatory influences; to recognize and to place the highest value on such intangibles as love, peace, and justice is a task that will not be undertaken by everyone. The poet, however, will excuse no one because the task requires a degree of discipline and commitment we rarely see, except perhaps in times of crisis, in ourselves or in others. But this unwavering and high level of commitment, and nothing less, is what the poet, in his faith, passion, and optimism, calls upon us to make.

In the first two lines and in others throughout the poem, we hear Whitman's voice singing sweetly of the "varied carols" and of the "strong, melodious songs" of each American.[10] But the poet asks that each American do more than sing. He also asks that we "crash the barrier to the next higher form" (214). By invoking a process that is almost Darwinian in its development and movement, the poet declares, in a tone that is insistent, impatient, and filled with the certainty of one gripped by a life-giving vision, that

> Beyond plants are animals,
> Beyond animals is man,
> Beyond man is the universe.
> The Big Light,
> Let the Big Light in!
>
> (214)

The Big Light, the beginning and ultimate source of self-knowledge and spiritual possibilities, should be our goal, and the poet calls upon the "Radiant Incorporeal," a kind of divine intermediary between man and the Big Light and a figure more powerful than the Being in *The Sacred Factory*, to assist us in our effort to move forward to the next higher form. The poet tells us that the Mississippi River, like the Ganges, "Is waiting to become / . . . a sacred river." Thus, the fate of the land seems inextricably linked with the fate of its inhabitants. Everyone—

> priest, clown, scientist, technician . . .
> Men of the East, men of the West . . .
> Americans and all countrymen

—must heed the call of the poet and understand that "Growth is by admixture from less to more." As we grow, so urges the poet, we must obey the same laws and move toward the same goal: higher consciousness, that "far-distant objective."

The poet's vision of a new America includes one of a more ancient America led by "old gods" who have perished and "old peoples" who have likewise perished and from whose dust, phoenixlike, rises a "New World in America." We, the inhabitants of this new world, are the sum of "all the peoples of the earth." These peoples—Europeans, Africans, and Native Americans—are, as a consequence of the racial mixing that has taken place in this country for generations, the new American race of which Toomer believed himself to be both a member and a symbol. In a fascinating section of one of his autobiographies, Toomer outlined his views on race, his effort to include them in the initial draft of "The Blue Meridian," then entitled "The First American," as well as the disappointing response to the poem by one of its first readers:

True, they [all people living in the United States] were conscious of being anything but American. Yet, underlying what they were aware of, underlying all the discussions, I had observed what seemed to me to be authentic—namely, that a new type of man was arising in this country—not European, not African, not Asiatic—but American. And in this American I saw divisions mended, the differences reconciled— saw that (1) we would in truth be a united people existing in the United States, saw that (2) we would in truth be once again members of a united human race.

Now all of this, needless to say, did not get into the poem. Years were to pass before that could happen, before the germ of "The First American" could grow and ripen and be embodied into "The Blue Meridian." But into "The First American" I did put something of my actuality, something of my vision of America—though it needed explaining.

Soon after I had written it I read it to a friend of that time, a colored fellow of more than ordinary mental grasp. . . . I read the poem, and he looked blank. I explained it, and he looked puzzled. So I plunged in and gave him my position and my experiences at some length. At the end he said three words, "You're white."

"What are you?" I asked.

"Colored."

I threw up my hands. "After all I've said you still don't get the point. I am not talking about whites or blacks. I am talking about Americans. I am an American. You are an American. Everyone is an American. Don't you see what I mean?" [11]

The sense of frustration Toomer felt after attempting to explain his racial views and position to his friend corresponds to the sense of frustration and even bewilderment that followed his efforts to enlighten Waldo Frank. Of course, the important difference between these confidences is that in the first Toomer was labeled "white," in the second "Negro." Although Toomer never succeeded in convincing his readers of the plausibility and potential benefits of his racial views, he was never discouraged. In fact, he accepted what he perceived as the shortsightedness of his generation as a challenge to which he had to continuously respond. As an artist who believed in the liberating power of the imagination, his responses assumed many different guises, but "The Blue Meridian" was Toomer's most successful effort to combine the theories of the Gurdjieff system with his theories on race. Plainly, the Americans described in this long dramatic poem are American in the exact sense that Toomer is American, that is to say, "neither black nor white," but a "new type of man." The sweep of this utopian vision encompasses us all.

In some of the most dramatic and memorable sections of the poem, Toomer describes the settlement of America by the ancestors of what are now the new Americans. It is an America of rapid, unprecedented expansion, but ironically it is the unwitting victim of its own progress. The poet begins his recollection, his history lesson, with the arrival of the Europeans:

> The old peoples—
> The great European races sent wave after wave
> That washed the forests, the earth's rich loam
> Great towns with the seeds of giant cities,

Made roads, laid silver rails,
Sang of their swift achievement
And perished, displaced by machines
Smothered by a world too huge for little men,
Too empty for life to breath in.
They say that near the end
It was a chaos of crying men and hard women,
A city of goddam and Jehovah
Baptized in finance
Without benefit of saints,
Of dear defectives
Winnowing their likeness from synthetic rock
Sold by national organizations of undertakers.

(215–16)

Even granting free reign to the poetic imagination, there are two glaring, disturbing inaccuracies in this imagined historical fragment. First, the poet wrongly gives the descendants of European immigrants full credit for the creation of the modern, industrial state. The westward expansion, or expansion in any direction for that matter, was not solely a European achievement. The descendants of Africans and Asians were an integral part of America's growth and development. Like their European brothers and sisters, both were the foundation for "the seeds," from which grew, fertilized by their labor and blood, the "giant cities." The second inaccuracy is the implication that European-Americans were the only group affected by the encroachment and eventual collapse of the industrial state, a veiled reference to the stock market crash of 1929. Disappointingly, the three voices that follow this recollection of the plight and fate of European-Americans contain only the anguish of this historically privileged group, yet plainly their devastation engulfs far more than the poet's vision allows.

The second part of this history lesson, which is an element, a feature, in the poet's vision of an America that has essentially destroyed itself, is the arrival of the Africans. This section is considerably shorter than the first and also contains, by omission, another inaccuracy:

The great African races sent a single wave
And singing riplets to sorrow in red fields,

Sing a swan, to break rocks
And immortalize a hiding water boy.

I am leaving the shining ground, brothers,
I sing because I ache,
I go because I must,
I am leaving the shining ground;
Don't ask me where,
I'll meet you there,
Brothers, I am leaving the shining ground.

But we must keep keep keep
the watermelon—
He moaned, O Lord, Lord,
This bale will break me—
But we must keep keep keep
the watermelon.

(216–17)

What is troubling about these stanzas is that they do not explain how the Africans came to be in America. The crime of the European slave trade is ignored, the peculiar form the peculiar institution assumed in America is ignored, and how slavery may have contributed to the erosion, to the destruction, of the republic of the poet's vision is ignored. Since the poet encourages us, by the facts and allusions of his vision, to draw certain historical parallels, we expect, perhaps without foundation, that these parallels will correspond to actual historical events. But this expectation, as we have seen, remains largely, like the dream and potential of the republic of the poet's vision, a thing to be fulfilled. Moreover, the suffering, to say nothing of the accomplishments, of the African in the new world, in America, is inadequately documented. The stanza, however, that contains the voice of a slave who has decided to leave the "shining ground," the region of his captivity, to escape to freedom does suggests something of the African's desolation.

The third and final part of the imaginative reconstruction of the settlement of America describes briefly the life of Native Americans and suggests, however vaguely, their fate in a changing America. As in the other two sections, the poet continues to speak in unrhymed, declarative statements and preserves the serious, almost solemn, tone of one who seems to be, as he seeks to order and explain a vision, delivering a verdict:

> The great red race was here.
> In a land of flaming earth and torrent-rains,
> Of red sea-plains and majestic mesas,
> At sunset from a purple hill
> The Gods came down;
> They serpentined into pueblo,
> And a white-robed priest
> Danced with them five days and nights;
> But pueblo, priest and Shalakos
> Sank into the sacred earth
> To fertilize the seven regions of America.
>
> (217)

What is distressing about this section of the poem, as is true of the two preceding it, is its historical inversion. It is both disturbing and peculiar that a vision that purports to mirror the history of the settlement of America would conclude rather than begin with documenting the culture and contribution of Native Americans. Here again and at a moment when we least expect it, we are reminded that the official history of America does not begin, as logic and morality indicate that it must, with Native Americans but with the arrival of the Europeans. Sadly, the poet is guilty not only of a skewed sense of history but also of cultural chauvinism. Additionally, while the appearance and disappearance of Native Americans is mentioned, there is no attempt to explain their decline, that is, to reveal the Europeans' effort to destroy a culture and a people for the possession and ownership of land. Such references would have added considerable force and authority to the poet's vision, but the omission of these and other telling facts to some extent diminishes an otherwise arresting vision. But in spite of these and other gaps in the poet's vision, it is astoundingly clear that the new America is the sum—both racially and culturally—of the three groups that emerge in his vision. The poet advocates cultural and racial pluralism as well as a new spiritualism of prodigious transformational powers.

As the poet unravels his vision, as it unfolds and expands in the same manner as America did in its infancy, we discover that the new Americans, this "new type of man," who have gathered in this new place "by the snatch of accident" and with the "speed of fate" and whose actual ancestry is as varied as the land itself, are not whole. We have not been made one, and here, as elsewhere, the poet appeals to the "Radiant Incorporeal" to "blend our bodies to one flesh / And blend this body to mankind" (218). Although we have not achieved the harmony for which the poet yearns, the land itself, "Reconciling force / And generator of symbols" (218), contains the promise of wholeness and is essential to our attainment of it. Although our progress through the ages has been slow, the poet's belief in this new America is steadfast, his commitment to it is unwavering, and he is prepared to make the most poignant, altruistic gesture to ensure its survival:

> I would give my life to see inscribed
> Upon the arch of our consciousness
> These aims: Growth, Transformation, Love,
> That we might become heart-centered towards
> one another,
> Love-centered towards God, dedicated to the creation of
> a higher type of man, growing up to Him.
>
> (219)

The poet is willing to commit a noble act to achieve a noble aim. Even though we may be blind to the exalted purpose of this sacrifice by the "habits, blights, and greeds" of our past, even though our hedonism—the "Bold Bitch of Babylon"—may keep us in darkness, even though our political, educational, and religious institutions may sometimes position the veil that distorts our vision more firmly into place, the poet, in his unshakable faith and optimism, remains undaunted: "We are made to grow, and by growing attain, / Rising in new birth to live in love" (223). "The kingdom," that place on earth—America—where there is the possibility for men and women to achieve a fullness of being, "exists and is," so proclaims the poet, "to be entered."

Although the poet is certain of the existence of this kingdom, that is, a whole and redeemed America, we cannot enter it, so he tells us in the second section of the poem, until we purge ourselves of

what Gurdjieff would regard as our wrongful attachment to wealth
and power. Beginning with questions that are largely rhetorical, the
poet tells us that we will make no progress as long as we continue to
place temporal successes above everything else:

> What value this, paper of the past,
> Engraved, ingrained, but meaningless?
> What life, that for words and figures,
> For power to spend and rear vain monuments,
> Two hold guns and the rest are destitute?
> Let go—and we'll carry all America in our hearts.
> This is no ship we want to sink with,
> But wreckage;
> This is no ark through deluge into the future,
> But wreckage manned by homesick ghosts.
> Let go!
> Let it go that we may live.
>
> (224)

We must, as the poet admonishes us, abandon the mad impulse for
money and power as well as the impulse to wage war. If we do, promises the poet, then we will "carry all of America in our hearts"; if we
ignore his warning, then America will become, not the ark on which
we will sail protected from the "deluge into the future," but "wreckage
manned by homesick ghosts" on which we, the nation, will perish.

We must also, so the poet advises us, "Let go!" of our desire for
money—"paper of the past"—and for all the superficial trappings of
success—"A fine suit . . . / A modern office"—for such things do not
lead to hope, knowledge, and faith, but to "pessimism . . . disillu-
sion, / . . . despair." We who have power, chastises the poet, "are
less than we should be" (224). In a strong, clear voice he urges us
to join—if we are to avoid the fate of the protagonists in such pieces
as "Seventh Street," "Rhobert," "The Gallonwerps," and *The Sacred
Factory*—

> that staff whose left hand is
> Demolishing defectives,
> Whose right is setting up a mill
> And a wheel therein, its rim of power,

> Its spokes of knowledge, its hub of conscience—
> And in that same heart we will hold all life.
>
> (224–25)

The purposeful activity of this "staff" of course prefigures the dance of the Blue Meridian in the third and last section of the poem, in which the poet delivers his final, passionate call to the life of the spirit.

But in the second section, the poet declares that not only must we cast off all the vanities of this world but we must also, if we wish to pass through the gates of the glorious kingdom he has described for us, undergo a further transformation of attitude, or, as Whitman lyricizes in "Song of the Open Road," be "loos'd of limits and imaginary lines" and divested of "holds that would hold" us. For the poet of "The Blue Meridian," these limits, lines, and holds are "prejudices and preferences," nationalism, regionalism, sexism, class antagonisms, and religious factionalism. In some of the best writing of the poem, Toomer reveals to us the absurdity of these man-made divisions and in the process reminds us of our true relationship not only to ourselves but also to each other:

> Unlock the races,
> Open this pod by outgrowing it,
> Free men from this prison and this shrinkage,
> Not from the reality itself
> But from our prejudices and preferences
> And the enslaving behavior caused by them,
> Eliminate these—
> I am, we are, simply of the human race.
>
> (225–26)

This is Toomer at his best and strongest. He is calling for nothing less than a total and complete transformation of American society. In the stanzas that follow he urges us to

> Uncase the nations,
> . . . We are of the human nation.
> Free the sexes. . . .
> Because we are male and female.

Unlock the classes. . . .
I am, we are, simply of the human class.
(226)

The lofty sentiments expressed in these stanzas were first expressed in *Essentials,* in which Toomer, in lines that are epigrammatic and spare by comparison, set forth an idealized vision of himself that in "The Blue Meridian" became the standard and values of a society:

> I am of no particular race. I am of the human race, a man at large in the human world, preparing a new race. I am of no specific region. I am of earth. I am of no particular class. I am of the human class, preparing a new class. I am neither male nor female nor in-between. I am of sex, with male differentiations. I am of no special field. I am of the field of being (xxiv).

There is no fundamental difference between the thoughts and opinions expressed here or those expressed, six years later, in "The Blue Meridian." The uniformity of thought further underscores the consistency of Toomer's philosophical formulations as well as his thematic concerns.

The artificial divisions enumerated here and which Toomer treated in *Cane,* "The Gallonwerps," "Transatlantic," and *The Sacred Factory* must be leveled. The poet urges us to "Uncase, unpod, whatever blocks" our path until

> Having realized pure consciousness of being,
> Knowing that we are beings
> Co-existing with others in an inhabited universe,
> We will be free to use rightly with reason
> Our own and other human functions—
> Free men, whole men, men connected
> With one another and with Deity.
> (226)

This "pure consciousness of being," that is, a sense of wholeness, is the Gurdjieffian ideal to which Toomer committed not only his entire being but also his enormous gifts and powers as a poet. This

Gurdjieffian statement of belief is followed by an appeal to the "Matrons of Shrinkage," that wide net of societal controls here personified as women possessed of crippling powers, to "Cut the binds of apron-strings" that impede the progress of the "young gods"—the new Americans—who populate and feed upon the land of this "new America."

In order to affirm and reveal the depth of his own humanity as well as to indicate his own expansion of consciousness, the poet momentarily speaks of events that are both past and personal. He becomes a character in this national epic of growth and possibilities. In the act of recounting his vision, of proclaiming the failures of one nation and the potential of another, the poet enters a reflective mode and shares with us private failures and successes that reflect and correspond to (the difference of course is one of scale) the nation's floundering and its imminent recovery: "I held a fair position as men rate things, / Even enviable." In his meditations on an impressive but brief professional success, the poet insists that he found "A river flowing flowing backward to its source" (228). Later, in what appears to have been the single, most significant love relationship of his life—"I met a woman— / Much that I am I owe to her"—the poet asserts that he, though failing to achieve the degree of intimacy and compatibility he felt certain was possible, discovered "the task of man." The first of these digressions is a faintly disguised allusion to Toomer's early but short-lived success following the publication of *Cane.* The second is an allusion to his involvement with Margaret Naumburg, the wife of Waldo Frank, who, claimed Toomer, "gave me a sense of myself, an awareness of the world and of values, which transcended even my dreams of high experience." [12] Here, as in other works, Toomer the man boldly enters the narrative. His own experiences, however private or painful, become his subject and are used not merely to entertain, but, more important, to instruct. We have here a form of personal testimony in which Toomer creates a feeling of intimacy in order to advance the larger purpose of his poem.

For awhile longer, the poet remains in this reflective mode. In this intensely subjective state he uses his own varied musical tastes—Bach, Duke Ellington, Eddy Duchin—to suggest the complex, multifaceted nature of his own being and also to suggest that although each of the musicians named created a particular kind of music, the music remains, with all its differences, of one piece. Although each may "Sing the flow of I," the music (or currents) passes through one "water wheel," a metaphor for all the longings that make our shared humanity patent and irrefutable. Here Toomer restates a belief delivered with considerable conviction and grace in previous stanzas:

> We are of the human nation.
> We are of Earth.
> We are beings.
>
> (226)

Translated and stated plainly, the poet believes that in his face we will discover again the faces of our sister and brother, in his voice we will hear the voices of our mother and father.

From this point, the poet goes on to restate the lessons and lasting effects of what appears to be the only real union with another human being: love. In these musings on romantic love—"Girl of the mesas and the great red plains"—we discern a change of emphasis. The poet's attention begins to move away from himself and return to the larger questions and themes of his vision. This shift in focus is revealed in the following lines:

> It is a new world,
> A new America
> To be spiritualized by each new American.
>
> (229)

Interspersed between stanzas, these lines return us to the poem's theme and signal subtle, important changes in mood and in particular events that previously seemed fixed and immutable.

The poet begins to recast the settlement of America, to retell the rise and fall of the America of his first vision, and into his passionate retelling creep new developments. It seems that there has been a transformation of great dimensions and with spiritual effects, a transformation that has occurred solely because the spirits of the departed old gods—"an inverted Christ, / A shaved Moses"—have entered the souls of the new Americans. The result of these visitations is that man is "at last triumphant over not-man," that those who have died, both in their bodies and in their souls, are

alive again
To demonstrate the worth of individuals,
The purpose of the commonwealth.

(230)

Now blood "does mix," whereas before it did not, "with the stuff upon our boards," and the descendants of the "old peoples"—the Europeans, the Africans, and the Native Americans—are now able to fulfill not only their individual destinies but the destiny of the nation as well. The poet declares:

> We are the new people,
> Born of elevated rock and lifted branches,
> Called Americans,
> Not to mouth the label but to live the reality,
> Not to stop anywhere, to respond to man,
> To outgrow each wider limitation,
> Growing towards the universal Human Being;
> And we are the old people, witnesses
> That behind us there extends
> An unbroken chain of ancestors,
> Ourselves linked with all who ever lived,
> Joined with all future generations;
> Of millions of fathers through as many years
> We are the breathing receptacles.

(232)

This is a glorious, extraordinary vision full of life and the hope of a new nation. There is a seriousness and a sense of purpose here that bespeaks the eventual triumph (that is our hope) of a new order of man and a new order of government. But the new man and the new government of the poet's vision, this new American and this new place called America, are, if we look closely at them, neither new nor even unfamiliar to us. They are nothing less than the government and the people of the United States in harmony, for the first time it seems, not only with the spirit of the outlandishly idealistic documents that govern them—the Declaration of Independence and the Constitution—but also with an ideal of man, a mode of being (enter Gurdjieff) that has instilled them with a new sense of themselves as vital human beings of limitless potential. Here again, the principles of a nation and the mission of a spiritual reformer, social critic, and poet converge and are transfigured.

At the conclusion of this section, the poet once again, as he has in earlier sections, enters the poem and declares, without bravado or a trace of insincerity, that he is a servant, indeed a willing sacrifice, to the mode of being revealed to him in his vision:

> My life is given to have
> Realized in our consciousness
> Actualized in life without celebrity,
> This real: wisdom empowered: men growing
> From womb to birth, from birth to rebirth
> Up arcs of brightness to the resplendent source.
>
> (233)

The reference here to arcs is not to be overlooked, for we are reminded of the arcs in *Cane*, the arcs that suggest the book's design and theme. The arcs in *Cane* and in "The Blue Meridian," however, signify two discrete and different views of man's spiritual and psychological condition. In the first, they symbolize modern man's lack of and search for wholeness; in the second, they imply the presence of a consciousness rapidly moving toward completion.

The poet's faith in our ability to achieve completion, that is, a state of wholeness, is total and unwavering. No force, so he states with the confidence and certainty of a true believer, can thwart the realization of this Gurdjieffian goal:

> No split spirit can divide,
> No dead soul can undermine thee,
> Thou, great coasts and harbors,
> Mountains, lakes and plains,
> Thou art the majestic base
> Of cathedral people;
> America,
> The seed which started thee has grown.
>
> (233)

Such destructive, worrisome facts as a "split spirit" or a "dead soul," those who are spiritually and psychologically fragmented, cannot hin-

der the emergence of the "cathedral people": the new Americans of
the poet's vision.

In the third and final section of the poem, the poet shares with
us the final phase of his vision, the vision of the Blue Meridian, as
he awakes and dervishes with "the seven regions / of America, and
all the world" (234). In contrast to the other two figures who are re-
spectively "sleeping" and "waking," the third has plainly shaken off
the deleterious effects of his, or our, Gurdjieffian sleep. He achieves
the high level of thought, feeling, and action for which his name is
a symbol. Infected by the grace and power of the dance of the Blue
Meridian, the poet, in his excitement, exclaims:

> Lift, lift thou waking forces!
> Let us have the power of man,
> The tender power of the loving hand,
> The irresistible urge
> Of brain and heart and limbs
> Moving on and on
> Through the terms of life on earth
> And then beyond
> To aid the operations of the cosmos.
>
> (234)

In the last lines of the poem, the poet makes yet another appeal to
the "Radiant Incorporeal," the distant, resplendent, apparently omniscient and omnipotent being for whom the Blue Meridian dances.
Keenly aware of the differences between our state and that of the
dancing Blue Meridian, the poet entreats the "Radiant Incorporeal" to
place above our "waking limbs" "Spirit-torsos of exquisite strength."
He asks the powerful being to endow us with the transcendent knowledge that animates the Blue Meridian and that will, when received
by us, also compel us to dance and to dervish. At this moment the
poet, like the reaper in "Harvest Song," stands waiting, poised, for a
reply that will, given the spirit of hope that pervades the work, certainly come. Far from being the deaf, blind, mute figure of "Harvest
Song," the poet of "The Blue Meridian" seems prepared to assume
his place alongside the dancing, whole Blue Meridian. He does not
hunger, because he has found direction, nourishment, and peace in
his vision.

"The Blue Meridian" is a decidedly optimistic work, mercifully free of the sermonizing and Gurdjieffian cant that is so characteristic of Toomer's other works. In this poem, Toomer achieves a balance between his purpose as a Gurdjieff devotee and his duties as a poet. Although he condemns the customs and institutions that keep us, as Gurdjieff would say, "asleep," in his righteous condemnation he does not forget that he is a poet. Thus above his judgments we discover a hopeful vision of mankind that dulls the bite of his pointed criticisms. During the writing of "The Blue Meridian," Toomer was plainly "possessed of his possessions." He was in the throes of that liberating knowledge of man and man's possibilities that is the promise of the Gurdjieff system. In this great poem, Toomer sought to demonstrate to us, as he wrote in *Essentials,* that "our aim is to spiritualize the actual and to actualize the potential" (v). Possessing an unshakable faith and a deep optimism in the possibilities of American life, Toomer urged us to awaken our dormant potentialities as individuals and as a nation.

Conclusion

"WITH CERTAIN NOTABLE exceptions, every one of my main ideas has a Gurdjieff idea as its parent."[1] Toomer made this statement in 1930, at the apex of his involvement with the Gurdjieff work. Although Toomer later distanced himself from Gurdjieff the man, who was, in his ways with all people, frequently bizarre, demanding, and exploitative, the Russian psychologist and philosopher was undeniably, as Toomer's familial, progenitive pronouncement makes plain, the most potent figure of his mind and imagination. But the workings of Toomer's mind and imagination or his insistence upon Gurdjieff's high place in both would mean little to us without some substantial, formal corroboration, that is, without the works themselves. These works—the novels, drama, and poetry—are, as I have shown, far from scarce, as many have supposed, and after 1923 all contain the indelible imprint of Gurdjieff's psychological system. Plainly, Toomer's deferential, almost self-effacing statement is not only one of belief but also one of fact.

And it is a fact that does not offer much comfort, for fewer collaborations have had such disastrous consequences for American literature. By 1925 the perceptive, androgynous philosopher-poet of *Cane* was fading quickly from view. The poet who wrote forcefully and lyrically of the women of Sparta, Georgia, the poet who provided us with one of the first views of the interior life of African-American women, the poet who extended and improved upon Gertrude Stein's efforts to explore black female sexuality and personhood in "Melanctha," would continue, even after these successes, his search for the "intelligible scheme" that would give his life definition and meaning. Moreover, the poet who refused to romanticize American race relations; the poet, like Charles Chesnutt in such works as *The Marrow of Tradition*, who

wrote in opposition to the plantation school of American letters; the
poet, like James Weldon Johnson in *The Autobiography of an Ex-Coloured
Man,* who clarified further the pressures and compromises endured
by African-Americans, would seek solutions to the problems of race
in extraliterary constructs. Finally, the poet, like W. E. B. Du Bois in
The Souls of Black Folk, who celebrated and mourned the passing of an
African-American folk culture, the poet who employed the distinctive
language of the group to suggest more clearly something of the history
and experience of the group, the poet who experimented with the application of musical forms to literature, would abandon these values
and interests after 1923 when the "intelligible scheme" assumed a
recognizable, tangible form in the person of George I. Gurdjieff.

Within one year of his fateful visit to Fontainebleau, the poet of *Cane*
had largely disappeared and in his place appeared the determined,
confident social critic and spiritual reformer whose voice dominates
"The Gallonwerps" and "Transatlantic." When he wrote these novels,
the search for the "intelligible scheme" was behind Toomer. With the
enthusiasm and unshakable optimism of a Gurdjieffian evangelist,
Toomer attempted to describe in these novels the emptiness and aim-
lessness of modern life. In "The Gallonwerps," Toomer set out to fulfill
his Gurdjieffian charge to promote higher development and to instill higher consciousness in his readers. Not wishing to discourage
his readers by the distressing facts of their modern circumstances,
not wishing to overwhelm them with the difficulty of the necessary
work they must undertake to improve a deteriorating spiritual and
psychological condition, Toomer employed satire as a vehicle for delivering his Gurdjieffian pronouncements and prophecies. But we do
not chuckle or even smile when we discover that the marriage of
Wisthold and Wimepime Gallonwerp is based not on love but on
habitual, mechanical contact. We are amused neither by Prince Klondike's antics and disguises nor by Wimepime's faintly ridiculous effort
to create a forum, regardless of how contrived, for the expression of
her husband's ideas and opinions. Although it was certainly part of
the novel's original design, there is little humor in "The Gallonwerps."
What could have been pointed, instructive satire emerges finally as a
dry, disconnected narrative held together by a disciple's faithful rep-
lication of his teacher's pronouncements and beliefs. The teacher was
Gurdjieff, and the disciple, Jean Toomer, created a spokesman, Prince

Klondike, who is essentially an idealized version of Toomer himself. For all its intended humor, "The Gallonwerps" is a cheerless novel from the first to the last paragraph. Unlike its progenitor *Cane*, "The Gallonwerps" is not a novel born of an inspiring and inspired vision, but it is a novel with a thesis that is rooted in Gurdjieff's psychological system.

"Transatlantic" proceeds forward as cheerlessly as does "The Gallonwerps." Of course, the important difference between these two novels is that in "Transatlantic" Toomer did not intend to write a satire, but a naturalistic novel with experimental narrative techniques. In spite of the differences between the two novels, however, the chief source of inspiration for both was Gurdjieff's psychological system. Of all Toomer's novels, "Transatlantic" was the most ambitious and the one in which Toomer invested the greatest part of himself. Although this novel, like "The Gallonwerps," was never accepted for publication, it was the work Toomer hoped would have the widest circulation. Like Nathan Merilh of *Natalie Mann*, Dan Moore of *Cane*, and Prince Klondike of "The Gallonwerps," Hugh Langley of "Transatlantic" is yet another idealized version of Jean Toomer. He is Toomer at his most articulate and inspiring.

As the *Burgundy's* resident spiritual reformer, Langley guides his fellow passengers through a series of lessons and revelations that produce in them a keen awareness of their principal strengths and weaknesses. Of course, all Langley's teaching situations are carefully orchestrated, and all are framed by Gurdjieff's theories and precepts. Like Prince Klondike, Hugh Langley functions to promote personal development and to instill in his fellow passengers a sense of their spiritual possibilities. We recall Langley's success in aiding Hod and Barbara Lorimer to realize their deficiencies as well as their potentialities. Often the Lorimers do not suspect that they are being led down a particular path, and Langley, careful not to reveal his purposes and always in search of opportunities to deliver his Gurdjieffian message, transforms each crisis into an opportunity for renewal, teaching, and learning.

While we may be impatient with Toomer's undisguised enthusiasm for Gurdjieff's theories and disappointed by the awkward, fumbling manner in which they are integrated into his narrative, nonetheless we must admire his faith in the possibilities of human development. Although the differences between *Cane* and "The Gallonwerps" and

"Transatlantic" are great, although we mourn particularly the disappearance of an African-American presence and a racial consciousness, the vital link that joins these three works is theme. Toomer's great theme of human development places these works in the same dynamic current of creative expression. Each work marks Toomer's struggle as an artist to achieve the sense of wholeness that he imparted to many of the men and women who inhabit his fictional universe.

The confident, urgent, sometimes zealous voice of the spiritual reformer and Gurdjieffian disciple we hear so often and so clearly in "The Gallonwerps" and in "Transatlantic" is happily modulated in *The Sacred Factory*. Of Toomer's several plays, *The Sacred Factory* is plainly the most important because he achieved within this expressionist, four-act drama a balance between his goals as a promoter of the Gurdjieff system and his responsibilities as a dramatist. The Gurdjieffian elements emerge as organic parts of Toomer's drama. We are interested in the conflict between John and Mary because Toomer created a situation that inspires empathy. We are interested in the function and power of the Being because Toomer created a situation that is compelling and dramatic. In this particular work, the theories of the Gurdjieff system extend and amplify Toomer's concerns and preoccupations as a dramatist. They increase the depth and range of meaning. Toomer did not make the mistake, as he did in "A Drama of the Southwest" and in "Pilgrims, Did You Say?" of burdening the work with the technical, specialized terminology of the Gurdjieff system. *The Sacred Factory* is devoid of Gurdjieffian cant, banter, and undisguised propaganda. Action and dialogue rise unfettered, unencumbered, to the level of meaning and ritual.

Like *Balo* and "Kabnis," *The Sacred Factory* is a drama deserving production and scholarly study. In these works, the poet of *Cane* demonstrated his potential and ability as a dramatist. We do not find in these plays, as we do in many of the others, the awkward musings of an amateur dramatist or the extremely confident, faintly patronizing pronouncements of a Gurdjieffian devotee. Instead we find dramatizations of what might be termed the three stages of Toomer's own quest for wholeness, for an "intelligible scheme." These three stages—meditation, search, and discovery—are subtexts within larger texts that possess abiding relevance and profound implications for our own spiritual odyssey.

As in *The Sacred Factory*, in "The Blue Meridian" Toomer maintained a balance between his duties as a poet and his objectives as a disciple of Gurdjieff. "The Blue Meridian" is the most important of Toomer's poems and after *Cane* the most important work in his canon. With the exception of his autobiographies, "The Blue Meridian" is perhaps the most complete, self-conscious expression of Toomer's philosophical convictions as a disciple of Gurdjieff and also as a poet deeply concerned about the values and direction of American life. Like Whitman's *Leaves of Grass* and Crane's "The Bridge," "The Blue Meridian" is nothing less than a national epic, an extraordinary effort to meld history and the possibilities of a young nation with the vision and faith of a wildly optimistic poet.

As he recounts the settlement and history of this nation, Toomer suggests something of the gifts each racial and ethnic group has contributed to its growth and expansion. For Toomer these gifts are both our national and spiritual inheritance. Moreover, they represent a hoped-for political harmony and a coalescence of spiritual values and beliefs that is symbolized by the transformation of the Black and White meridians into the dancing, dervishing Blue Meridian. The Black and White meridians symbolize the various ethnic and racial groups in this country, and their metamorphosis into the Blue Meridian symbolizes the birth of the Americans—the new racial group of which Toomer considered himself both a member and a symbol.

But the three meridians symbolize not only America's ethnic and racial diversity, the attainment of harmony in our national politics and the new race Toomer believed was emerging in America, but also the first three stages of consciousness possible for man in the Gurdjieff system. Of course, it is no coincidence that the history of the groups who established the place called America and spiritual enlightenment are the subjects of the same poem. Plainly, Toomer suggests that we as a nation can attain the level of humanity and knowledge of the Blue Meridian if we affirm and celebrate not only the ideals on which this republic was founded and in which it finds its hope and direction but also the diversity and sense of possibility in ourselves.

Plainly, all of Toomer's works written after 1923 were highly dependent upon and greatly influenced by the theories of Gurdjieff's psychological system. For many years, Toomer was never troubled by the potential negative effects of his Gurdjieffian experiments, for, like all seekers of the truth, Toomer felt that the truth, or what passed for it, was all that mattered. Toomer's immersion in the Gurdjieff work, which we regard as an intrusion and a terrible disturbance in the creative life of a gifted writer, was for Toomer a much welcomed, indeed ineluctable, transition. But this transition dramatically altered the face, character, and voice of everything Toomer would ever write. The mannered, self-conscious, arcane language of Prince Klondike and Hugh Langley is disappointing proof of Toomer's movement away from art to propaganda for the Gurdjieff system.

But in spite of the fissures his devotion to the Gurdjieff system created in his work, Toomer never stopped thinking of himself as a poet, the poet whose work became the inspiration for an entire generation of American writers and whose work remains the standard by which their work and the work of succeeding generations of writers has been and continues to be judged. In "Remember and Return," a massive unpublished collection of definitions and aphorisms, Toomer described himself in the following manner: "I am not less poet; I am more conscious of all that I am, am not, and might become."[2] It is possible that Toomer, after having been tested once and then again by the imperious Gurdjieff, discovered truths about himself that the writing of poetry only obscured. It is possible that Toomer, after immersing himself in the theories of the Gurdjieff system, discovered new personal truths concerning his potential and mission as a poet. But one discovery surely must have been, though a certain blindness and vanity on Toomer's part seems to have diminished for him its scale and importance, that after 1923 he became less of a poet, not more of one.

It is not clear how Toomer defined the word "poet," and it will not be necessary to attempt a definition here. It need only be said that the word raises in all of us certain expectations, expectations that Toomer, after a certain point in his writing career and in specific instances, failed to meet. Many of the later works are distressing proof of his precipitous fall from more to less. The lyricism of *Cane*, its seductive prose and verse rhythms, the spectacular union of sense with sound, of meaning with ambiguity, is supplanted by a voice riddled with jargon and platitudes, a voice with discordant features, a voice shouting a thesis. Although we may bicker endlessly over the definition of a poet—he or she must be this and this and certainly not that—we need only compare the opening lines of *Cane* to many of the works that followed it to discover that the qualities, sometimes intangible and sometimes not, that we have grown to expect from a writer who calls himself a poet are not present in their original force and clarity. These qualities have undergone a process of dilution, because after Toomer discovered Gurdjieff, dogma became more important than any aesthetic standard. Many of the works after *Cane* do not contain, in the best sense of the word, a theme, but a thesis. And, as I have stated before, they are all, even the best efforts, a kind of literary propaganda for the Gurdjieff work.

Although it is clear that Toomer's involvement in the Gurdjieff system weakened his talent as a poet, it is also clear that it gave him the things he needed most: a vision of mankind as psychologically and spiritually whole as well as a method of achieving this much desired state. Throughout his life, Toomer had been in search of what he termed "an intelligible scheme." He found this scheme in the Gurdjieff system, and soon afterward, in the didactic, self-conscious, and at times self-congratulatory manner of the seeker who has at last found the truth, he set out to bring this new truth into the world. Now, we may not be interested in the theories of the Gurdjieff system or even in our own spiritual possibilities, but throughout his long life Toomer remained interested in both. It is this unwavering commitment to these matters that distinguishes him from other writers of his generation.

Although Toomer may have been part of what Stein called that lost generation of writers—Pound, Eliot, Fitzgerald, and Hemingway— he certainly did not share their fatalistic, defeatist outlook. Toomer's vision of America was a hopeful one full of power, knowledge, and potential. He did not linger over the impotence, stupidity, and despair of his generation as did so many others. It is because he did not dwell on man's darker side that he perhaps escaped the fate of Crane and Hemingway and avoided the unspeakable, tragic mistakes of Pound. Toomer believed, like the Transcendentalists, in the life and the power of the spirit—in our potentiality. This emphasis upon things spiritual, this preoccupation with our psychological and spiritual development—human development—is Toomer's great strength and theme, a theme that ascends in outline in *Cane* and descends, in the years following Gurdjieff, fully formed in "The Blue Meridian."

Although most of Toomer's work remains unpublished, his accomplishment in *Cane, Essentials,* and "The Blue Meridian" has established him as a seminal figure in American letters not only for writers of his own generation but also for those of succeeding generations. "I look upon *Cane* as one of the most influential forces in the artistic awakening of the Negro and as one of the most beautiful and moving books of contemporary American literature." This statement by Sterling A. Brown, who, as Michael S. Harper dutifully reminds us, is a "trustee of consciousness and a national treasure," appears in a letter Brown wrote to Toomer requesting permission to reprint portions of *Cane* in *The Negro Caravan* (1941). Brown is only one of many writers who achieved national prominence during the twenties and thirties for whom *Cane* was an "influential . . . beautiful and moving" book.[3] Even though Toomer had embraced the arcane psychological theories of the Gurdjieff system only months after his celebrated work appeared in bookstores, his extremely sophisticated, sensual, and frank portrayal of African-American life forged new literary possibilities for the writers of the New Negro movement.

It will not be necessary to cite again here the panegyrics penned by the then younger generation of African-American writers—Hughes, Cullen, Faucett, and Hurston—who were dazzled by the mood and style of *Cane*. Nor will it be necessary to repeat the measured, but laudatory, pronouncements of the then older generation of African-American writers—Du Bois, Locke, Johnson, and Braithwaite—who discovered in the pages of Toomer's luminous book language and images that signaled a dramatic change in the treatment of African-American subjects. We are all familiar with these often-quoted accolades, and McKay's accurate and representative summation of them in the last pages of her fine study on Toomer makes their repetition here unnecessary. What would be more useful and interesting in my effort to demonstrate the accuracy and prophetic nature of Brown's assessment of *Cane*'s influence on African-American writers (an assessment with which I am in complete agreement) is specificity, that is, examples of works by African-American writers that build upon and extend Toomer's seminal accomplishments. But before identifying some of the works by African-American authors who have in textual ways absorbed and reinterpreted Toomer's highly instructive example in verse, fiction, and aphoristic writing, it is important to suggest something of the scope and possible boundaries of Toomer's example.

For writers in search of guidance in craftsmanship as well as a system of values by which to compare and evaluate their own, the lessons of *Cane* are many. Three of its most important ones are that African-American folk culture is compelling, complex, and deserving of serious treatment; that traditional narrative techniques and forms are points at which a writer can begin, knowing that more expressive forms and methods may emerge through experimentation; and that a writer's concerns are both formal and philosophical and that he or she is the creator of forms and the interpreter of situations that nourish the intellect and the spirit. These are the principal elements that give Toomer's call its significance and force. There were many writers during the twenties and thirties who heard and responded to this call, but foremost among them was Langston Hughes.

Hughes complained of Toomer's aloofness in his letters to Noel Sullivan and derided Toomer's Gurdjieffian conversion in "A House in Taos" and in *The Big Sea*, but the poet laureate of the New Negro movement had the greatest respect for Toomer's achievement in *Cane*. Certainly Hughes sensed the potential of modernism before reading *Cane*, but after studying Toomer's stories and poems he doubtless felt far more confident about applying its methods to African-American subjects. The influence of Toomer's example upon the impressionable Hughes is felt in many places, but perhaps most acutely in *The Weary Blues* (1926). There are many poems in this volume that reveal Hughes's awareness of Toomer's three-point aesthetic resolution, but more than most, "Jazzonia" suggests something of Hughes's debt to Toomer.

"Jazzonia" is a stylized tribute to the rigorous, infectious nature of jazz as well as an impressionistic rendering of Harlem cabaret life. It would not be an exaggeration to assert that after studying "Karintha," "Blood-Burning Moon," "Seventh Street" and "Theatre," in which Toomer employed language influenced by sacred, jazz, and blues rhythms to introduce, extend, and complete an imagined conflict, Hughes discovered a model for "Jazzonia," a model that affirmed his impulse to join musical forms to literary forms. On this point, Toomer's influence extends beyond *The Weary Blues* to such experimental, musically based works of Hughes as *Ask Your Mama* and *Montage of a Dream Deferred*.

In addition to suggesting to Hughes the rich implications that music would have for his verse, Toomer also reminded Hughes that African-

American folk culture is a vital resource for literature. Like the moon-struck characters in "Blood-Burning Moon," the heroine in Hughes's "Aunt Sue's Stories" is keenly aware of the power of African-American folklore. The stories Aunt Sue shares with the "dark-faced child" come, so Hughes tells us, "right out of her own life," and they are testi-monies to the "black slaves" who sang "sorrow songs on the banks of a mighty river." [4] Aunt Sue establishes a pattern in Hughes's writing that emerged not only from his reading of *Cane* but also from *The Souls of Black Folk,* a pattern that rejects the belief that African-American lit-erature need only reflect the concerns and values of the black mid-dle class.

Plainly, *Cane* was an important work for the young Hughes, but Toomer's influence extends beyond the verse of the poet who also gave us "The Cat and the Saxophone (2 A.M.)," a poem whose title comes right out of the pages of "Bona and Paul." Toomer's influence emerges again in the verse of a contemporary poet who draws upon all the varied strains of American, African, and European cultures and in the process returns to us gifts from and for the spirit. The poet is Michael S. Harper, whose "Cryptograms" in *Nightmare Begins Responsibility* (1975) are based upon his inspired reading of Toomer's *Essentials.*

Harper's seventeen "Cryptograms" are preceded by selections from *Essentials,* selections that ably suggest not only the range of issues Toomer addressed in *Cane* and in *Essentials* but also those issues Harper himself addresses in this section of his fifth book of verse. Several of Harper's "Cryptograms" are comments on, further explora-tions of, and vehicles for returning to moments in *Cane.* For example, in "Outer Visions" Harper writes:

> Heaven is below one's waist;
> hell above one's neck.
> Split infinitives
> reduced to form(s).[5]

Surveying the chaos that is the consequence of sexual excess and un-regulated living, Harper conjures images and characters from such stories in *Cane* as "Karintha," "Carma," "Fern," and "Avey," in which the themes of hedonism and sexual excess predominate. Additionally, in "Form" Harper criticizes the impulse to reduce human beings to objects, to systematically strip away the humanity of others through an inversion of language and values. In "Rhobert" and in "Calling Jesus," in which the protagonists have yielded to a belief system that celebrates materialism and technology instead of such values as kinship and community, we witness this process of dehumanization, what Harper tersely and densely describes as

> the decadent
> reduction
> to the inhuman
> in
> nonfunctional
> terms.[6]

Also, in "The Book of Names" Harper, by urging us all to recall and be redeemed by our ancestral ties and national history, evokes the challenge and triumph of Ralph Kabnis. "By habit / cultivate your name;" writes Harper, "the dead spoken / remembered habitual."[7] As we recall, Kabnis eventually learns to "cultivate" his "name," that is to say, to embrace the past, the "dead," the history that has come down to him through his name. This capacity to embrace and internalize history ("History is your own heartbeat" writes Harper) will, as Toomer and Harper believe, renew and sustain us.

In addition to recasting and recalling in the cryptic, allusive manner of an Ezra Pound the chief preoccupations and themes of *Cane*, Harper also in "Surrender: Toomer(s)" offers us a concentrated, critical assessment of Toomer's literary career and racial position. Harper writes:

> Earth
> Art
> Music
> unchained
> mulatto
> remains.[8]

Employing the economy of haiku and Imagist poetry, Harper not only evokes and pays tribute to Toomer's literary achievement but also evokes the pronouncements of those who have been critical of

Toomer's effort to transcend race through art, an effort that Harper, understanding deeply the ideology of race in America, suggests was futile. Throughout "Cryptograms" Harper is epigrammatic, illuminating and existing always in a state of kinship, remembrance, and knowledge, as he skillfully links the trials of our era with those of Toomer's. This act of kinship in language extends the duration and scope of human experience and affirms the spiritual values by which Toomer lived. Moreover, in "Cryptograms" we discover, because of the depth and range of Harper's transcendent vision, new sources of strength and endurance in our journey toward what Toomer called "the radiant plateau" in "Transatlantic," or to what Harper calls "high modes" in *History Is Your Own Heartbeat*.

But there is yet another contemporary writer, one whom Harper honors in his poem "Alice," whose work is in many ways a direct response to Toomer's call.[9] I am thinking of Alice Walker, who not only celebrates Toomer's treatment of the trials endured by black women in her landmark essay "In Search of Our Mothers' Gardens" but also makes manifest again the importance of Toomer's achievement in *Cane* and in "The Blue Meridian" by employing them both as frames and guides in *Meridian*, her much underrated second novel.

In *Meridian*, Walker evokes not only the spirit of a particular place and time—the South during the 1960s—but also the spirit and the spiritual place of a particular writer—Jean Toomer. An awareness of this fact deepens our appreciation of the power of Walker's novel, a power that gathers its peculiar elements and proportions from a place and a work dear to Toomer.

As we know, Meridian Hill is the name of the heroine in Walker's novel, but there is also a beautiful spot in northwest Washington, D.C., called Meridian Hill Park, a park often visited by young Jean Toomer. Toomer, who as a child lived within walking distance of the park, was doubtless drawn there by its splendid vista. On this bluff he could see with one glance the White House, the Washington Monument, the Potomac River, and the hills of Virginia. Meridian Hill Park was a special place for Toomer because it was here that he, inspired by the vista, dreamed of becoming a poet.

The name of Walker's heroine calls to mind not only a place known to Toomer but also a major work by him—"The Blue Meridian." In this long Whitmanesque poem, Toomer described not only the settlement of North America but also the metamorphosis of the White and Black meridians into the Blue Meridian. For Toomer, the Blue Meridian represented not only the new American race of which he considered himself a member but also the highest point in our spiritual and psychological development. Based upon Toomer's lifelong study of Gurdjieff's psychological system, the poem functions as a challenge to our complacency as well as a model for our spiritual possibilities. Not surprisingly, Walker's novel and its heroine function in precisely the same manner.

Meridian Hill's example of self-knowledge through self-sacrifice, of clarity through an involvement in a righteous cause, is both powerful and inspiring. One of Walker's most important and complex fictional creations, Meridian Hill is born of Walker's love for and admiration of the women of *Cane*. Meridian's bizarre falling sickness and her intense spirituality remind us of Fernie May Rosen's occult powers and spiritual affliction. Toomer wrote that men "took Fern" but "got no joy from it"; afterward, they "felt bound to her." This curious sexual predicament is reenacted with extraordinary effects in *Meridian*. Like the foolish men who misinterpret the meaning in Fern's eyes, Truman Held is held by and "bound to" Meridian. Quite "unlike [his] hit and run with other girls," Truman can neither free himself from the woman he exploits and abandons nor influence her, since she reserves herself for the work of the people, the important work of struggle and commitment to which Truman later dedicates himself.

But the influence of *Cane* upon *Meridian* goes much deeper than the resemblance in temperament that one character bears to another. Indeed, it goes as deep as structure and theme. Like *Cane*, *Meridian* contains a three-part structure with conflicts that follow a pattern of South-North-South. Additionally, much of the meaning of *Meridian* is encapsulated in brief sketches that echo the mood and lyricism of such pieces as "Fern," "Esther," and "Calling Jesus." Thematically, Walker's novel inverts Toomer's theme in *Cane*. The characters of *Cane* yearn for a sense of wholeness but are caught in an age and circumstances in which fragmentation of the psyche and the soul is the expected condition. Meridian Hill, however, achieves through her work for the people a sense of purpose and wholeness that Toomer only suggests is possible in *Cane*.

Throughout *Meridian*, Walker displays a deep respect for the folk whose vanishing culture Toomer sought to capture and preserve in *Cane*. It is well known that one of Walker's most important teachers of African-American folklore and folk culture was the novelist and anthropologist Zora Neale Hurston. I would not be exaggerating Toomer's influence, however, by claiming that part of Walker's sensitivity to folk culture and her awareness of its value for literature stem from her reading of *Cane*. Through Meridian's love for the stories of the Sojourner and her grief after its razing, Mr. Hill's (Meridian's father's) reverence for the history and culture of Native Americans, and Meridian's work as a teacher and freedom fighter in the rural areas of Georgia, Walker reaffirms her respect for the old ways of thinking and doing and chides the modern temperament that questions their relevance.

Walker's use of folklore, her experimentation with various narrative techniques, and her commitment to portray in vivid, revealing language the trials and victories of African-American women are evidence of her admiration for Toomer's example in *Cane*. In Walker, the South-North-South pattern of Toomer's call in *Cane* comes full circle. Unlike the circle in *Cane*, which remains broken and serves as Toomer's symbol for the spiritual and psychological fragmentation of his time and ours, the great circle of literary kinship—Hughes, Harper, Walker—is joined, strengthened by the bonds of authorship.

There are certainly other African-American writers whose original offerings bear the unmistakable imprint of Toomer's influence— Ernest J. Gaines's *The Autobiography of Miss Jane Pittman* and Gloria Naylor's *The Women of Brewster Place*, to name only two—but the examples of Hughes, Harper, and Walker will support my claim of Toomer's influence and growing legacy. *Cane*, *Essentials*, and "The Blue Meridian" are Toomer's most important works, and we see them emerging again and again in the work of the most talented contemporary writers. This, I suppose, is one measure of the value of an author's work, since it cannot rest solely in the writer's own particular effort and achievement but also in the effort and achievement of other writers.

> Greatness in life is spending
> it for something that will out last life,
> and be life renewed in other lives. . . .[10]

These lines, fashioned by Harper for "The Essential Tree" in "Cryptograms," aptly describes Jean Toomer's achievement and the artistic process his achievement has set in motion in other writers.

The irony, however, is that Toomer's reputation as a writer reposes upon *Cane*, the work he later rejected, and not upon those works— "The Gallonwerps," "Transatlantic," *The Sacred Factory, Essentials*, and "The Blue Meridian"—by which he felt certain he would leave his mark. Many of these later works, for reasons well known to us now, fall short of the high standard created by the first. Although we may not admire all of them, we are inspired nonetheless by the psychological and spiritual struggle from which they emerged as well as the vision of American life they seek to honor and to make permanent. And although we expected more from the poet who had such a brilliant, auspicious beginning, Toomer still remains, in the words of his friend Gorham Munson, "a dynamic symbol of what all artists of our time should be doing, if they are to command our trust."[11] We have the large body of work, impressive and uneven, and we also have the example of the life, highly instructive and enigmatic. That is our legacy.

Notes

CHAPTER 1. *Cane:* The Search for an Ideal of Man

1. Alfred Kreymborg, *Our Singing Strength* (New York: Coward-McCann, 1929), 575.
2. Darwin T. Turner, ed., *The Wayward and the Seeking: A Collection of Writings by Jean Toomer* (Washington, D.C.: Howard University Press, 1980), 108.
3. Kreymborg, *Our Singing Strength*, 575.
4. Box 66, Folder 8, Jean Toomer Collection, Fisk University, Nashville, Tenn.
5. Carl Jung, *The Undiscovered Self* (New York: Mentor Books, 1957).
6. Robert Bone, *Down Home: A History of Afro-American Short Fiction from Its Beginnings to the End of the Harlem Renaissance* (New York: G. P. Putnam's Sons, 1975), 229.
7. Darwin T. Turner, *In a Minor Chord: Three Afro-American Writers and Their Search for Identity* (Carbondale: Southern Illinois University Press, 1971), 30.
8. S. P. Fullwinder, *The Mind and Mood of Black America* (Chicago: Dorsey Press, 1969), 137.
9. Turner, *The Wayward and the Seeking*, 40, 62.
10. Ibid., 63.
11. I am indebted to Darwin Turner for the term "spiritual reformer." See Turner, *The Wayward and the Seeking*, 3.
12. Ibid., 41, 43.
13. Ibid., 73–74.
14. Ibid., 75.
15. Ibid., 74.
16. Box 67, Folder 5, Toomer Collection.
17. Turner, *The Wayward and the Seeking*, 76.
18. Ibid., 89.
19. Ibid., 90.
20. Ibid., 101.

21. Ibid., 105.

22. Ibid., 119.

23. Ibid., 120.

24. Turner, *In a Minor Chord*, 37.

25. Arna Bontemps, "The Negro Renaissance: Jean Toomer and the Harlem Writers of the 1920's," in *Anger and Beyond*, ed. Herbert Hill (New York: Harper and Row, 1966), 23.

26. Bone, *Down Home*, 207; Nathan Huggins, *The Harlem Renaissance* (New York: Oxford University Press, 1971), 180.

27. Turner, *The Wayward and the Seeking*, 123.

28. Robert Bone, *The Negro Novel in America* (New Haven: Yale University Press, 1958), 81; Turner, *In a Minor Chord*, 14.

29. Turner, *In a Minor Chord*, 125.

30. E. M. Forster, *Aspects of the Novel* (New York: Harcourt, Brace and Co., 1927), 17. I am aware of recent theories of the novel set forth in such representative studies as *The Theory of the Novel* (London: Merlin Press, 1971) by Georg Lukacs, and *The Dialogic Imagination* (Austin: University of Texas Press, 1981) by Mikhail Bakhtin. For all the fascinating questions these studies raise about form, I have not abandoned my own, albeit conservative, definition of the novel: a fiction chiefly of prose of a certain length that achieves unity through the development and resolution of a central conflict. *Cane* does not possess such a conflict, and thus I do not call it a novel. It is important to remember, however, that Toomer did not conceive of *Cane* as a novel; therefore, it is not, as some might think, a work containing a structural flaw.

31. Bernard Bell, "A Key to the Poems in *Cane*," *College Language Association Journal* 14 (1970): 253–54.

32. Charles T. Davis, "Jean Toomer and the South: Region and Race as Elements Within a Literary Imagination," *Studies in the Literary Imagination* 7: 31, 30.

33. Letter to Waldo Frank, 12 December 1922, Box 3, Folder 6, Toomer Collection.

34. Robert B. Stepto, *From Behind the Veil* (Urbana: University of Illinois Press, 1979).

35. Northrop Frye, *Anatomy of Criticism* (Princeton: Princeton University Press, 1957), 5.

36. Jean Toomer, *Essentials* (Chicago: Lakeside Press, 1931), 11. Further references to this edition will appear in the text and cite page numbers only.

37. Turner, *The Wayward and the Seeking*, 20.

38. Jean Toomer, *Cane* (New York: Boni and Liveright, 1923), 134. Further references to this edition will appear in the text and cite page numbers only.

39. Ralph Ellison, *Invisible Man* (New York: Signet Books, 1952), 231.

40. William Carlos Williams, *In the American Grain* (New York: New Directions, 1956), 39.

41. Turner, *The Wayward and the Seeking*, 20.

42. In his essay "Jean Toomer's Ralph Kabnis: Portrait of the Negro Artist as a Young Man," *Phylon* 30 (Spring 1969): 72–85, William J. Goede briefly compares Becky to Hester Prynne, but he does not develop the comparison.

43. Houston A. Baker, Jr., *Singers of Daybreak: Studies in Black American Literature* (Washington, D.C.: Howard University Press, 1974), 58.

44. Sterling A. Brown, *The Negro in American Fiction* (New York: Arno Press, 1937).

45. Forster, *Aspects of the Novel*, 124.

46. Ernest J. Gaines, *Bloodline* (New York: Dial Press, 1968).

47. P. D. Ouspensky, *Talks with a Devil* (New York: Pocket Books, 1972), 126.

48. *The Complete Works of Ralph Waldo Emerson* (New York: AMS Press, 1968), 1: 11.

49. Richard Wright, *American Hunger* (New York: Harper and Row, 1977), 135.

50. Davis, "Jean Toomer and the South," 34.

CHAPTER 2. The Years with Gurdjieff

1. Jean Toomer to Waldo Frank, April 1922, Waldo Frank Collection, University of Pennsylvania, Philadelphia, Pa.

2. See Frank's foreword to *Cane* (New York: Boni and Liveright, 1923), vii. For all his praise of Toomer as a poet, Frank's identification of Toomer as an African-American poet disturbed Toomer.

3. Box 66, Folder 8, Toomer Collection.

4. Box 66, Folder 8, Toomer Collection.

5. Turner, *The Wayward and the Seeking*, 128.

6. Alice Walker, *In Search of Our Mothers' Gardens* (New York: Harcourt, Brace and Jovanovich, 1983), 376.

7. Turner, *The Wayward and the Seeking*, 128.

8. Box 27, Folder 2, Toomer Collection.

9. Box 1, Folder 5, Toomer Collection.

10. Turner, *The Wayward and the Seeking*, 91, 92.

11. Ibid., 93, 121.

12. Box 1, Folder 3, Toomer Collection.

13. Ralph Ellison, "The World and the Jug," in *Shadow and Act* (New York: Random House, 1953).

14. Nellie Y. McKay, *Jean Toomer, Artist: A Study of His Literary Life and Work, 1894–1936* (Chapel Hill: University of North Carolina Press, 1984), 180–81.

15. Box 1, Folder 3, Toomer Collection.

16. Box 1, Folder 5, Toomer Collection.

17. Box 1, Folder 5, Toomer Collection.

18. McKay is surprised that Toomer reacted so angrily to Liveright's inquiries about his racial background and position, but it is important to remember that Toomer thought of Liveright not only as his publisher but also as a friend. Liveright's request that Toomer feature himself as "Negro" shocked Toomer, since he had been so careful to explain his racial position and Liveright had led him to believe that he understood and respected it. Toomer could receive Barnett's inquiry with what McKay terms "equanimity" for the simple reason that Barnett was a stranger. See McKay, *Jean Toomer, Artist*, 181.

19. Walker, *In Search of Our Mothers' Gardens*, 65.

20. Box 66, Folder 8, Toomer Collection.

21. Box 67, Folder 5, Toomer Collection.

22. Turner, *The Wayward and the Seeking*, 121.

23. James Moore, *Gurdjieff and Mansfield* (London: Routledge and Kegan, 1980), 19.

24. G. I. Gurdjieff, *Meetings with Remarkable Men* (New York: E. P. Dutton, 1969), 50.

25. Ibid., 65.

26. Ibid., 270.

27. Box 67, Folder 5, Toomer Collection.

28. Box 67, Folder 5, Toomer Collection.

29. G. I. Gurdjieff, *Views from the Real World* (New York: E. P. Dutton, 1973), 108.

30. Moore, *Gurdjieff and Mansfield*, 198.

31. Box 53, Folder 26, Toomer Collection.

32. Box 26, Folder 45, Toomer Collection.

33. Box 66, Folder 8, Toomer Collection.

34. Box 53, Folder 26, Toomer Collection.

35. Box 66, Folder 8, Toomer Collection.

36. Box 53, Folder 27, Toomer Collection.

37. Ibid.

38. Box 67, Folder 3, Toomer Collection.

39. Ibid.

40. Ibid.

41. Ibid.

42. Box 67, Folder 5, Toomer Collection.

43. Box 67, Folder 3, Toomer Collection.

44. Box 67, Folder 5, Toomer Collection.

45. Ibid.

46. Ibid.

47. Ibid.

48. Langston Hughes, *The Big Sea* (New York: Hill and Wang, 1963), 241.

49. Box 24, Folder 25, Toomer Collection.

50. Box 67, Folder 5, Toomer Collection.

51. P. D. Ouspensky, *The Psychology of Man's Possible Evolution* (New York: Vintage Books, 1974), 6.

52. Ibid., 8.

53. Gurdjieff, *Views from the Real World*, 44.

54. Ouspensky, *The Psychology of Man's Possible Evolution*, 13.

55. Gurdjieff, *Views from the Real World*, 44.

56. Ouspensky, *The Psychology of Man's Possible Evolution*, 13.

57. Ouspensky, *In Search of the Miraculous: Fragments of an Unknown Teaching* (New York: Harcourt, Brace and Jovanovich, 1949), 155, 117.

58. Box 24, Folder 25, Toomer Collection.

59. P. D. Ouspensky, *The Fourth Way* (New York: Vintage Books, 1971), 30.

60. Ouspensky, *The Psychology of Man's Possible Evolution*, 35.

61. Ouspensky, *The Fourth Way*, 30.

62. Box 67, Folder 3, Toomer Collection.

63. Ibid.

64. Ibid.

65. Ibid.

66. McKay, *Jean Toomer, Artist*, 193.

67. Box 24, Folder 14, Toomer Collection.

68. Box 66, Folder 8, Toomer Collection.

69. Ibid.

CHAPTER 3. I Would Rather Form a Man Than Form a Book

1. Box 66, Folder 8, p. 49, Toomer Collection.

2. Box 66, Folder 8, Toomer Collection.

3. Box 66, Folder 8, p. 49, Toomer Collection.

4. Gorham Munson, *Destinations* (New York: J. H. Sears, 1928), 185.

5. Turner, *The Wayward and the Seeking*, 123.

6. Ibid., 19.

7. These three unpublished manuscripts are housed in the Toomer Collection.

8. Since Toomer was known as an African-American writer, his marriage to a white woman caused quite a scandal. For public reactions to this event see the New York *Amsterdam News*, 21 March 1932, and the New York *Daily News*, 26 March 1932.

9. Box 39, Folder 1, p. 1, Toomer Collection. All further references to "The Gallonwerps" will cite page numbers only.

10. Turner, *The Wayward and the Seeking*, 93, 92.

11. Box 15, Folder 3, Toomer Collection.

12. Turner, *The Wayward and the Seeking*, 93.

13. Ibid., 126.

14. Frank, foreword to *Cane*, vii.

15. Turner, *The Wayward and the Seeking*, 126.

16. Ibid.

17. Box 14, Folder 1, Toomer Collection.

18. In an undated letter to Frank, Toomer complained of Anderson's habit of referring to him as Negro. Frank Collection.

19. *Memoirs of Waldo Frank*, ed. Alan Trachtenburg (Amherst: University of Massachusetts Press, 1973), 107.

20. Turner, *The Wayward and the Seeking*, 132.

21. Letter to Cunard, 8 February 1930, Toomer Collection.

22. Turner, *The Wayward and the Seeking*, 91–94.

23. Walker, *In Search of Our Mothers' Gardens*, 60–65.

24. Ouspensky, *The Psychology of Man's Possible Evolution*, 9.

25. In the Gurdjieff system, to become individualized or to attain individuality means that one possesses unity and volition. These are traits of individuals who have attained what Gurdjieff called self-consciousness, the third state of consciousness in his scheme of higher development.

26. Ouspensky, *The Fourth Way*, 22.

27. Toomer, *Cane*, 1.

28. See Arna Bontemps's introduction to the second edition of *Cane* (New York: Harper and Row, 1969), viii–ix.

29. See the Milwaukee *Sentinel*, 20 March 1932, and the New York *Daily News*, 26 March 1932. James Weldon Johnson Memorial Collection, Beinecke Rare Book and Manuscript Library, Yale University, New Haven, Conn.

30. Turner, *In a Minor Chord*, 52.

31. Ibid., 53.

32. Box 34, Folder 3, p. 381, Toomer Collection. All further references to the novel "Transatlantic" will cite page numbers only.

33. Turner, *The Wayward and the Seeking*, 126–27.

34. Laurie Lisle, *Portrait of an Artist: A Biography of Georgia O'Keeffe* (New York: Seaview Books, 1980).

35. Ouspensky, *The Fourth Way*, 63.

36. Ouspensky, *In Search of the Miraculous*, 138.

37. Ibid., 154–55.

38. Turner, *In a Minor Chord*, 52.

39. Flannery O'Connor, *Mystery and Manners*, ed. Sally Fitzgerald and Robert Fitzgerald (New York: Farrar, Straus, and Giroux, 1957), 66, 67–68.

40. Letter to Sherwood Anderson, January 1924, Box 2, Folder 1, Toomer Collection.

41. Box 25, Folder 35, Toomer Collection.

CHAPTER 4. *The Sacred Factory:* Drama as Development

1. Turner, *The Wayward and the Seeking*, 16.

2. Box 49, Folder 5, Toomer Collection.

3. Box 49, Folder 16, Toomer Collection.

4. Ibid.

5. Box 66, Folder 8, Toomer Collection.

6. Sterling A. Brown, *Negro Poetry and Drama* (1937; rpt. New York: Atheneum, 1969), 112.

7. Huggins, *The Harlem Renaissance*, 289.

8. Turner, *The Wayward and the Seeking*, 109.

9. Ibid., 104, 107.

10. Box 15, Folder 3, Toomer Collection.

11. George Bernard Shaw, *Complete Plays with Prefaces*, Vol. 1 (New York: Dodd, Mead and Co., 1963), 191, 206.

12. George Bernard Shaw, *Nine Plays* (New York: Dodd, Mead and Co., 1948), 194, 514.

13. Turner, *The Wayward and the Seeking*, 108.

14. Box 49, Folder 16, Toomer Collection.

15. Turner, *The Wayward and the Seeking*, 19.

16. For my discussion of "Kabnis," which will not be repeated in this chapter, I refer the reader to chapter 1. Additionally, I am aware that I am violating the chronology of my study by including *Natalie Mann* (c. 1922), *Balo* (1922), and "Pilgrims, Did You Say?" (c. 1940), but the decision to include these works was not arbitrary. The first two plays were added because, in order to demonstrate the force of Gurdjieff's influence on Toomer's development as a dramatist, it was essential to examine works written before the discovery of Gurdjieff. The last play was included not only because it illustrates the continued influence of Gurdjieff's thought on Toomer's writing but also because of the thematic unity it gives to Toomer's canon.

17. Darwin T. Turner, "The Failure of a Playwright," *College Language Association Journal* 10 (June 1967): 309, 243.

18. Ibid., 278, 262.

19. Ibid., 324.

20. Ibid., 257.

21. Ibid., 278.

22. Ibid., 17.

23. Ibid., 87.

24. Brown, *Negro Poetry and Drama*, 121; Alain Locke and Montgomery Gregory, eds., *Plays of Negro Life* (New York: Harper and Brothers, 1927), 407; Turner, "The Failure of a Playwright," 314.

25. Brown, *Negro Poetry and Drama*, 115.

26. Box 49, Folder 8, Toomer Collection.

27. Forster, *Aspects of the Novel*, 105.

28. Richard Samuel, *Expressionism in German Life, Literature, and the Theatre* (Cambridge: W. Heffer and Sons, 1939), 146–70. See also Egbert Krispyn, *Style and Society in German Literary Expressionism* (Gainesville: University of Florida Press, 1964), 45.

29. Walter H. Sokel, ed., *An Anthology of Expressionist Drama* (New York: Anchor Books, 1963), xii.

30. Box 49, Folder 4, Toomer Collection.

31. Box 49, Folder 4, p. 6, Toomer Collection.

32. Box 49, Folder 4, p. 36, Toomer Collection.

33. Ouspensky, *The Fourth Way*, 22.

34. Box 49, Folder 4, p. 35, Toomer Collection.

35. Toomer Collection, uncataloged.

36. In an interview with Marjorie Content Toomer on 5 November 1983, I learned that Toomer had long wished to visit India and spent several weeks there just before the outbreak of World War II. According to Mrs. Toomer, Jean Toomer visited the northern part of India in the hope of meeting an Indian guru who was said to possess enormous spiritual powers. Gurdjieff also traveled in India, but it is impossible to determine if he and Toomer were in the same villages. It is likely, though, that they visited the same region, as Gurdjieff traveled extensively throughout the East.

37. Cynthia E. Kerman and Richard Eldridge, *The Lives of Jean Toomer: A Hunger for Wholeness* (Baton Rouge: Louisiana State University Press, 1987), 245.

38. Turner, *The Wayward and the Seeking*, 327–410.

39. Sokel, *Expressionist Drama*, xv.

40. Turner, *The Wayward and the Seeking*, 327.

41. Sokel, *Expressionist Drama*, xii.

42. H. F. Garten, *Modern German Drama* (Fair Lawn, N.J.: Essential Books, 1959), 116.

43. Turner, *The Wayward and the Seeking*, 354, 361.

44. Ibid., 387.

45. Ibid., 404.

46. Ibid., 408.

47. Ouspensky, *The Fourth Way*, 16.

48. Turner, *The Wayward and the Seeking*, 409–10.

49. Exodus 3:6.

50. Turner, "The Failure of a Playwright," 308–18.

51. Box 49, Folder 16, Toomer Collection.

CHAPTER 5. "The Blue Meridian": Poetry as Development

1. Box 25, Folder 20, Toomer Collection.

2. Box 66, Folder 8, Toomer Collection.

3. McKay, *Jean Toomer, Artist*, 213–14.

4. Ibid., 214.

5. R. W. B. Lewis, *The Poetry of Hart Crane: A Critical Study* (Princeton: Princeton University Press, 1967), 28.

6. Brom Weber, ed. *The Complete Poems and Selected Letters and Prose of Hart Crane* (New York: Liveright, 1933), 4.

7. Turner, *The Wayward and the Seeking*, 126, 121.

8. My intention is to cast Toomer as an independent artist and visionary, since it is all too easy, given Crane's prominence in modern American poetry, to perceive Toomer's efforts as merely derivative.

9. Jean Toomer, "The Blue Meridian," in Turner, *The Wayward and the Seeking*, 214–34. All further references to this poem will appear in parentheses in the text.

10. Walt Whitman, "I Hear America Singing," in *Leaves of Grass* (New York: Doubleday, Doran and Company, 1940), 16.

11. Turner, *The Wayward and the Seeking*, 121.

12. Turner, *The Wayward and the Seeking*, 126.

Conclusion

1. Turner, *In a Minor Chord*, 37.

2. Portions of "Remember and Return" have been published in Turner, *The Wayward and the Seeking*, 433.

3. Sterling A. Brown to Jean Toomer, 13 August 1941, Box 1, Folder 6, Toomer Collection; Michael S. Harper, ed., *The Collected Poems of Sterling A. Brown* (New York: Harper and Row, 1980), xii.

4. Langston Hughes, *The Weary Blues* (New York: Alfred Knopf, 1926), 57.

5. Michael S. Harper, *Nightmare Begins Responsibility* (Urbana: University of Illinois Press, 1975), 47.

6. Ibid., 45.

7. Ibid., 52.

8. Ibid., 60.

9. Harper's poem "Alice" appears in *Images of Kin: New and Selected Poems* (Urbana: University of Illinois Press, 1977), 66.

10. Harper, *Nightmare Begins Responsibility*, 58.

11. Munson, *Destinations* (New York: J. H. Sears, 1928), 185.

Bibliography

Works by Jean Toomer

BOOKS

Cane. New York: Boni and Liveright, 1923.
Essentials. Chicago: Lakeside Press, 1931.

SHORT STORIES

"Drachman." Unpublished. Jean Toomer Collection, Fisk University, Nashville, Tenn.
"Easter." *Little Review,* 11 (Spring 1925), 3–7.
"Love on a Train." Unpublished. Jean Toomer Collection, Fisk University, Nashville, Tenn.
"Mr. Costyve Duditch." *Dial* 85 (December 1928): 6.
"Mr. Costyve Duditch." In *The Wayward and the Seeking: A Collection of Writings by Jean Toomer,* edited by Darwin T. Turner, 182–96. Washington, D.C.: Howard University Press, 1980.
"Mr. Limph Krok's Famous L'Pride." Unpublished. Jean Toomer Collection, Fisk University, Nashville, Tenn.
"Two Professors." Unpublished. Jean Toomer Collection, Fisk University, Nashville, Tenn.
"Winter on Earth." In *The Second American Caravan: A Yearbook of American Literature,* edited by Alfred Kreymborg, Lewis Mumford, and Paul Rosenfeld, 166–81. New York: Macauley Company, 1928.
"Withered Skin of Berries." In *The Wayward and the Seeking: A Collection of Writings by Jean Toomer,* edited by Darwin T. Turner, 139–65. Washington, D.C.: Howard University Press, 1980.
"York Beach." In *The New Caravan,* edited by Alfred Kreymborg, Lewis Mumford, and Paul Rosenfeld. New York: Macauley Company, 1929.

POETRY

"As the Eagle Soars." *Crisis* 39 (April 1932): 116.

"The Blue Meridian." In *The New Caravan,* edited by Alfred Kreymborg, Lewis Mumford, and Paul Rosenfeld. New York: W. W. Norton and Company, 1936.

"The Blue Meridian." In *The Wayward and the Seeking: A Collection of Writings by Jean Toomer,* edited by Darwin T. Turner, 214–34. Washington, D.C.: Howard University Press, 1980.

"Bride of Air." Unpublished. Jean Toomer Collection, Fisk University, Nashville, Tenn.

"Brown River, Smile." *Pagany* 3 (January–March 1932), 29–33.

"Gum." *Chapbook,* 36 (April 1923).

"White Arrow." *Dial* 86 (July 1929): 596.

DRAMA

Balo. In *Plays of Negro Life,* edited by Alain Locke and Montgomery Gregory, 269–86. New York: Harper and Row, 1927.

"A Drama of the Southwest." Unpublished. Jean Toomer Collection, Fisk University, Nashville, Tenn.

"Man's Home Companion." Unpublished. Jean Toomer Collection, Fisk University, Nashville, Tenn.

Natalie Mann. In *The Wayward and the Seeking: A Collection of Writings by Jean Toomer,* edited by Darwin T. Turner, 243–325. Washington, D.C.: Howard University Press, 1980.

"Pilgrims, Did You Say?" Unpublished. Jean Toomer Collection, Fisk University, Nashville, Tenn.

The Sacred Factory. In *The Wayward and the Seeking: A Collection of Writings by Jean Toomer,* edited by Darwin T. Turner, 327–410. Washington, D.C.: Howard University Press, 1980.

AUTOBIOGRAPHY

"Autobiography," 1936. Unpublished. Jean Toomer Collection, Fisk University, Nashville, Tenn.

"Earth Being," 1930. Unpublished. Jean Toomer Collection, Fisk University, Nashville, Tenn.

"Incredible Journey," 1945. Unpublished. Jean Toomer Collection, Fisk University, Nashville, Tenn.

"Outline of an Autobiography," 1946. Unpublished. Jean Toomer Collection, Fisk University, Nashville, Tenn.

MISCELLANEOUS

The Flavor of Man. William Penn Lecture, 1949. Repr. Philadelphia, 1974, 1979. Pamphlet.

"Oxen Cart and Warefare." *Little Review* 10 (Autumn-Winter 1924–25), 44–48. Criticism.

"Race Problems and Modern Society." In *Man and His World,* edited by Baker Brownell. New York: D. Van Nostrand, 1929.

"Reflections." *Dial* 86 (April 1929): 314. Aphorism.

Selected Secondary Sources

Antonides, Chris. "Jean Toomer: The Burden of Impotent Pain." Ph.D. diss., Michigan State University, 1975.

Baker, Houston A., Jr., *Singers of Daybreak: Studies in Black American Literature.* Washington, D.C.: Howard University Press, 1974.

Bell, Bernard W. "A Key to the Poems in *Cane.*" *College Language Association Journal* 14 (March 1971): 251–58.

——— . "Jean Toomer's 'Blue Meridian': The Poet as Prophet of a New Order of Man." *Black American Literature Forum* 14 (Summer 1980): 77–80.

——— . "Portrait of the Artist as High Priest of the Soul: Jean Toomer's *Cane.*" *Black World* 23 (September 1974): 4–19, 92–97.

Benson, Brian Joseph, and Mabel Mayle Dillard. *Jean Toomer.* Twayne Monograph, no. 389. Boston: G. K. Hall, 1980.

Bone, Robert. *Down Home: A History of Afro-American Short Fiction from Its Beginning to the End of the Harlem Renaissance.* New York: G. P. Putnam's Sons, 1975.

——— . *The Negro Novel in America.* New Haven: Yale University Press, 1958.

Bontemps, Arna. Introduction to *Cane,* by Jean Toomer. New York: Harper and Row, 1969.

——— . "The Harlem Renaissance." *Saturday Review of Literature* 30 (22 March 1947): 12–13, 44.

——— . *The Harlem Renaissance Remembered.* New York: Dodd, Mead and Company, 1972.

——— . "The Negro Renaissance: Jean Toomer and the Harlem Writers of the 1920's." In *Anger and Beyond: The Negro Writer in the United States,* edited by Herbert Hill, 20–36. New York: Harper and Row, 1966.

Braithwaite, William Stanley. "The Negro in American Literature." *Crisis* 28 (September 1924): 204–10.

Bricknell, Hersell. "On *Cane.*" *Literary Review* 8 December 1923: 333.

Brooks, Cleanth, and Robert Penn Warren. *The Scope of Fiction.* New York: Appleton-Century-Crofts, 1960.

Brown, Sterling A. *Negro Poetry and Drama.* 1937. Repr. New York: Atheneum, 1969.

————. *Southern Road.* New York: Harcourt, Brace and Company, 1932.

Bush, Ann Marie, and Louis D. Mitchell. "Jean Toomer: A Cubist Poet." *Black American Literature Forum* 17 (Fall 1983): 106–18.

Byrd, Rudolph P. "Jean Toomer and the Writers of the Harlem Renaissance: Was He There With Them?" In *The Harlem Renaissance: Revaluations,* edited by Amritjit Singh, William S. Shiver, and Stanley Brodwin, 209–19. New York: Garland Publishing, 1989.

Callahan, John F. *In the African-American Grain: The Pursuit of Voice in Twentieth-Century Black Fiction.* Urbana: University of Illinois Press, 1988.

Christian, Barbara. "Spirit Bloom in Harlem: The Search for a Black Aesthetic During the Harlem Renaissance: The Poetry of Claude McKay, Countée Cullen, and Jean Toomer." Ph.D. diss., Columbia University, 1970.

Collins, Paschal. "Jean Toomer's *Cane:* A Symbolist Study." Ph.D. diss., University of Florida, 1978.

Crewdson, Arlene J. "Invisibility: A Study of the Works of Jean Toomer, Richard Wright, and Ralph Ellison." Ph.D. diss., Loyola University of Chicago, 1974.

Davenport, Franklin. "Mill House." *Banc* 2, 2 (1972): 6–7.

Davis, Charles T. "Jean Toomer and the South: Region and Race as Elements Within a Literary Imagination." *Studies in the Literary Imagination* 7:23–37.

Dillard, Mabel M. "Jean Toomer: Herald of the Negro Renaissance." Ph.D. diss., Ohio University, 1967.

Dorris, Ronald. "The Bacchae of Jean Toomer." Ph.D. diss., Emory University, 1979.

Du Bois, W. E. B. "The Younger Literary Movement." *Crisis* 27 (1924): 161–63.

Durham, Frank, ed. *The Merrill Studies in Cane.* Columbus, Ohio: Charles E. Merrill, 1971.

Eldridge, Richard. "Jean Toomer's *Cane:* The Search for the American Roots." Ph.D. diss., University of Maryland, 1977.

————. "The Unifying Images in Part One of Jean Toomer's *Cane.*" *College Language Association Journal* 22 (1979): 187–214.

Ellison, Ralph. *Invisible Man.* New York: Signet Books, 1952.

Forster, E. M. *Aspects of the Novel.* New York: Harcourt, Brace and Company, 1927.

Frank, Waldo. Foreword to *Cane,* by Jean Toomer. New York: Boni and Liveright, 1923.

Frye, Northrop. *Anatomy of Criticism.* Princeton: Princeton University Press, 1957.

Fullwinder, S. P. "Jean Toomer, Lost Generation or Negro Renaissance?" *Phylon* 27 (1966): 396–403.

———. *The Mind and Mood of Black America*. Homewood, Ill.: Dorsey Press, 1969.

Gaines, Ernest J. *Bloodline*. New York: Dial Press, 1968.

Garten, H. F. *Modern German Drama*. Fair Lawn, N.J.: Essential Books, 1959.

Gayle, Addison, Jr. *The Way of the New World: The Black Novel in America*. Garden City, N.Y.: Anchor Press, 1975.

Gibson, Donald B. *The Politics of Literary Expression: A Study of Major Black Writers*. Westport, Conn.: Greenwood Press, 1981.

Gloster, Hugh M. *Negro Voices in American Fiction*. Chapel Hill: University of North Carolina Press, 1948.

Goede, William J. "Jean Toomer's Ralph Kabnis: Portrait of the Negro Artist as a Young Man." *Phylon* 30 (Spring 1969): 72–85.

Griffin, John C. "Jean Toomer: American Writer (A Biography)." Ph.D. diss., University of South Carolina, 1976.

Gurdjieff, G. I. *Meetings with Remarkable Men*. New York: E. P. Dutton, 1969.

———. *Views from the Real World*. New York: E. P. Dutton, 1973.

Gysin, Fritz. *The Grotesque in American Negro Fiction: Jean Toomer, Richard Wright, and Ralph Ellison*. Cooper Monograph, no. 22. Bern: Francke, 1975.

Hartman, Thomas de. *Our Life with Mr. Gurdjieff*. New York: Cooper Square Publishers, 1964.

Holmes, Eugene. "Jean Toomer, Apostle of Beauty." *Opportunity* 10 (August 1932): 252–54, 260.

Huggins, Nathan I. *Harlem Renaissance*. New York: Oxford University Press, 1971.

Hughes, Langston. *The Big Sea*. New York: Hill and Wang, 1963.

Jackson, Blyden. "Jean Toomer's *Cane*: An Issue of Genre." In *The Twenties: Fiction, Poetry, and Drama*, edited by Warren French, 317–33. Deland, Fla.: Everett/Edwards, 1974.

Jung, Carl. *The Undiscovered Self*. New York: Mentor Books, 1957.

Jung, Udo. "Die Dichtung Jean Toomer und die Negerrenaissance." In *Black Literature: Zur Afrikanischen und Afroamerikanischen Literatur*, edited by Eckhard Bretinger, 295–316. Kritische Information, no. 73. Munich: Fink, 1979.

———. "Jean Toomer: 'Fern'." In *The Black American Short Story in the Twentieth Century: A Collection of Critical Essays*, edited by Peter Brunck, 53–69. Amsterdam: Guner, 1977.

Kerman, Cynthia E. "Jean Toomer? Enigma." *Indian Journal of American Studies* 7 (1977): 67–68.

Kerman, Cynthia E., and Richard Eldridge. *The Lives of Jean Toomer: A Hunger for Wholeness*. Baton Rouge: Louisiana State University Press, 1987.

Kraft, James. "Jean Toomer's *Cane*." *Markham Review* 2 (1970): 61–63.

Kransky, Michael. "Jean Toomer and the Quest for Consciousness." Ph.D. diss., University of Wisconsin, 1972.

Kreymborg, Alfred. *Our Singing Strength*. New York: Coward-McCann, 1929.

Lewis, David L. *When Harlem Was in Vogue*. New York: Alfred A. Knopf, 1979.

Lewis, R. W. B. *The American Adam*. Chicago: University of Chicago Press, 1955.

Littlejohn, David. *Black on White: A Critical Survey of Writing by American Negroes*. New York: Grossman, 1966.

Locke, Alain. "From Native Son to Invisible Man: A Review of the Literature of the Negro for 1952." *Phylon* 14 (1953): 34–44.

Locke, Alain, and Montgomery Gregory, eds. *Plays of Negro Life*. New York: Harper and Brothers, 1927.

Lukacs, Georg. *The Theory of the Novel*. London: Merlin Press, 1971.

McKay, Nellie Y. *Jean Toomer, Artist: A Study of His Literary Life and Work, 1894–1936*. Chapel Hill: University of North Carolina Press, 1984.

McNelly, Darrell. "Jean Toomer's *Cane* and Sherwood Anderson's *Winesburg, Ohio*: A Black Reaction to the Literary Conventions of the Twenties." Ph.D. diss., University of Nebraska, 1974.

Margolies, Edward. *Native Sons: A Critical Study of Twentieth-Century Negro American Authors*. Philadelphia: J. B. Lippincott, 1968.

Miller, Ruth, and Peter J. Katopes. "The Harlem Renaissance: Arna W. Bontemps, Countée Cullen, James Weldon Johnson, Claude McKay, and Jean Toomer." In *Black American Writers: Bibliographic Essays*. Vol. 1, *The Beginnings Through the Harlem Renaissance and Langston Hughes*, edited by Thomas M. Inge, et al., 161–86. New York: St. Martin's Press, 1978.

Moore, James. *Gurdjieff and Mansfield*. London: Routledge and Kegan, 1980.

Munson, Gorham B. *Destinations: A Canvass of American Literature Since 1900*. New York: J. H. Sears, 1928.

Nwankwo, Nkem. "Cultural Primitivism and Related Ideas in Jean Toomer's *Cane*." Ph.D. diss., Indiana University, 1982.

O'Connor, Flannery. *Mystery and Manners*, edited by Sally Fitzgerald and Robert Fitzgerald. New York: Farrar, Straus, and Giroux, 1957.

Ouspensky, P. D. *The Fourth Way*. New York: Vintage Books, 1971.

―――. *The Psychology of Man's Possible Evolution*. New York: Vintage Books, 1974.

―――. *In Search of the Miraculous: Fragments of an Unknown Teaching*. New York: Harcourt, Brace and Jovanovich, 1949.

Oxley, Thomas L. G. "The Negro in World's Literature." *New York Amsterdam News*, 28 March 1928: 8.

Payne, Ladell. *Black Novelists and the Southern Literary Tradition*. Athens, Ga.: University of Georgia Press, 1981.

Perry, Margaret. *Silence to the Drums: A Survey of the Literature of the Harlem Renaissance*. Westport, Conn.: Greenwood Press, 1976.

Peters, Fritz. *Boyhood with Gurdjieff*. New York: E. P. Dutton, 1964.

Rankin, William. "Ineffability in the Fiction of Jean Toomer and Katherine Mansfield." In *Renaissance and Modern: Essays in Honor of Edwin M. Moseley*, edited by Murray J. Levitt, 160–71. Saratoga Springs, N.Y.: Skidmore College, 1975.

Redding, Saunders J. *To Make a Poet Black*. Chapel Hill: University of North Carolina Press, 1939.

Rosenblatt, Roger. *Black Fiction*. Cambridge, Mass.: Harvard University Press, 1974.

Rosenfeld, Paul. "Jean Toomer." In *Men Seen*. 27–36. New York: Dial Press, 1925.

Rusch, Frederick L. "Every Atom Belonging to Me as Good Belongs to You: Jean Toomer and His Bringing Together of the Scattered Parts." Ph.D. diss., State University of New York at Albany, 1976.

Samuel, Richard. *Expressionism in German Life, Literature, and the Theatre*. Cambridge: W. Heffer and Sons, 1939.

Scruggs, Charles W. "Jean Toomer: Fugitive." *American Literature* 47 (1975): 84–96.

———. "The Mark of Cain and the Redemption of Art: A Study in Theme and Structure of Jean Toomer's *Cane*." *American Literature* 44 (1972): 276–91.

Shaw, Brenda Joyce Robinson. "Jean Toomer's Life Search for Identity as Realized in *Cane*." Ph.D. diss., Middle Tennessee State University, 1975.

Singh, Amritjit. *The Novels of the Harlem Renaissance: Twelve Black Writers, 1923–33*. University Park: Pennsylvania State University Press, 1976.

Sokel, Walter H., ed. *An Anthology of Expressionist Drama*. New York: Anchor Books, 1963.

Solard, Alain. "The Impossible Unity: Jean Toomer's 'Kabnis.'" In *Myth and Ideology in American Culture*, edited by Regis Furand, 175–94. Cahiers Américains, no. 1. Villeneuve d'Ascq: Université de Lille III, 1975.

Stepto, Robert B. *From Behind the Veil*. Urbana: University of Illinois Press, 1979.

Taylor, Carolyn. "'Blend Us With Thy Being': Jean Toomer's Mill House Poems." Ph.D. diss., Boston College, 1977.

Trachtenburg, Alan, ed. *Memoirs of Waldo Frank*. Amherst: University of Massachusetts Press, 1973.

Turner, Darwin T. "The Failure of a Playwright." *College Language Association Journal* 10 (June 1967): 308–18.

———. In *A Minor Chord: Three Afro-American Writers and Their Search for Identity*. Carbondale: Southern Illinois University Press, 1971.

————. Introduction to *The Wayward and the Seeking: A Collection of Writings by Jean Toomer*. Washington, D.C.: Howard University Press, 1980.

Twombly, Robert C. "A Disciple's Odyssey: Jean Toomer's Gurdjieffian Career." *Prospects: An Annual Journal of American Cultural Studies* 2 (1976): 437–62.

Wagner, Jean. *Black Poets of the United States: From Paul Laurence Dunbar to Langston Hughes*. Urbana: University of Illinois Press, 1973.

Walker, Alice. *In Search of Our Mothers' Gardens*. New York: Harcourt, Brace and Jovanovich, 1983.

Weinstein, Norman. *Gertrude Stein and the Literature of the Modern Consciousness*. New York: Frederick Ungar Publishing Company, 1970.

Whitman, Walt. *Leaves of Grass*. New York: Doubleday, Doran, and Company, 1940.

Wright, Richard. *American Hunger*. New York: Harper and Row, 1977.

Index